Math and Logic Puzzles That Make Kids Think!

Grades 6–8

Math and Logic PUZZLES

That Make Kids Think!

Jeffrey J. Wanko

 PRUFROCK PRESS INC.
WACO, TEXAS

Copyright © 2010, Prufrock Press Inc.
Edited by Lacy Compton
Cover and Layout Design by Marjorie Parker

ISBN-13: 978-1-59363-416-2

Printed in the United States of America.

At the time of this book's publication, all facts and figures cited are the most current available. All telephone numbers, addresses, and website URLs are accurate and active. All publications, organizations, websites, and other resources exist as described in the book, and all have been verified. The author and Prufrock Press Inc. make no warranty or guarantee concerning the information and materials given out by organizations or content found at websites, and we are not responsible for any changes that occur after this book's publication. If you find an error, please contact Prufrock Press Inc.

Prufrock Press Inc.
P.O. Box 8813
Waco, TX 76714-8813
Phone: (800) 998-2208
Fax: (800) 240-0333
http://www.prufrock.com

Contents

Chapter 1
Introduction

Sudoku puzzles have been a mainstay in the United States since 2005. They are based on Latin Squares, which were popularized by Leonard Euler in the 18th century. Latin Squares were simply arrangements of numbers or letters (originally, they contained Latin characters which gave rise to their name) in a square so that each character appeared exactly once in each row and column (see Figure 1). These were not necessarily considered puzzles—they were actually a mathematical curiosity that Euler observed and made use of in different areas of mathematics.

In 1979, Howard Garns published the first Sudoku puzzle—then called Number Place—in which the basic rules of Latin Squares are used with the additional constraint of bordered regions, which also contain each character exactly once in the solution (see Figure 2). In his puzzle, he omitted some of the numbers and challenged the solver to deduce the missing numbers so that the rules of the puzzle were met (each number had to appear exactly once in each row, each column, and each bordered region).

By 1986, the Japanese puzzle magazine *Nikoli* had adapted the Number Place puzzles—giving

5	8	1	4	6	3	2	9	7
4	9	8	2	3	1	7	5	6
2	1	5	6	7	9	4	8	3
3	4	2	8	5	6	1	7	9
8	5	9	1	4	7	3	6	2
6	7	4	3	9	2	8	1	5
7	6	3	5	1	8	9	2	4
1	3	7	9	2	5	6	4	8
9	2	6	7	8	4	5	3	1

Figure 1. Example 9 × 9 Latin Square.

4	3	9	1	8	6	2	5	7
7	1	5	2	4	3	8	6	9
6	2	8	9	5	7	1	4	3
5	6	7	4	1	5	3	9	2
2	4	3	7	9	8	6	1	5
8	9	1	3	6	2	4	7	8
1	8	6	5	2	9	7	3	4
9	7	2	6	3	4	5	8	1
3	5	4	8	7	1	9	2	6

Figure 2. Example 9 × 9 completed Sudoku.

them some additional constraints (like limiting the amount of starting numbers and arranging the starting numbers so that there is rotational symmetry—see Figure 3) and renaming them *Sudoku* (translated as "single number"). When computer programs were developed in the 1990s to generate Sudoku puzzles, they became more popular and were soon featured in newspapers and puzzle books around the world.

Sudoku puzzles have an undeniable appeal. Their rules are easy to understand, yet puzzles can range from very easy to extremely difficult. They also are a type of language-independent and culture-independent logic puzzle—that is, once the basic rules are understood, neither language nor culture is a barrier to the solver. This is very different from the most popular type of puzzle that exists—the crossword puzzle. With crosswords, the solver must know not only the language of the puzzle to read the clues and provide answers, but also aspects of the appropriate culture. Sudoku puzzles transcend language and culture, enabling the solver to pick up a Sudoku puzzle from Japan, Germany, India, or any place in the world and know the goals and rules of the puzzle.

Language-independent logic puzzles have gained in popularity throughout the world over the past few decades. Today, there is even a World Puzzle Federation (WPF), an organization that advocates language-independent puzzles across the globe. The WPF sponsors a World Puzzle Competition every year in which teams of solvers from a number of countries meet to solve puzzles in friendly competition. One popular type of puzzle that appears in the competition every year is the Sudoku puzzle and its many variations.

Some people mistakenly believe that Sudoku puzzles are mathematical because they use numbers. But although numbers are the most typical characters used in Sudoku puzzles, they are not at all necessary. There are Sudoku puzzles that use letters, symbols, or even pictures as the elements that are placed in the grid (see Figure 4 for a Word Sudoku puzzle in which a nine-letter word appears in the solution). Nevertheless, Sudoku puzzles are extremely mathematical—in the number of possible placements of characters, the symmetry of the starting grids, and in the deductive reasoning that is used in finding the solution to a puzzle.

This book contains a few variations of Sudoku puzzles and Latin Squares that have additional

Figure 3. Example 9 × 9 Sudoku with starting numbers arranged in a rotationally symmetric pattern (see the answer key for the solution to this puzzle).

Figure 4. Word Sudoku puzzle (see the answer key for the solution to this puzzle).

Math and Logic Puzzles That Make Kids Think

mathematical elements in support of school mathematics. Each of the puzzle types included here involves a mathematical concept (or concepts) that contributes to the solution strategies for the puzzles. Some of these solution strategies are discussed in the opening section of each puzzle type, but other strategies are left for you and your students to discover and devise.

The puzzles in each section are assigned general difficulty levels. These levels represent our best attempt at classifications, but individual solvers may approach a puzzle with different strategies that might indicate a different difficulty level. This is a good thing and solvers are encouraged to explore the underlying mathematics and logic of the puzzles to find alternative strategies for solving. With each puzzle, there is exactly one solution—but there may be more than one way to arrive at that solution.

Using the Puzzles in Your Classroom

There are many ways in which these and other language-independent logic puzzles can be used in your classroom. At the most basic level, students can be challenged as solvers to find solutions to the puzzles. This is what we do when we pick up a puzzle magazine and work on puzzles—it's a solitary endeavor that can lead to some new insight about strategies and methods, but not always.

Another approach is to have students work collaboratively on puzzles or to have conversations about their solving methods. These approaches help students devise problem-solving strategies and develop their deductive and spatial reasoning skills by making arguments (about what they know and how they know it) to their peers. This practice forms the foundation of mathematical proof and argumentation—skills that become more important for students as they interact with more advanced levels of mathematics. With this approach, teachers often allow students to work together or independently on puzzles, while mediating conversations about the students' solving strategies. Questions that often are used as prompts in these conversations include:

- What is the first number that you filled in and how do you know that it must be placed there?
- Is there a row, column, or bordered region that looks like it might be one of the first ones that you may be able to complete and why?
- What are all of the different starting moves that you can make in a puzzle without knowing any information other than what is originally given?
- Is there a unique strategy that can be used in this puzzle and what about this puzzle allows for this strategy to be possible?

The most common question that is asked in this conversation is simply:

- How do you know that?

This basic prompt indicates to students that they must supply a sound mathematically deductive reason for a particular step. The explanation must be easy to follow, must account for any other possibilities, and must be defensible—conditions that students will be addressing when they are writing formal proofs in geometry and other mathematics classes.

These suggestions address the important logical aspect of the puzzles—the left-brain activities that are a natural part of most mathematical endeavors. But there also is a right-brain aspect of puzzles that can appeal to the creative nature of your students as well. After solving and discussing these puzzles, students also can be encouraged and challenged to create puzzles of their own for their peers to solve. Good puzzle design starts with an understanding of the underlying structure of the particular type of puzzle. From there, puzzle designers are challenged to find new approaches or new variations for solvers to experience. This is how the puzzles in Chapter 3—Shapedoku—came about. My colleague and I were exploring the different aspects of Sudoku variations and proposed a new puzzle type that forced the solver to look at the placements of a set of numbers while considering the geometric shape created by connecting the numbers in that set. We played around with that idea until we had developed Shapedoku—a variation that uses not the values of the numbers themselves (as with the other types in this book), but the figure created by the placement of the numbers.

Students don't have to create their own variation of Sudoku to use right-brain thinking strategies. They should start by picking one of the Sudoku variations included here and creating new examples. They will learn that the process is not an easy one—that even through their best efforts, it is not uncommon to create a puzzle that has more than one solution or does not have enough information to solve it. Information is included near the end of the introduction in each chapter about how students might approach designing puzzles of that type. As a teacher, you might have students solve one another's puzzles to check for uniqueness of solutions and devise a rating system for the difficulty of each puzzle. Students' puzzles could then be collected in a class puzzle book that could be shared with parents and other students.

Chapter 2

Greater Than Sudoku

The first variation is known as Greater Than Sudoku. It uses the basic rules of Sudoku puzzles (each number appears exactly once in each row, each column, and each bordered region) but also capitalizes on the ordering of the numbers that are used. Within each bordered region, greater than (and less than) signs are placed between any adjacent squares, indicating which of the two numbers is greater than the other (see the completed puzzle in Figure 5). The solver is originally given the grid with only the greater than signs placed throughout (see Figure 6) and is challenged to find the unique solution.

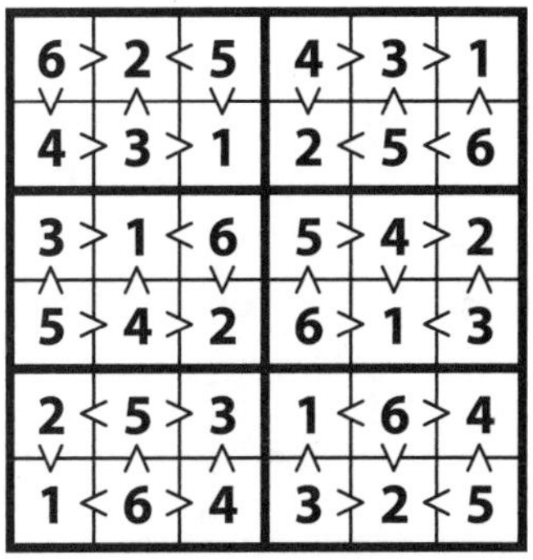

Solving the Example Puzzle

One of the easiest ways to start solving a Greater Than Sudoku is to consider the extremes—the highest and lowest values in the grid. In a 6 × 6 puzzle, the numbers range from 1 to 6, so it's helpful to consider which squares within each bordered region could have a 1 or a 6. In this example, we will look at the potential 6s in each bordered region. Because 6 is the largest number in this grid, each 6 must always have the ordering symbols pointing away from it. These squares (the potential 6s) have been marked

Figure 5. Example 6 × 6 Greater Than Sudoku solution.

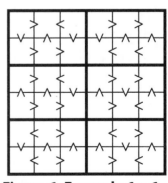

Figure 6. Example 6 × 6 Greater Than Sudoku starting grid.

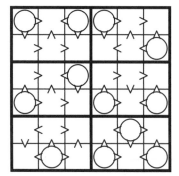

Figure 7. Potential 6s.

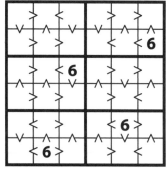

Figure 8. Some 6s.

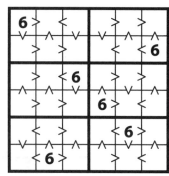

Figure 9. All 6s.

with a circle (Figure 7). Because there has to be a 6 in each row and column, there is only one choice for a 6 in the second row, the third row, the second column, and the fifth column (Figure 8). The remaining 6s are thus constrained by the need to have exactly one 6 in each row, column, and bordered region (Figure 9).

A similar approach can be used for locating the 1s in this puzzle. When all of the squares that have ordering symbols only pointing toward them are marked as potential 1s with a smaller inset square (Figure 10), the only 1 that can be immediately determined is at the bottom left, because it is the only square in which a 1 can be placed in the first column (Figure 11). The rest of the 1s can be determined by methodically eliminating each of the inset squares that would conflict with a 1 that is already placed, resulting in a solution with all 6s and 1s correctly determined (Figure 12).

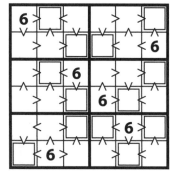

Figure 10. Potential 1s.

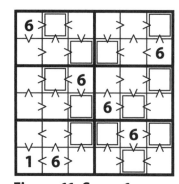

Figure 11. Some 1s.

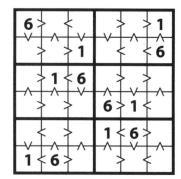

Figure 12. All 1s.

Next, we can turn our attention to the 5s. In the bordered region at the bottom right of the puzzle, the 5 cannot appear to the right of the 6 because it would then have to have another number greater than it appearing below it, so it must appear somewhere in the bottom row. We know it's not in the middle of the bottom row in this region, but it could be in either of the other two squares. This means that in the region at the bottom left of the puzzle, the 5 must appear in the *top* row. Looking at the ordering symbols in this row, we know that it has to appear in the middle. The only square in the left-center region of the puzzle that could contain a 5 is at the bottom left, forcing the 5 into the third column in the top-left region of the puzzle. The ordering symbols place it in the top row of the third column (Figure 13). The 5s on the right side of the puzzle can now be uniquely determined, using the given ordering symbols and the standard Sudoku rules—keeping exactly one 5 in each row, column, and region (Figure 14).

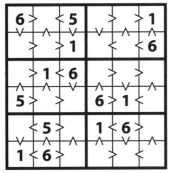

Figure 13. Three 5s.

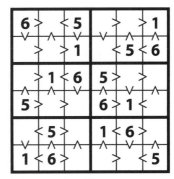

Figure 14. All 5s.

Similar logic can now be used for placing all of the 4s, starting with the regions on the right side of the puzzle. In the top region, a 4 must appear at the top left corner to satisfy all of the ordering symbols in that region. Consequently, in the top left region, the 4 must appear directly below the 6 (Figure 15). The rest of the 4s can now be uniquely determined, starting with the middle left region while using both the ordering symbols and the standard Sudoku rules (Figure 16).

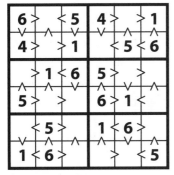

Figure 15. Some 4s.

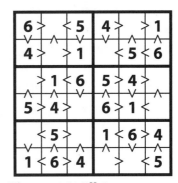

Figure 16. All 4s.

There are now three regions in the puzzle in which there are two connected squares left for the 2 and 3 in those regions (Figure 17). In each one, the 3 must be placed so that the ordering symbols point toward the 2. The remaining 3s can be uniquely determined according to the standard Sudoku rules (Figure 18).

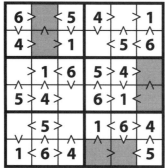

Figure 17. Shading for 2s and 3s.

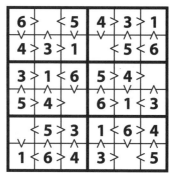

Figure 18. All 3s.

The rest of the grid can now be filled in with 2s to obtain the unique solution to the puzzle (see Figure 19).

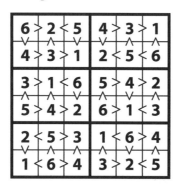

Figure 19. Solution to Greater Than Sudoku example puzzle.

These strategies—as well as others that are waiting to be discovered—can be used to solve the Greater Than Sudoku puzzles in this chapter. In each case, students are challenged to consider the ordering of numbers, the maximum and minimum values that can be used (even as those values shift while working on solutions to the puzzles), and the geometric placements of the numbers in the regions.

Creating Greater Than Sudoku Puzzles

Students also can be challenged to create Greater Than Sudoku puzzles for their classmates. One approach is to start by creating a Sudoku puzzle solution, then adding the appropriate ordering symbols. It must be noted, though, that this does not ensure a unique solution. The puzzle must be tested by solving it, using logic to check for uniqueness. For example, the puzzle below (Figure 20) may look like it has great potential as a Greater

Than Sudoku puzzle—but the final placement of 2s and 3s reveals a common problem that arises when creating these puzzles. In this case, there are four squares left unfilled (Figure 21). The placement of the ordering symbols creates the possibility of two different solutions (Figure 22). Either solution satisfies all of the conditions of the puzzle, but the puzzle is not actually solvable because more than one solution exists.

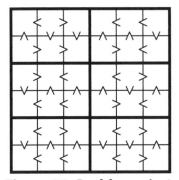

Figure 20. Problematic 6 × 6 Greater Than Sudoku puzzle.

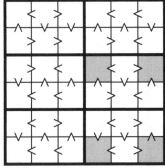

Figure 21. Trouble spots.

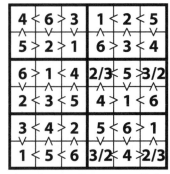

Figure 22. Two possible solutions.

Another approach to creating Greater Than Sudoku puzzles is to plan ahead for situations such as these and avoid them by deliberately placing numbers so that one solution exists. This approach takes time and is more difficult to master, but it forces the puzzle creator to think like a puzzle solver throughout the entire creation process. The best way to plan ahead for situations like this would be to have multiple instances of consecutive numbers appear in adjacent squares in the grid. In the previous example, had the shaded squares in Figure 21 appeared next to each other in the regions, the 2s and 3s would be uniquely determined.

Greater Than Sudoku–Level 1

Puzzle 1

Puzzle 2

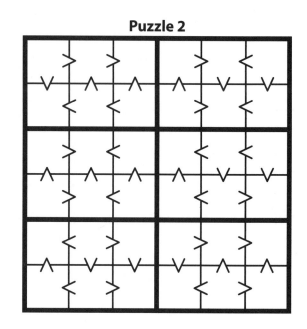

Puzzle 3

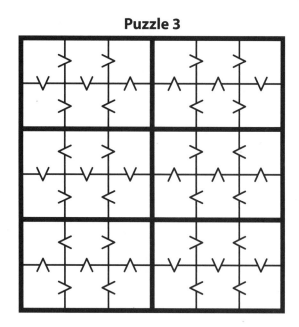

Puzzle 4

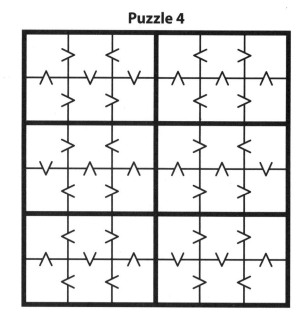

Greater Than Sudoku–Level 1

Puzzle 5

Puzzle 6

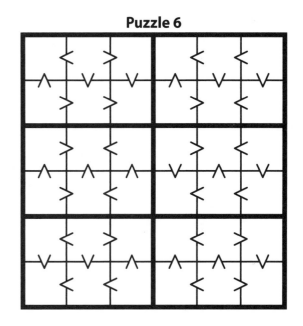

Puzzle 7

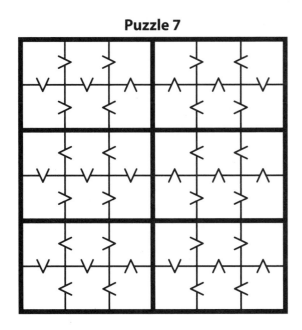

Puzzle 8

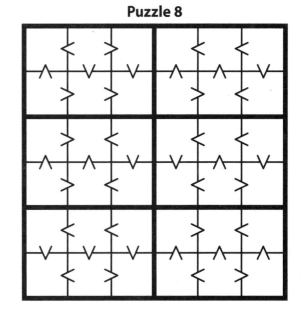

Greater Than Sudoku–Level 1

Puzzle 9

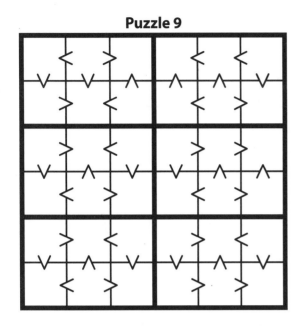

Puzzle 10

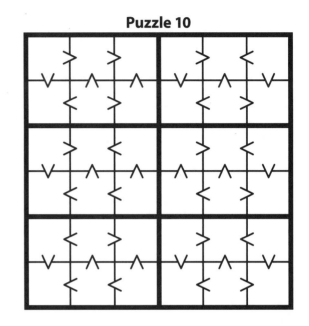

Greater Than Sudoku–Level 2

Puzzle 1

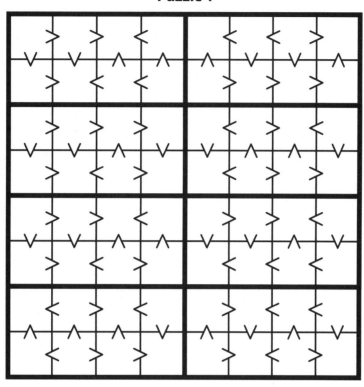

Puzzle 2

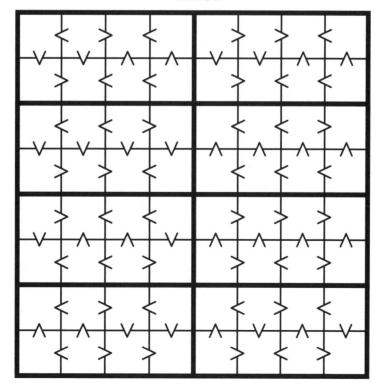

Name:_____ Date:_____

Greater Than Sudoku–Level 2

Puzzle 3

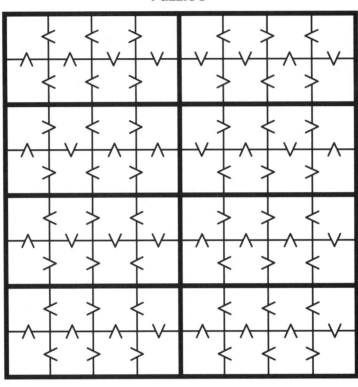

Puzzle 4

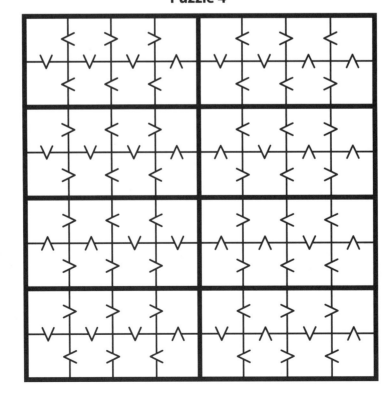

Math and Logic Puzzles That Make Kids Think © Prufrock Press Inc. • Permission is granted to photocopy or reproduce this page for single classroom use only.

Greater Than Sudoku–Level 2

Puzzle 5

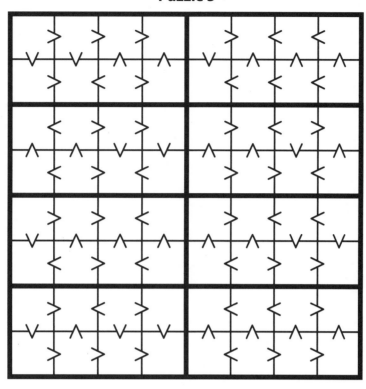

Puzzle 6

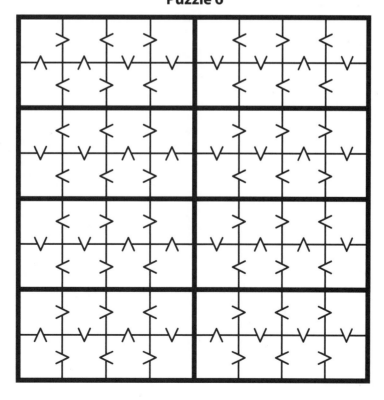

Greater Than Sudoku–Level 2

Puzzle 7

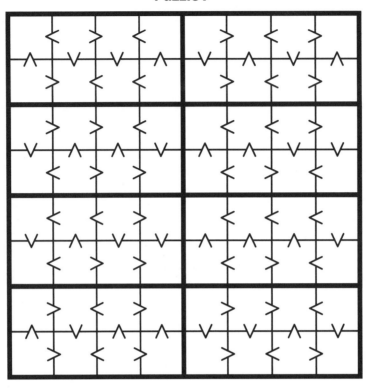

Puzzle 8

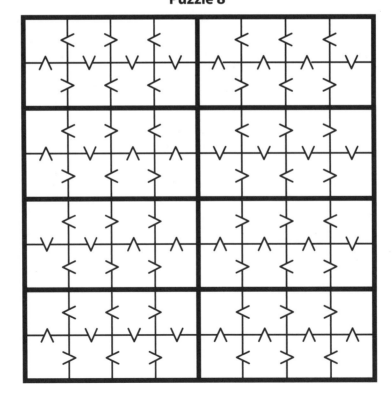

Greater Than Sudoku–Level 2

Puzzle 9

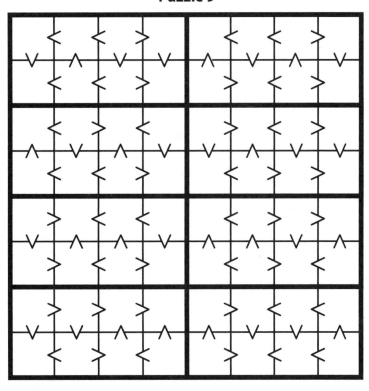

Puzzle 10

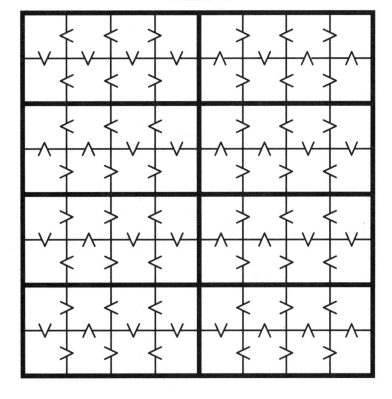

Greater Than Sudoku–Level 3

Puzzle 1

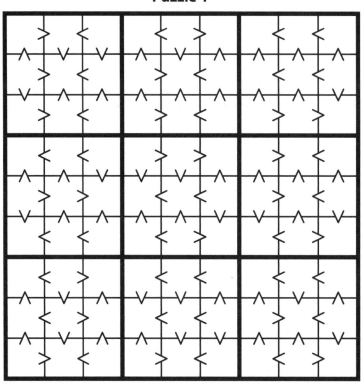

Puzzle 2

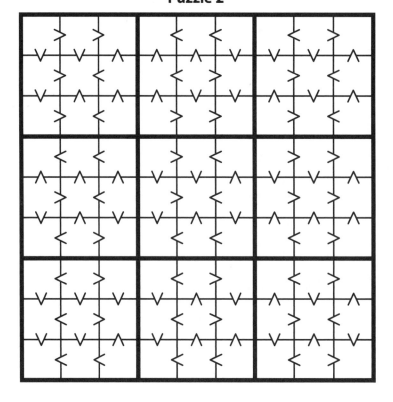

Greater Than Sudoku-Level 3

Puzzle 3

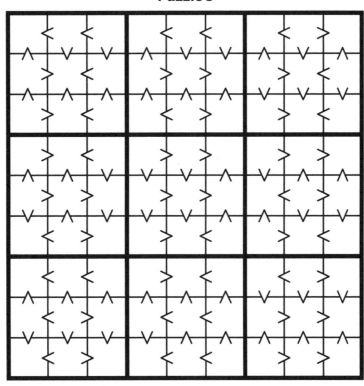

Puzzle 4

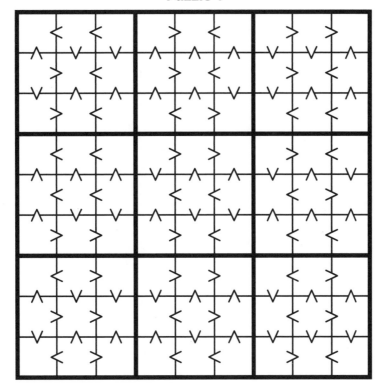

Greater Than Sudoku–Level 3

Puzzle 5

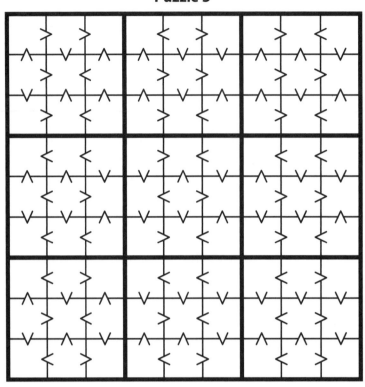

Puzzle 6

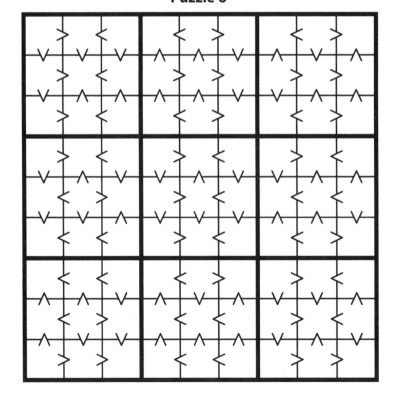

Greater Than Sudoku—Level 3

Puzzle 7

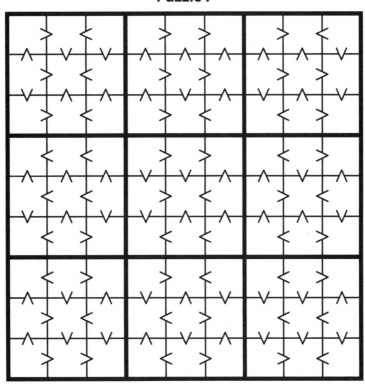

Puzzle 8

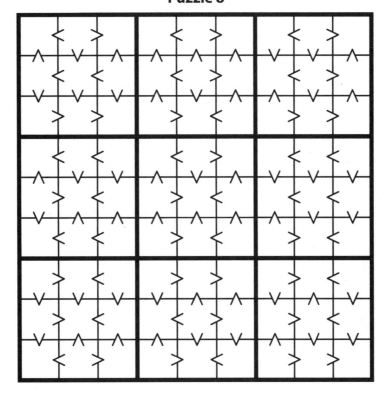

Greater Than Sudoku—Level 3

Puzzle 9

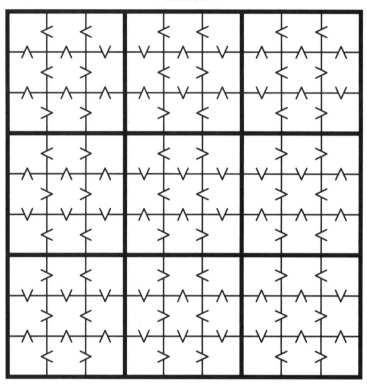

Puzzle 10

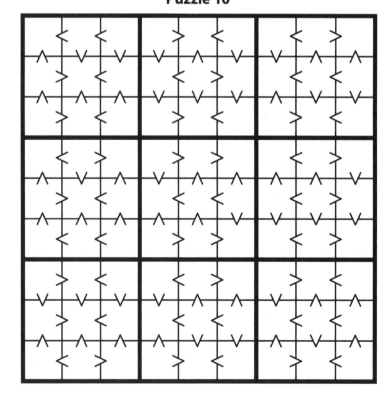

Chapter 3

Shapedoku

This puzzle type is based on the Latin Square design—each number appears exactly once in each row and in each column. In Shapedoku puzzles, there are no bordered regions to provide additional constraints on number placement. Instead, you are given clues about the shape that is made by connecting numbers in the grid.

				④
		①		
			④	
③		②		⑤

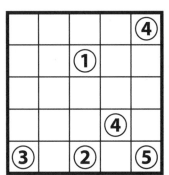

1–Quadrilateral
2–Parallelogram
3–Rectangle
4–Isosceles right triangle
5–Rectangle

Figure 23. Shapedoku example.

In the 5 × 5 in Figure 23, you are given a starting grid with six circled numbers already placed. You also are given a list of shapes that are created by connecting the centers of the squares containing all of the *noncircled numbers* of each kind in the solution (Figure 24). The shape names that are given are the *most specific names* that could be used. For example, the parallelogram and rectangles also are quadrilaterals, but they have additional attributes that allow them to be called by these more specific names. A detailed description of these attributes is given following the discussion of the solution strategy for this puzzle.

2	1	5	3	④
4	2	①	5	3
5	3	4	2	1
1	5	3	④	2
③	4	②	1	⑤

Figure 24. Shapedoku example solution.

Solving the Example Puzzle

In solving this puzzle, it is best to start with some of the standard

Sudoku rules, filling in numbers so that each number appears exactly once in each row and column. In this case, the bottom row still needs a 1 and a 4. Since there already is a 4 in the fourth column, there is one way to fill in the bottom row (Figure 25). The third column needs a 4 and there is only one open row that doesn't already have a 4. This leaves one square in the first column without a 4—which also completes the placement of the three 4s, creating an isosceles right triangle (Figure 26).

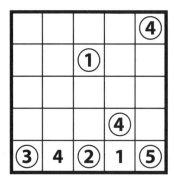

Figure 25. Bottom row completed.

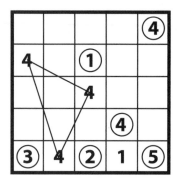

Figure 26. All 4s.

With one 1 already filled in, it seems like the 1s would be the next logical set to work on. However, the shape created by the 1s is defined only as a quadrilateral—thus giving us no additional clues about what the shape looks like, other than the fact that it must have four sides. Instead, we might want to consider our possibilities with the 3s, which must make a rectangle. When we eliminate the first column and bottom row—which already include a 3 as a given in the starting grid—we can get a clearer picture of which squares we have to work with, the nonshaded ones in Figure 27. Because no two 3s can appear in the same row or column, we know that the rectangle cannot be oriented with horizontal and vertical sides—it must appear on a slant. After some exploration, we find that the only way this can be done so that all of the 3s appear in empty squares is as shown in Figure 28.

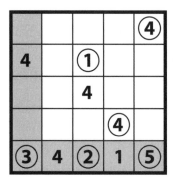

Figure 27. Possible placement of 3s.

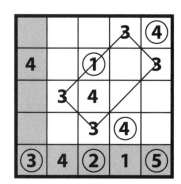

Figure 28. All 3s.

We can follow the same approach to locate the 5s that also are arranged as a rectangle, eliminating the row and column in which the circled 5 already appears (Figure 29) and finding the only way to place the 5s so that they form a rectangle (Figure 30).

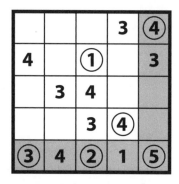

Figure 29. Possible placement of 5s.

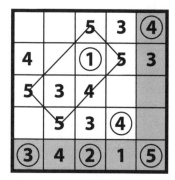

Figure 30. All 5s.

The rest of the puzzle can now be filled in following the standard Sudoku rules. It is helpful to note that the four noncircled 2s can be connected to make a parallelogram (Figure 31), albeit a very narrow one. This can be verified by noting that the opposite sides are congruent and parallel (they have the same slope). You also can see that the figure created by connecting the noncircled 1s (Figure 32) is a quadrilateral with no other noteworthy characteristics (i.e., no parallel sides, no congruent sides). It does happen to have a right angle (at the bottom left) but that is not enough to classify it as any other type of quadrilateral.

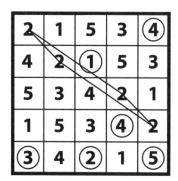

Figure 31. All 2s.

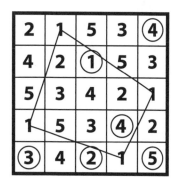

Figure 32. All 1s.

It is important to understand the definitions and properties of the various shapes that are used in Shapedoku puzzles. They are:

Triangle: A three-sided polygon

Isosceles Triangle: A triangle with exactly two congruent sides

Right Triangle: A triangle with one right angle

Isosceles Right Triangle: A triangle with exactly two congruent sides and a right angle

Quadrilateral: A four-sided polygon

Parallelogram: A quadrilateral with two pairs of parallel opposite sides (opposite sides are congruent)

Rectangle: A parallelogram with four right angles

Rhombus: A parallelogram with four congruent sides

Square: A parallelogram with four right angles and four congruent sides

Kite: A quadrilateral with two pairs of adjacent congruent sides

Trapezoid: A quadrilateral with exactly one pair of parallel opposite sides[1] (which are not congruent)

Right Trapezoid: A trapezoid with two right angles

Isosceles Trapezoid: A trapezoid with congruent nonparallel sides

Creating Shapedoku Puzzles

As you will see in the rest of this chapter, larger Shapedoku puzzles are not necessarily more difficult. There are some interesting challenges that arise with 4 × 4 Shapedoku puzzles. Your students may want to experiment with different sizes of grids to see which puzzles are more challenging to create.

Once a grid size has been chosen, there are several ways to approach the creation of Shapedoku puzzles—either placing all of the numbers first and then identifying some shapes that can be found in the puzzle or creating a puzzle with specific shapes and arrangements in mind. Either way, a puzzle must be checked to ensure that there is exactly one solution.

---

1   Some sources use a different definition of trapezoid—one that allows for more than one pair of parallel opposite sides. This book uses the definition that is used most frequently in U.S. classrooms.

Shapedoku—Level 1

Puzzle 1

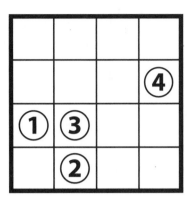

1—Right triangle
2—Triangle
3—Isosceles triangle
4—Isosceles right triangle

Puzzle 2

1—Isosceles right triangle
2—Isosceles triangle
3—Isosceles triangle
4—Isosceles right triangle

Puzzle 3

1—Isosceles triangle
2—Isosceles triangle
3—Right triangle
4—Isosceles right triangle

Puzzle 4

1—Isosceles right triangle
2—Isosceles triangle
3—Isosceles triangle
4—Isosceles triangle

Shapedoku–Level 1

Puzzle 5

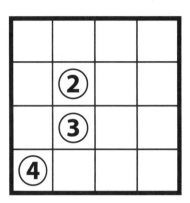

1—Quadrilateral
2—Isosceles triangle
3—Isosceles triangle
4—Isosceles triangle

Puzzle 6

1—Isosceles triangle
2—Isosceles right triangle
3—Triangle
4—Quadrilateral

Puzzle 7

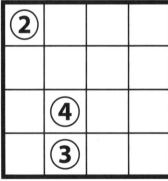

1—Quadrilateral
2—Isosceles triangle
3—Isosceles right triangle
4—Isosceles triangle

Puzzle 8

1—Rhombus
2—Right triangle
3—Rectangle
4—Isosceles triangle

Shapedoku–Level 1

Puzzle 9

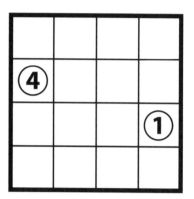

1—Isosceles right triangle
2—Rhombus
3—Square
4—Isosceles right triangle

Puzzle 10

1—Triangle
2—Square
3—Rhombus
4—Isosceles triangle

Shapedoku–Level 2

Puzzle 1

④		①		
	⑤			②
③				⑤

1—Parallelogram
2—Parallelogram
3—Rhombus
4—Rhombus
5—Isosceles triangle

Puzzle 2

⑤				②
		④		
③	⑤			①

1—Rectangle
2—Square
3—Rectangle
4—Rectangle
5—Isosceles triangle

Puzzle 3

⑤				
③		①		②
		④		
④			②	

1—Quadrilateral
2—Right Triangle
3—Quadrilateral
4—Isosceles right triangle
5—Square

Puzzle 4

			①	
		②	③	
		③		
⑤		④		

1—Quadrilateral
2—Rectangle
3—Isosceles triangle
4—Parallelogram
5—Rectangle

Shapedoku–Level 2

Puzzle 5

⑤				
		⑤	④	②
③	②			①

1—Rhombus
2—Right triangle
3—Rhombus
4—Isosceles trapezoid
5—Isosceles triangle

Puzzle 6

			③	
④	②			
	①		④	
				③
⑤				①

1—Isosceles triangle
2—Quadrilateral
3—Right isosceles triangle
4—Right triangle
5—Quadrilateral

Puzzle 7

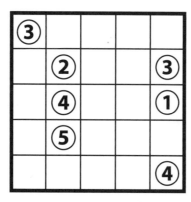

③				
	②			③
	④			①
	⑤			
				④

1—Parallelogram
2—Isosceles trapezoid
3—Isosceles triangle
4—Isosceles triangle
5—Kite

Puzzle 8

				⑤
⑤				
		④	①	
②				③

1—Quadrilateral
2—Square
3—Rectangle
4—Square
5—Isosceles triangle

Shapedoku–Level 2

Name:_____   Date:_____

Puzzle 9

1—Square
2—Quadrilateral
3—Parallelogram
4—Isosceles triangle
5—Isosceles triangle

Puzzle 10

1—Right isosceles triangle
2—Isosceles trapezoid
3—Quadrilateral
4—Isosceles triangle
5—Isosceles trapezoid

Shapedoku—Level 3

Puzzle 1

1—Parallelogram
2—Square
3—Quadrilateral
4—Square
5—Quadrilateral
6—Rectangle

Puzzle 2

1—Parallelogram
2—Quadrilateral
3—Parallelogram
4—Parallelogram
5—Quadrilateral
6—Quadrilateral

Puzzle 3

1—Square
2—Quadrilateral
3—Trapezoid
4—Quadrilateral
5—Quadrilateral
6—Rectangle

Shapedoku—Level 3

Puzzle 4

					⑤
⑤	④				
	⑥	③		①	
		⑥	③		
	②				
②				④	①

1—Parallelogram
2—Rectangle
3—Rectangle
4—Quadrilateral
5—Square
6—Quadrilateral

Puzzle 5

④					
⑥	①				
③		②	⑥		
			①		
					⑤
⑤	③		②		④

1—Quadrilateral
2—Parallelogram
3—Parallelogram
4—Rectangle
5—Rectangle
6—Right trapezoid

Puzzle 6

	①				③
④			①		
			③	⑥	②
		⑥		⑤	
		④			
②	⑤				

1—Quadrilateral
2—Parallelogram
3—Isosceles trapezoid
4—Quadrilateral
5—Quadrilateral
6—Quadrilateral

Shapedoku–Level 3

Puzzle 7

		⑥			⑤
⑤			②		
		③			④
			③	④	
			⑥		①
①	②				

1—Square
2—Quadrilateral
3—Square
4—Parallelogram
5—Square
6—Quadrilateral

Puzzle 8

④			②		
		②	①		
					⑤
	④			⑤	①
	⑥			③	
⑥			③		

1—Quadrilateral
2—Parallelogram
3—Trapezoid
4—Quadrilateral
5—Parallelogram
6—Rectangle

Shapedoku–Level 3

Puzzle 9

	①				③
		⑥		④	
		⑤	②		
	⑤			③	
①					⑥
②		④			

1—Quadrilateral
2—Rectangle
3—Parallelogram
4—Right trapezoid
5—Quadrilateral
6—Quadrilateral

Puzzle 10

③		④			
					①
④			⑤		⑥
	③		②		
		①		②	
		⑤		⑥	

1—Parallelogram
2—Isosceles trapezoid
3—Parallelogram
4—Kite
5—Parallelogram
6—Quadrilateral

Chapter 4

Killer Sudoku

In this Sudoku variation, solvers must use their knowledge of basic addition and subtraction along with their deductive reasoning skills. Puzzle grids include the bordered regions, as in Sudoku puzzles, but they also include additional regions surrounded by dotted lines in which the sum of the numbers in each of the regions also is given. Finally, no number can be repeated in a dotted region.

At the right is an example of a 6 × 6 Killer Sudoku puzzle (Figure 33). In the solution to this puzzle, each of the numbers 1–6 is used once in each row, column, and bordered region. Also, no number is repeated in a dotted region (see Figure 34).

Solving the Example Puzzle

When solving a 6 × 6 Killer Sudoku puzzle, one of the most important pieces of information to know is that $1 + 2 + 3 + 4 + 5 + 6 = 21$. Because each row, column, and bordered region must contain each of the numbers 1–6, then you know that each row, column, and bordered region must sum to 21. This is helpful, for example, when considering the first column in the puzzle, which includes two of three numbers that sum to 9 (at the top), two

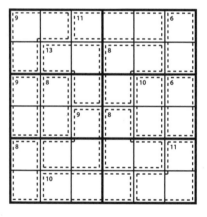

Figure 33. Killer Sudoku example.

<table>
<tr><td>¹⁹ 1</td><td>5</td><td>¹¹ 2</td><td>6</td><td>3</td><td>⁶ 4</td></tr>
<tr><td>3</td><td>¹³ 4</td><td>6</td><td>⁸ 1</td><td>5</td><td>2</td></tr>
<tr><td>⁹ 5</td><td>⁸ 6</td><td>3</td><td>2</td><td>¹⁰ 4</td><td>⁶ 1</td></tr>
<tr><td>4</td><td>2</td><td>⁹ 1</td><td>⁸ 3</td><td>6</td><td>5</td></tr>
<tr><td>⁸ 2</td><td>3</td><td>5</td><td>4</td><td>1</td><td>¹¹ 6</td></tr>
<tr><td>6</td><td>¹⁰ 1</td><td>4</td><td>5</td><td>2</td><td>3</td></tr>
</table>

Figure 34. Killer Sudoku example solution.

numbers that sum to 9 (in the middle), and two numbers that sum to 8 (at the bottom). Because 9 + 9 + 8 = 26 and since the first column must sum to 21, we know that the number in the dotted region at the top left of the puzzle that is not in the first column must be 5 (26 – 21). A similar situation with the sixth column shows that the fifth number in the bottom row is a 2 (Figure 35).

This is a good time to note that in most Killer Sudoku puzzles (including all of the ones in this book), there is a symmetry to the dotted regions. Typically, as it is in this example, the symmetry is 180° rotational—which means that the entire set of dotted outlines could be turned upside-down and matched onto itself (not the indicated sums or the numbers inside of the dotted regions, but the outlines of the dotted regions themselves). This can be helpful when solving Killer Sudoku puzzles, because a strategy that is used in one part of the puzzle, may be able to be used again in the part that is symmetrically opposite (as demonstrated in Figure 35).

With the 5 in the top row, the dotted region in which is it placed now needs two numbers that sum to 4. Our only option is a 1 and a 3 (you cannot use 2 + 2 because 2 cannot be repeated in a column or in a dotted region). We don't know which box contains which number yet (Figure 36), but eliminating the 1 and the 3 in the first column helps fill in some other information. Below that region is another dotted region with two numbers that sum to 9. With 1 and 3 out of the picture, that leaves only 4 and 5. Again, we don't know which number to place in which box (Figure 36), but their elimination in the first column leaves only 2 and 6 for the remaining boxes in the first column. If the 2 were placed in the bottom row, it would conflict with the 2 that is already in the puzzle, so the 6 must be placed in the bottom row with the 2 above it (Figure 36).

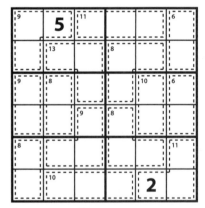

Figure 35. First move.

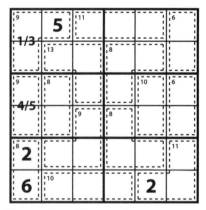

Figure 36. First column.

Continuing with the bottom row, we have placed a 2 and a 6. There also is a dotted region with a sum of 10—together these account for five squares with a sum of 18, leaving a 3 to be placed at the bottom right with a 6 above the 3 to complete the dotted region with a sum of 11 (Figure 37).

We turn our attention now to the middle region on the left side of the grid. The dotted region in the second column with a sum of 8 can only use a 2 and a 6 (in some order), leaving a 1 and a 3 also to be placed in this bordered region. If the 1 were to be placed in the third row, it would be part of a dotted region with a sum of 13—and there is no combination of two different numbers that could be used to complete this dotted region. So the 1 must be placed in the fourth row, leaving the 3 in the third row (Figure 38). To complete the dotted region in which the 3 is placed, a 4 and a 6 must be used—but the 6 cannot be in the second column, because it would conflict with a 6 that we already know has to appear in that column (Figure 38). This leaves a 2 to be placed in the top left bordered region (Figure 38).

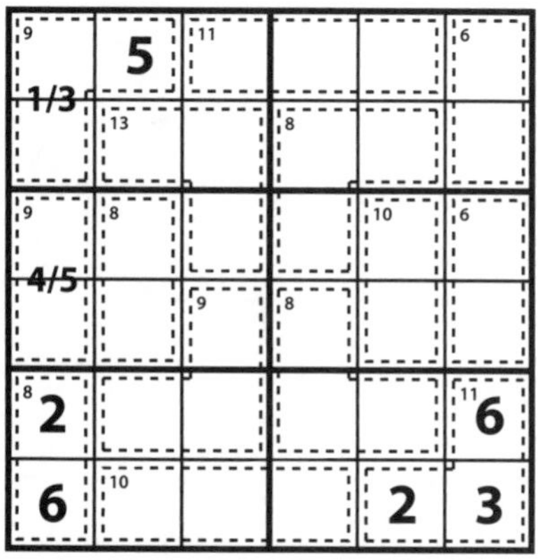

Figure 37. Bottom right corner.

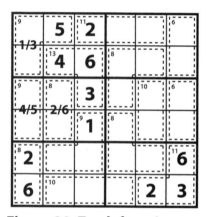

Figure 38. Top left region.

The second column still needs a 1 and a 3—only one placement of these will not conflict with the 3 already in the bottom row (Figure 39). The third column still needs a 4 and a 5. The 5 needs to be placed in the fifth row to create the sum of 9 in the dotted region (Figure 39).

The bottom row needs a 5 to complete it (and finish the dotted region with a sum of 10) (Figure 40). The bordered region at the bottom right

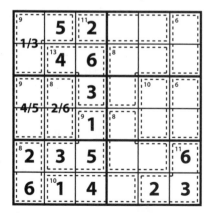

Figure 39. Bottom left region.

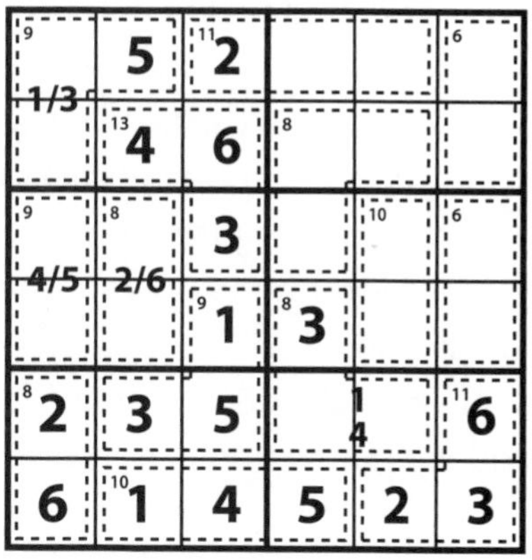

Figure 40. Bottom right region.

still needs a 1 and a 4, but their positions are not yet known. However, they are two of the three squares needed to sum to 8, which requires a 3 to be placed in the fourth row, fourth column (Figure 40).

In the top row, the dotted region with a sum of 11 already has one number placed, a 2. The other two squares need to sum to 9. They cannot be 4 and 5, because this would conflict with the 5 that is already in the top row, so they must be 3 and 6. The 3 must be placed in the fifth column to avoid conflicting with the 3 already in the fourth column (Figure 41). With the 3 in the top row, we now know how to arrange the 1 and 3 in the top left region (Figure 41).

We still need a 4 in the top row, leaving it for the top right corner. Because it sums to 6 with a 2, we place the 2 below it (Figure 42). This leaves a 1 and 5 needing to be placed in the sixth column. The 1 must go in the third row to avoid conflict with the 1 already in the fourth row (Figure 42). We also now know how to arrange the 4 and 5 in the first column (Figure 42).

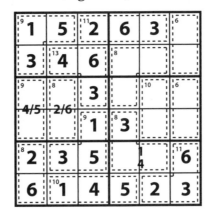

Figure 41. Top row.　　　　**Figure 42. Sixth column.**

The second row still needs a 1 and 5 and they must be placed in that order to avoid conflict with the 5 in the bottom row (Figure 43). They also appear in a dotted region that sums to 8, requiring a 2 to be placed in the third row, fourth column (Figure 43). This leaves a 4 and 6 in the middle-right bordered region and the 4 must be placed in the third row so it doesn't conflict with the 4 already in the fourth row (Figure 43).

To complete the puzzle the last two sets of undecided numbers need to be placed to avoid conflict with other numbers in their respective rows and columns (Figure 44).

In addition to knowing the sum of the numbers in each row, column, and bordered region for a given puzzle size, it also is helpful to know some combinations of numbers for specific sums. The tables of possible addends shown on p. 42 were created to be used with 6 × 6 Killer Sudoku

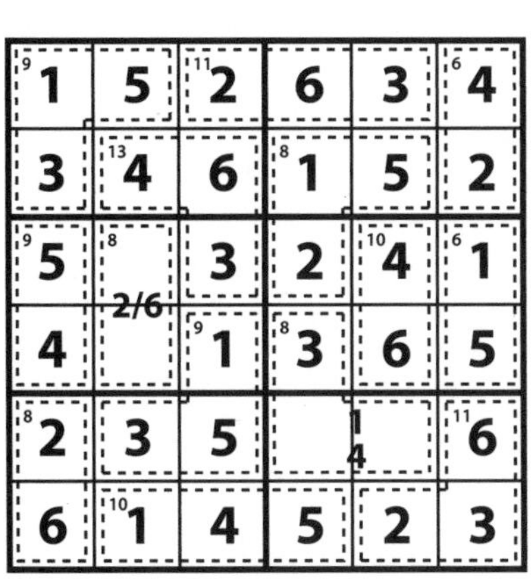

Figure 43. Middle right region.

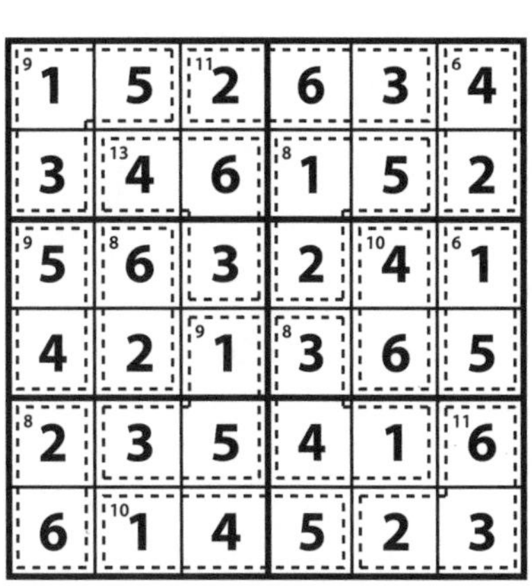

Figure 44. Completed puzzle.

puzzles. Students might be interested in creating their own tables of addends for other sizes of Killer Sudoku puzzles.

Creating Killer Sudoku Puzzles

Although symmetry of dotted regions is not a requirement for Killer Sudoku Puzzles, it generally is considered good form and good practice. This adds an extra challenge for creators of Killer Sudoku puzzles. Some creators choose to start with a legitimate Sudoku grid and then add the dotted regions in a symmetric pattern. The difficulty of the puzzle often is a reflection of the sizes of the dotted regions (smaller dotted regions tend to make for easier puzzles) and the amount of dotted regions that overlap the bordered regions in the grid (puzzles with a lot of dotted regions that overlap a number of bordered regions tend to be more difficult). Puzzles created this way also must be checked for solvability and unique solutions.

The other approach to creating Killer Sudoku puzzles is to build dotted regions in a symmetric pattern with specific solving strategies in mind. This is a more difficult way to create Killer Sudoku puzzles, but the puzzles that are created this way often are more satisfying and interesting.

Sum Combinations for 6 × 6 Killer Sudoku Puzzles

Two Addends

Sum			
3	1 + 2		
4	1 + 3		
5	1 + 4	2 + 3	
6	1 + 5	2 + 4	
7	1 + 6	2 + 5	3 + 4
8	2 + 6	3 + 5	
9	3 + 6	4 + 5	
10	4 + 6		
11	5 + 6		

Three Addends

Sum			
6	1 + 2 + 3		
7	1 + 2 + 4		
8	1 + 2 + 5	1 + 3 + 4	
9	1 + 2 + 6	1 + 3 + 5	2 + 3 + 4
10	1 + 3 + 6	1 + 4 + 5	2 + 3 + 5
11	1 + 4 + 6	2 + 3 + 6	2 + 4 + 5
12	1 + 5 + 6	2 + 4 + 6	3 + 4 + 5
13	2 + 5 + 6	3 + 4 + 6	
14	3 + 5 + 6		
15	4 + 5 + 6		

Four Addends

Sum			
10	1 + 2 + 3 + 4		
11	1 + 2 + 3 + 5		
12	1 + 2 + 3 + 6	1 + 2 + 4 + 5	
13	1 + 2 + 4 + 6	1 + 3 + 4 + 5	
14	1 + 2 + 5 + 6	1 + 3 + 4 + 6	2 + 3 + 4 + 5
15	1 + 3 + 5 + 6	2 + 3 + 4 + 6	
16	1 + 4 + 5 + 6	2 + 3 + 5 + 6	
17	2 + 4 + 5 + 6		
18	3 + 4 + 5 + 6		

Five Addends

Sum	
15	1 + 2 + 3 + 4 + 5
16	1 + 2 + 3 + 4 + 6
17	1 + 2 + 3 + 5 + 6
18	1 + 2 + 4 + 5 + 6
19	1 + 3 + 4 + 5 + 6
20	2 + 3 + 4 + 5 + 6

Killer Sudoku—Level 1

Puzzle 1

Puzzle 2

Puzzle 3

Puzzle 4

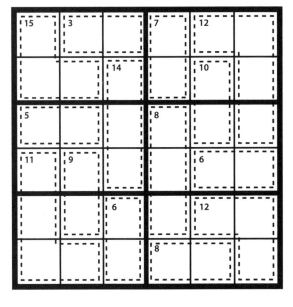

Killer Sudoku–Level 1

Puzzle 5

Puzzle 6

Puzzle 7

Puzzle 8

Killer Sudoku–Level 1

Puzzle 9

Puzzle 10

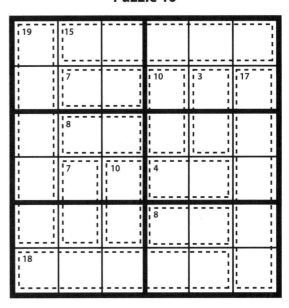

Killer Sudoku–Level 2

Puzzle 1

Puzzle 2

Math and Logic Puzzles That Make Kids Think © Prufrock Press Inc. • Permission is granted to photocopy or reproduce this page for single classroom use only.

Killer Sudoku–Level 2

Puzzle 3

Puzzle 4

Killer Sudoku-Level 2

Puzzle 5

Puzzle 6

Killer Sudoku–Level 2

Puzzle 7

Puzzle 8

Killer Sudoku-Level 2

Puzzle 9

12	22				18	3	9
	15						
13			3		26		
		14				9	
9		21		7		22	
			11		6		
14	5	15				27	7

Puzzle 10

16			9	4	8	21	
	11					9	
5		26			16		
11		13				14	
9				18		10	
14	14					5	
		9	10	10	8		18

Killer Sudoku–Level 3

Puzzle 1

Puzzle 2

Killer Sudoku–Level 3

Puzzle 3

Puzzle 4

Killer Sudoku–Level 3

Puzzle 5

Puzzle 6

Killer Sudoku–Level 3

Puzzle 7

Puzzle 8

Killer Sudoku–Level 3

Puzzle 9

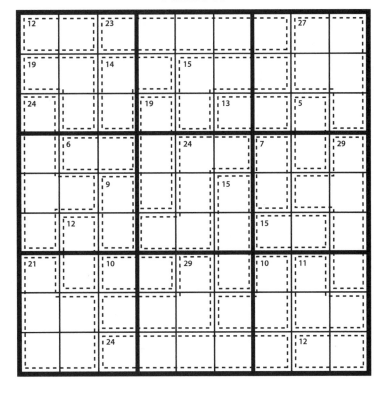

Puzzle 10

Chapter 5

Calcudoku

This variation is similar to the Killer Sudoku in that there are clues about how the numbers in different squares combine with a mathematical operation—except with Calcudoku, operations other than addition will be involved. This variation also is more closely related to a Latin Square than a Sudoku puzzle in that there are no additional bordered regions in which one number of every kind must appear. The bordered regions that do appear in Calcudoku simply group numbers together for each indicated mathematical operation and its outcome. Unlike Killer Sudoku, though, a number may be repeated in any of these regions (but not in a row or column).

Below is an example of a 6 × 6 Calcudoku puzzle (Figure 45). The operations that are used in a given Calcudoku always appear above and to the right of the puzzle. As you can see in the solution to this Calcudoku puzzle (Figure 46), each of the numbers 1–6 is used once in each row and column. Each bordered region includes an outcome and an operation—indicating the sum, difference, product, or quotient of the numbers in the bordered region. You also will note several examples of numbers being repeated in a bordered region—but never in a row or column (see the 1s in the region at the bottom left and the 4s in the region in the center of the grid).

Solving the Example Puzzle

The region at the bottom left corner actually provides a good starting

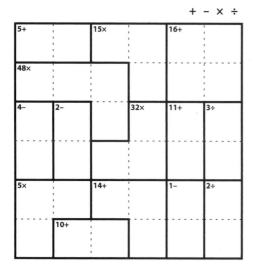

Figure 45. Calcudoku example.

Figure 46. Calcudoku example solution.

point for solving this puzzle. The three squares in this L-shaped region have a product of 5. Because 5 is a prime number, the only way to multiply three integers and result in a product of 5 is to use one 5 and two 1s. Because the 1s cannot appear in the same row or column, there is only one way to place them in the grid (Figure 47). The region in the middle of the first column uses two numbers with a difference of 4—which must be either 1 and 5 or 2 and 6. Because the 1 and 5 are already placed in this column, we know that the 2 and 6 are in this region (although we don't know their exact placement; see Figure 47). The region in the bottom row with a sum of 10 must be 4 and 6, although their exact placement is not yet known either (Figure 47). This strategy of making notes about possible placements is a very useful one with Calcudoku puzzles. Because the regions simply indicate the outcomes, we often can determine the numbers to be used in a region, but their exact placement may not be known until later in the solution process.

In the top left corner, there is a region of squares with a sum of 5. The two options for this possibility are 1 and 4 or 2 and 3. A 1 already appears in both the first and second columns, so it must be 2 and 3. Because a 2 already appears in the first column, there is only one way to place these numbers (Figure 48). Because we don't have a 4

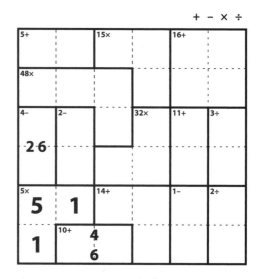

Figure 47. Bottom left corner.

Math and Logic Puzzles That Make Kids Think

yet in the first column, it must be placed in the second row (Figure 48).

In the center region in the top two rows, there are three squares with a product of 15. Because 15 is the product of two prime numbers, these three squares must contain 1, 3, and 5 (in some order). There already is a 3 in the first row, so the 3 in this region must appear in the square in the second row and the 1 and 5 must appear in some order in the top row (Figure 49). This leaves 4 and 6 to finish out the two open squares in the first row (Figure 49). The region in the top right corner of the grid contains four squares with a sum of 16—the top two squares contain 4 and 6—this leaves the bottom two with a sum of 6. The only possibilities that wouldn't conflict with the 4 already in the second row are 1 and 5 in some order (Figure 49).

The second row still needs 2 and 6. We place the 2 in the third column so that it doesn't conflict with the 2 already in the second column (Figure 50). We can finish the region that contains this 2 and 6 now—it covers four squares with a product of 48, leaving a 1 for the square in the third row, third column (Figure 50). This determines the order of the 1 and 5 in the top row (Figure 50). We also can indicate that 3 and 5 are the two remaining numbers to be placed in some order in the second column (Figure 50). The 4 and 6 in the bottom can also be fixed to avoid conflicting with 6 already in the second column.

In the third column, 3 and 4 have yet to be placed. The square in the fourth row is part of a region that has a product of 32. Because 4 is a factor of 32 and 3 is not, 4 is in the fourth row and 3 is in the fifth row (Figure 51). The region in the center with a product of 32 now has one square filled in. The remaining two squares must have a product of 8, so they must be 2 and 4. The 4 must be placed in the third row so that it doesn't conflict with the 4 in the fourth row (Figure 51). This determines the order of the 2

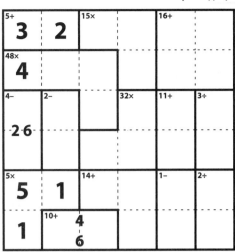

Figure 48. Top left corner.

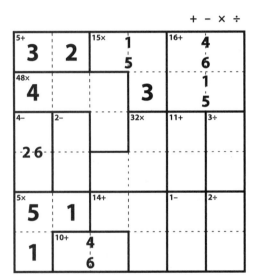

Figure 49. Top right corner.

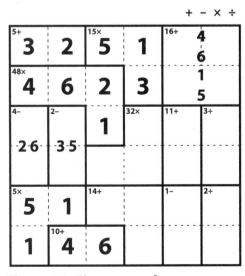

Figure 50. First two columns.

and 6 in the first column (Figure 51). The fourth column still needs a 5 and a 6—the 6 must be placed in the fifth row so that it doesn't conflict with the 6 already in the bottom row (Figure 51).

In the middle of the fifth column, there are two numbers with a sum of 11. The only possibility is 5 and 6—the 6 must be placed in the third row so that it doesn't conflict with the 6 already in the fourth row (Figure 52). This determines the order of the 3 and 5 in the second column (Figure 52). The third and fourth rows must be completed with a 3 and a 1 respectively (Figure 52). The 4 and 6 and the 1 and 5 are now uniquely determined in the top right corner of the puzzle. (Figure 52).

The squares in the bottom right corner are now uniquely determined, making sure that each number appears exactly once in each row and column (Figure 53).

This entire solution strategy demonstrates several important approaches when solving Calcudoku—but it is not the only series of steps that could be taken to solve this puzzle. For example, the two regions in the sixth column that use division could have been utilized earlier in the puzzle to determine the placements of some of the numbers. There are only several combinations of numbers in a 6 × 6 puzzle that have a quotient of 2 (1 and 2, 2 and 4, and 3 and 6) and there are fewer with a quotient of 3 (1 and 3, 2 and 6). Regions marked with division signs can be very helpful when solving Calcudoku puzzles.

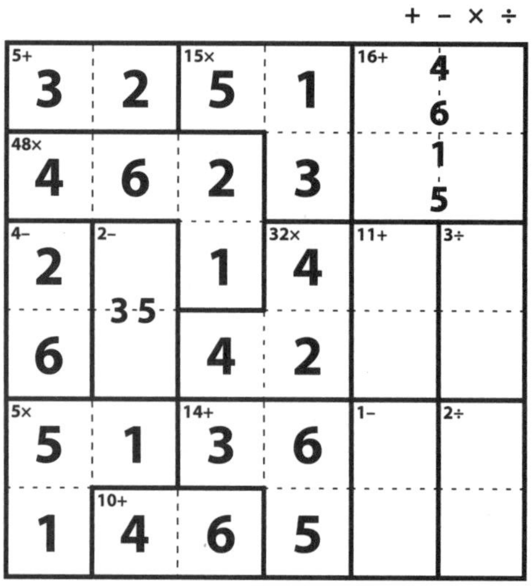

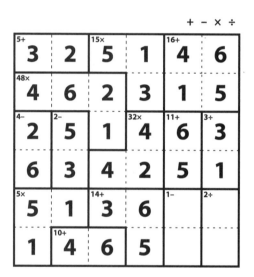

Figure 51. Middle two columns.

Figure 52. Middle two rows.

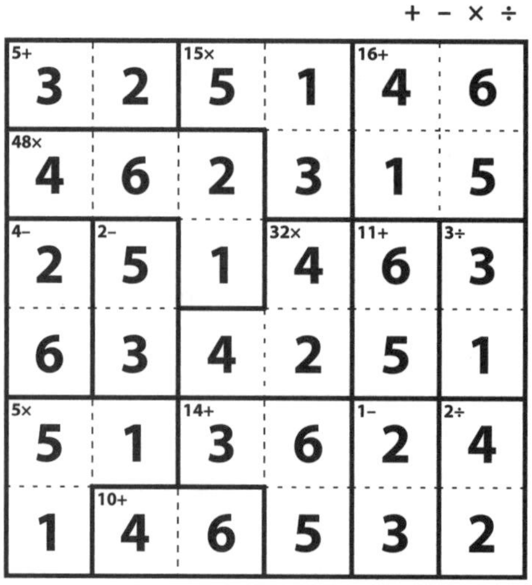

Figure 53. Completed puzzle.

Math and Logic Puzzles That Make Kids Think

Creating Calcudoku Puzzles

Unlike Killer Sudoku puzzles, Calcudoku puzzles do not necessarily utilize any symmetry of the regions defined by an operation. This does not make Calcudoku puzzles any more or less difficult to create, because other factors come into play.

Calcudoku puzzles can be created simply by making a Latin Square solution grid, and then outlining regions and choosing operations and their outcomes. But each puzzle must then be solved to check for uniqueness of the solution. As with other puzzle types, some of the better Calcudoku puzzles are created with specific solving methods and situations in mind—forcing the solver to consider possibilities that he or she may never have encountered before.

As mentioned earlier, Calcudoku puzzles also can be created with fewer than four operations included. When a puzzle creator decides to use only one or two specific operations or some particular shapes for the regions, the puzzles can be quite interesting and fun to solve. In some advanced versions of Calcudoku puzzles, some or all of the operation symbols may be omitted, leaving just the corresponding results. As you can imagine, these puzzles can be significantly challenging.

Calcudoku–Level 1

Puzzle 1

+ − × ÷

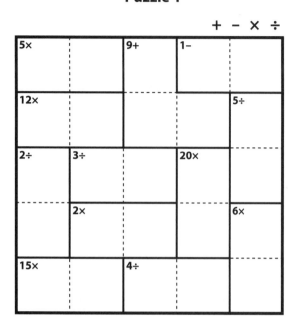

Puzzle 2

+ − × ÷

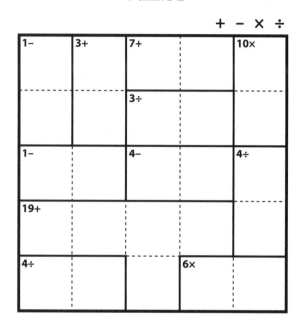

Puzzle 3

+ − × ÷

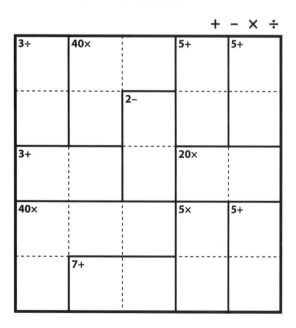

Puzzle 4

+ − × ÷

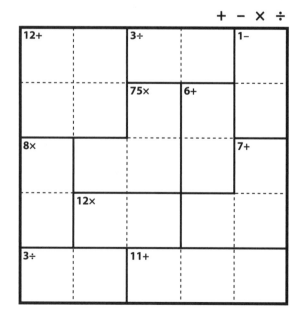

Calcudoku–Level 1

Puzzle 5

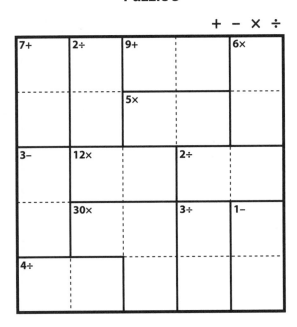

Puzzle 6

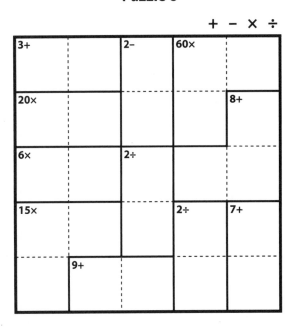

Puzzle 7

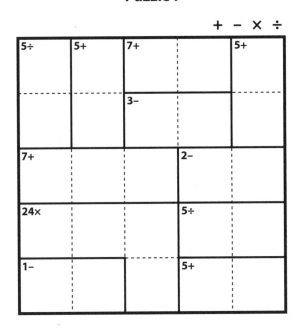

Puzzle 8

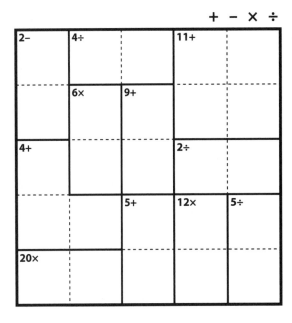

Calcudoku–Level 1

Puzzle 9

+ − × ÷

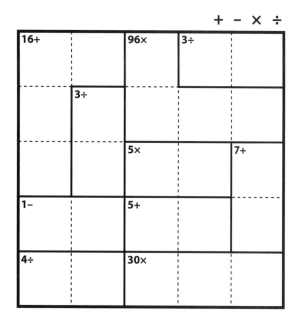

Puzzle 10

+ − × ÷

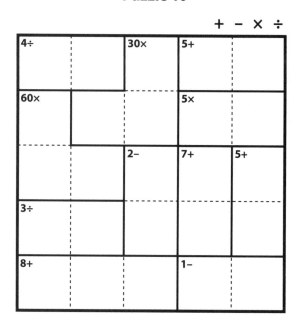

Calcudoku–Level 2

Puzzle 1

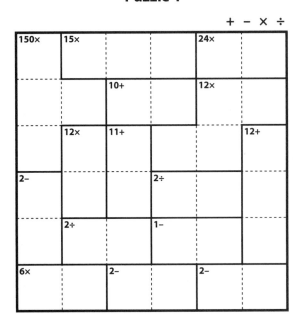

Puzzle 2

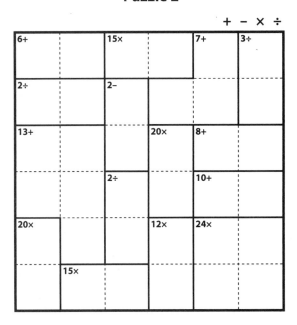

Puzzle 3

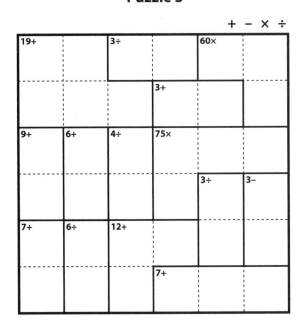

Puzzle 4

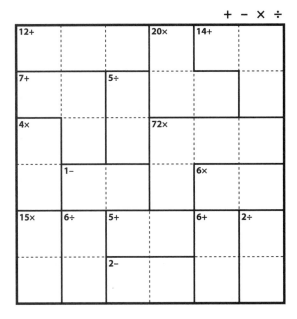

Calcudoku–Level 2

Puzzle 5

+ − × ÷

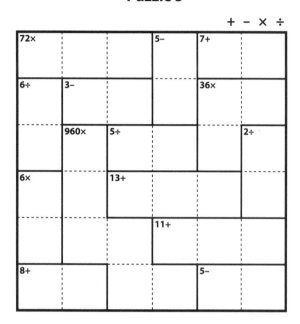

Puzzle 6

+ − × ÷

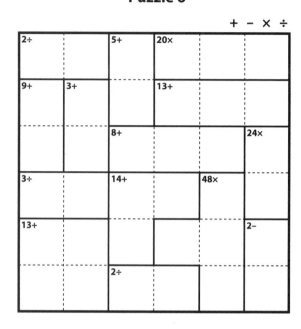

Puzzle 7

+ − × ÷

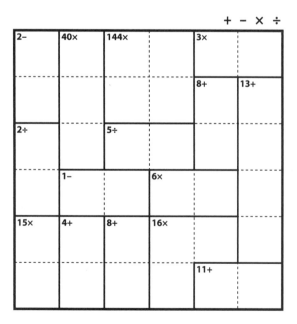

Puzzle 8

+ − × ÷

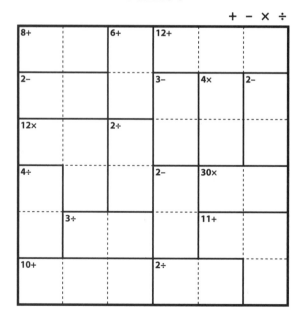

Calcudoku–Level 2

Puzzle 9

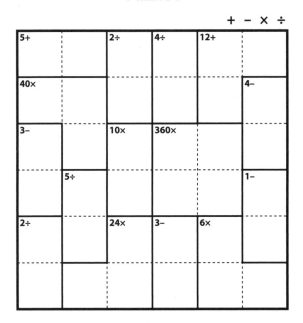

Puzzle 10

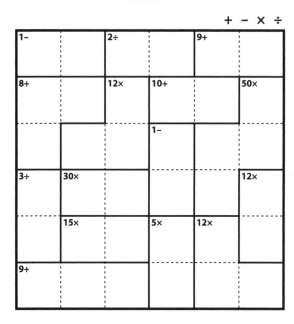

Calcudoku—Level 3

Puzzle 1

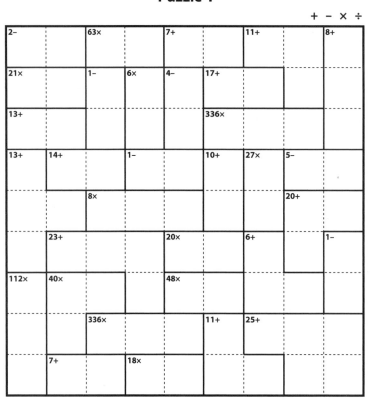

Puzzle 2

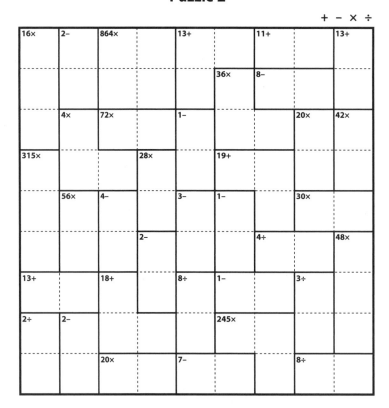

Calcudoku–Level 3

Puzzle 3

+ − × ÷

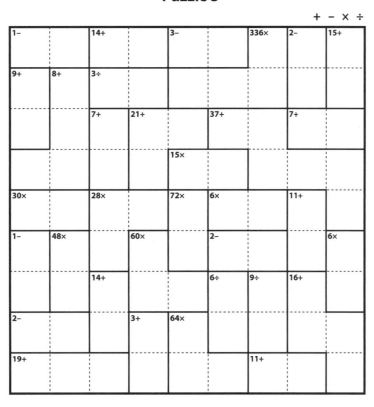

Puzzle 4

+ − × ÷

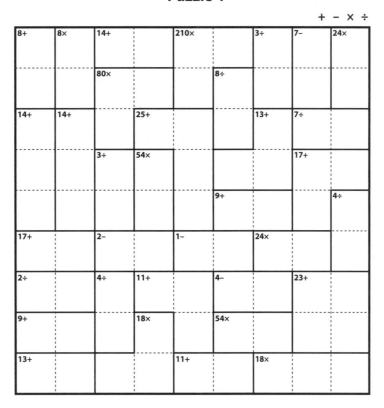

Calcudoku–Level 3

Puzzle 5

+ − × ÷

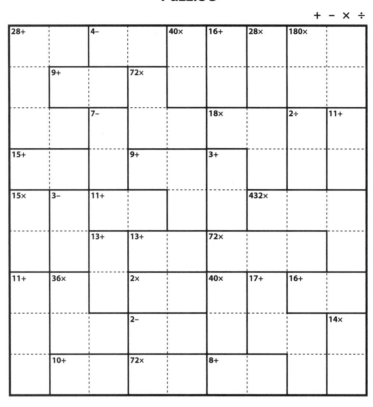

Puzzle 6

+ − × ÷

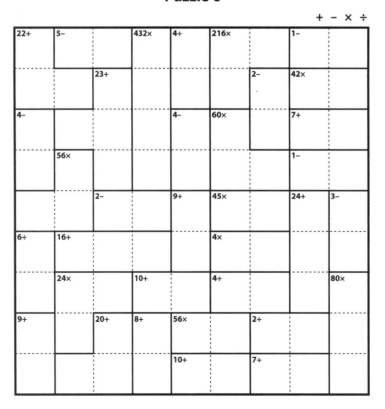

Math and Logic Puzzles That Make Kids Think © Prufrock Press Inc. • Permission is granted to photocopy or reproduce this page for single classroom use only.

Calcudoku–Level 3

Puzzle 7

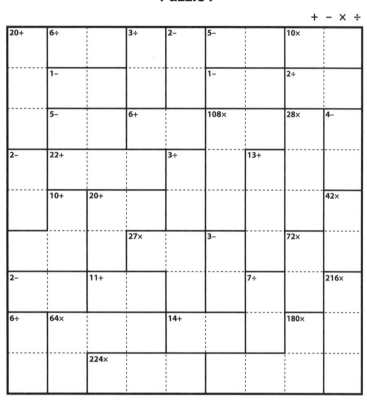

Puzzle 8

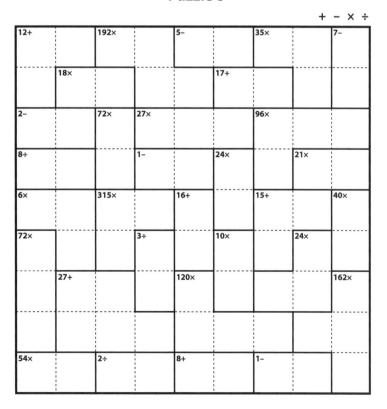

Calcudoku–Level 3

Puzzle 9

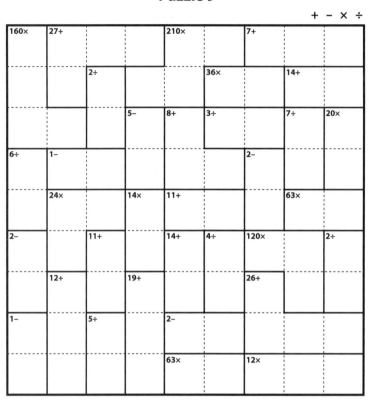

Puzzle 10

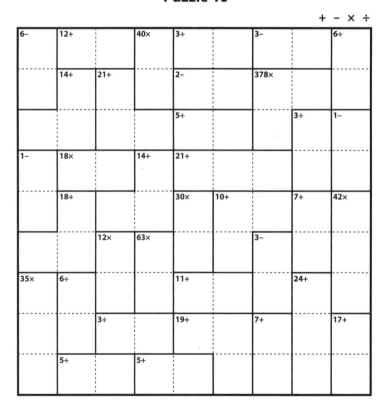

Math and Logic Puzzles That Make Kids Think © Prufrock Press Inc. • Permission is granted to photocopy or reproduce this page for single classroom use only.

Answer Key

Figure 3 Solution

6	8	9	7	1	3	4	5	2
4	7	2	6	5	8	3	9	1
5	3	1	2	4	9	8	7	6
1	5	8	9	2	4	7	6	3
3	2	4	8	7	6	5	1	9
9	6	7	1	3	5	2	4	8
8	4	5	3	6	1	9	2	7
7	1	3	5	9	2	6	8	4
2	9	6	4	8	7	1	3	5

Figure 4 Solution

L	A	T	I	S	G	C	O	N
O	S	I	A	C	N	T	G	L
C	N	G	O	L	T	I	S	A
S	C	O	L	I	A	N	T	G
I	G	N	C	T	S	L	A	O
T	L	A	G	N	O	S	C	I
N	O	S	T	A	L	G	I	C
A	T	C	N	G	I	O	L	S
G	I	L	S	O	C	A	N	T

Greater Than Sudoku—Level 1

Puzzle 1

5	1	2	4	3	6
3	4	6	2	1	5
6	3	1	5	4	2
2	5	4	1	6	3
1	2	3	6	5	4
4	6	5	3	2	1

Puzzle 2

6	3	1	4	2	5
2	4	5	6	1	3
4	1	3	2	5	6
5	2	6	3	4	1
1	6	4	5	3	2
3	5	2	1	6	4

Puzzle 3

6	5	1	4	3	2
4	2	3	5	6	1
3	6	5	2	1	4
2	1	4	3	5	6
1	3	2	6	4	5
5	4	6	1	2	3

Puzzle 4

4	3	6	1	5	2
5	2	1	3	6	4
6	1	3	4	2	5
2	5	4	6	3	1
1	6	2	5	4	3
3	4	5	2	1	6

Puzzle 5

6	2	5	4	1	3
3	1	4	5	6	2
4	5	6	3	2	1
2	3	1	6	5	4
1	6	3	2	4	5
5	4	2	1	3	6

Puzzle 6

1	5	3	2	4	6
6	4	2	5	1	3
3	1	4	6	2	5
5	2	6	1	3	4
4	6	1	3	5	2
2	3	5	4	6	1

Puzzle 7

6	4	2	3	1	5
5	1	3	4	6	2
4	5	6	1	2	3
3	2	1	6	5	4
2	6	4	5	3	1
1	3	5	2	4	6

Puzzle 8

4	6	3	1	2	5
5	2	1	6	3	4
2	1	5	3	4	6
6	3	4	2	5	1
3	5	6	4	1	2
1	4	2	5	6	3

Puzzle 9

4	5	2	1	3	6
3	1	6	2	5	4
6	3	5	4	2	1
2	4	1	3	6	5
5	2	4	6	1	3
1	6	3	5	4	2

Puzzle 10

5	2	1	6	3	4
4	6	3	1	5	2
6	1	4	3	2	5
2	3	5	4	6	1
3	4	2	5	1	6
1	5	6	2	4	3

Greater Than Sudoku–Level 2

Puzzle 1

7	5	2	4	3	6	8	1
3	1	6	8	7	5	4	2
8	6	3	2	4	7	1	5
5	4	7	1	2	8	6	3
6	3	1	5	8	4	2	7
4	2	8	7	1	3	5	6
1	7	4	6	5	2	3	8
2	8	5	3	6	1	7	4

Puzzle 2

5	6	2	3	8	7	1	4
4	1	7	8	3	2	5	6
6	7	8	5	1	3	4	2
3	2	1	4	5	6	7	8
8	3	5	7	6	4	2	1
2	4	6	1	7	5	8	3
1	5	4	6	2	8	3	7
7	8	3	2	4	1	6	5

Puzzle 3

1	3	8	6	4	5	2	7
2	5	7	4	3	1	8	6
7	4	5	2	8	3	6	1
8	1	6	3	5	7	4	2
4	7	3	8	6	2	1	5
6	2	1	5	7	8	3	4
3	6	2	7	1	4	5	8
5	8	4	1	2	6	7	3

Puzzle 4

2	8	6	3	5	7	1	4
1	4	5	7	2	3	8	6
7	3	8	4	1	5	6	2
5	1	2	6	8	4	7	3
3	2	7	8	6	1	4	5
6	5	4	1	7	2	3	8
8	7	3	2	4	6	5	1
4	6	1	5	3	8	2	7

Puzzle 5

7	6	5	2	8	1	3	4
4	1	8	3	2	5	6	7
1	7	6	5	4	2	8	3
2	8	3	4	7	6	1	5
6	2	1	7	5	3	4	8
3	5	4	8	6	7	2	1
8	3	7	6	1	4	5	2
5	4	2	1	3	8	7	6

Puzzle 6

3	1	6	5	2	8	4	7
7	8	2	4	1	3	5	6
4	5	7	1	8	6	3	2
2	3	8	6	4	5	7	1
5	7	3	2	6	4	1	8
1	6	4	8	5	7	2	3
6	4	1	7	3	2	8	5
8	2	5	3	7	1	6	4

Puzzle 7

3	5	4	6	7	1	8	2
8	1	2	7	4	3	6	5
4	3	1	8	2	5	7	6
2	7	6	5	3	8	1	4
5	6	7	4	1	2	3	8
1	8	3	2	5	6	4	7
6	4	5	1	8	7	2	3
7	2	8	3	6	4	5	1

Puzzle 8

5	6	3	8	1	2	4	7
7	1	2	4	6	5	8	3
2	4	1	5	3	8	7	6
8	3	7	6	2	1	5	4
6	8	4	2	7	3	1	5
1	7	5	3	8	4	6	2
3	5	8	7	4	6	2	1
4	2	6	1	5	7	3	8

Puzzle 9

2	3	8	7	1	4	6	5
1	4	6	5	7	2	8	3
4	8	1	3	6	5	7	2
5	6	7	2	4	8	3	1
7	1	3	8	2	6	5	4
6	2	5	4	3	7	1	8
8	7	2	1	5	3	4	6
3	5	4	6	8	1	2	7

Puzzle 10

5	7	8	2	4	3	6	1
3	4	6	1	5	2	8	7
1	2	7	8	6	4	5	3
6	5	4	3	8	7	1	2
7	6	3	5	2	1	4	8
2	8	1	4	7	5	3	6
8	1	5	7	3	6	2	4
4	3	2	6	1	8	7	5

Greater Than Sudoku–Level 3

Puzzle 1

7	6	8	5	9	1	2	3	4
9	1	4	7	2	3	5	6	8
3	2	5	8	4	6	9	7	1
1	3	6	9	8	5	4	2	7
8	4	2	1	3	7	6	5	9
5	7	9	4	6	2	1	8	3
2	9	1	6	7	8	3	4	5
4	8	3	2	5	9	7	1	6
6	5	7	3	1	4	8	9	2

Puzzle 2

9	7	3	1	2	6	4	8	5
8	1	4	7	9	5	3	2	6
6	2	5	8	4	3	7	1	9
2	3	6	9	5	7	8	4	1
7	4	9	6	1	8	5	3	2
5	8	1	2	3	4	6	9	7
4	9	8	5	6	2	1	7	3
3	6	2	4	7	1	9	5	8
1	5	7	3	8	9	2	6	4

Math and Logic Puzzles That Make Kids Think

Puzzle 3

3	8	9	1	5	6	2	7	4
6	1	4	7	3	2	8	5	9
7	2	5	8	9	4	6	1	3
8	3	6	9	7	1	5	4	2
9	5	2	6	4	3	1	8	7
4	7	1	5	2	8	9	3	6
2	6	7	3	1	5	4	9	8
5	9	8	4	6	7	3	2	1
1	4	3	2	8	9	7	6	5

Puzzle 6

9	6	7	3	5	4	2	8	1
8	1	4	7	6	2	9	5	3
3	2	5	8	9	1	6	7	4
5	3	6	9	1	8	4	2	7
4	9	2	5	3	7	1	6	8
1	7	8	4	2	6	3	9	5
2	5	9	1	7	3	8	4	6
6	8	3	2	4	5	7	1	9
7	4	1	6	8	9	5	3	2

Puzzle 4

3	6	8	2	1	5	9	7	4
9	1	4	7	3	6	8	2	5
7	2	5	8	9	4	1	3	6
2	3	6	9	5	1	7	4	8
4	7	9	3	6	8	2	5	1
8	5	1	4	2	7	3	6	9
1	9	7	5	4	2	6	8	3
6	4	2	1	8	3	5	9	7
5	8	3	6	7	9	4	1	2

Puzzle 7

7	6	9	5	2	1	8	3	4
8	1	4	7	6	3	9	5	2
3	2	5	8	4	9	6	7	1
2	3	6	9	5	4	1	8	7
5	7	8	3	1	6	4	2	9
4	9	1	2	7	8	5	6	3
1	8	2	4	3	5	7	9	6
6	5	7	1	9	2	3	4	8
9	4	3	6	8	7	2	1	5

Puzzle 5

8	6	3	1	9	4	5	2	7
9	1	4	7	5	2	8	6	3
7	2	5	8	3	6	9	1	4
1	3	6	9	4	7	2	5	8
5	9	2	6	8	3	7	4	1
4	7	8	2	1	5	6	3	9
2	5	1	4	7	9	3	8	6
6	4	9	3	2	8	1	7	5
3	8	7	5	6	1	4	9	2

Puzzle 8

4	8	7	1	5	3	6	9	2
5	6	9	2	7	4	1	8	3
3	2	1	8	6	9	7	5	4
1	5	6	4	8	2	3	7	9
9	3	4	7	1	5	2	6	8
2	7	8	9	3	6	4	1	5
8	4	5	6	2	1	9	3	7
7	1	2	3	9	8	5	4	6
6	9	3	5	4	7	8	2	1

Puzzle 9

2	4	9	6	7	8	1	3	5
5	6	1	2	9	3	4	8	7
8	7	3	4	1	5	2	9	6
4	5	2	3	8	7	9	6	1
9	8	7	1	4	6	5	2	3
1	3	6	9	5	2	7	4	8
7	2	5	8	3	4	6	1	9
3	1	4	7	6	9	8	5	2
6	9	8	5	2	1	3	7	4

Puzzle 10

1	5	9	8	3	7	2	6	4
3	2	4	5	9	6	1	7	8
8	6	7	2	1	4	9	3	5
2	9	1	7	4	3	5	8	6
4	3	6	1	5	8	7	9	2
5	7	8	9	6	2	3	4	1
9	4	5	6	7	1	8	2	3
6	1	2	3	8	9	4	5	7
7	8	3	4	2	5	6	1	9

Shapedoku–Level 1

Puzzle 1

2	4	1	3
3	1	2	**4**
1	**3**	4	2
4	**2**	3	1

Puzzle 2

2	**1**	3	4
4	**2**	1	3
1	3	4	2
3	**4**	2	1

Puzzle 3

3	2	**4**	1
1	4	2	3
2	**1**	3	4
4	**3**	1	**2**

Puzzle 4

3	1	2	**4**
4	2	3	1
1	3	4	2
2	4	**1**	3

Puzzle 5

1	4	2	3
3	**2**	1	4
2	**3**	4	1
4	1	3	2

Puzzle 6

1	2	3	4
4	3	1	2
2	1	4	**3**
3	4	**2**	**1**

Puzzle 7

2	1	4	3
3	2	1	4
1	**4**	3	2
4	**3**	2	1

Puzzle 8

4	2	3	1
2	1	4	3
3	4	1	**2**
1	3	2	**4**

Puzzle 9

1	3	4	2
4	2	1	3
3	4	2	**1**
2	1	3	4

Puzzle 10

4	1	2	3
2	3	1	4
1	4	3	2
3	2	4	1

Shapedoku–Level 2

Puzzle 1

4	2	1	5	3
5	1	3	2	4
1	5	4	3	2
2	3	5	4	1
3	4	2	1	5

Puzzle 2

5	4	1	3	2
4	2	5	1	3
1	3	4	2	5
2	1	3	5	4
3	5	2	4	1

Puzzle 3

5	1	2	4	3
3	4	1	5	2
2	5	3	1	4
1	2	4	3	5
4	3	5	2	1

Puzzle 4

3	2	5	1	4
2	5	1	4	3
1	4	2	3	5
4	1	3	5	2
5	3	4	2	1

Puzzle 5

5	4	2	1	3
4	1	3	2	5
2	5	1	3	4
1	3	5	4	2
3	2	4	5	1

Puzzle 6

2	5	1	3	4
4	2	3	1	5
3	1	5	4	2
1	4	2	5	3
5	3	4	2	1

Puzzle 7

3	1	2	4	5
4	2	5	1	3
2	4	3	5	1
1	5	4	3	2
5	3	1	2	4

Puzzle 8

1	4	3	2	5
5	2	1	3	4
3	5	4	1	2
4	3	2	5	1
2	1	5	4	3

Puzzle 9

2	1	3	4	5
5	3	4	1	2
1	4	5	2	3
3	2	1	5	4
4	5	2	3	1

Puzzle 10

5	1	2	4	3
3	4	1	5	2
2	5	4	3	1
1	3	5	2	4
4	2	3	1	5

Math and Logic Puzzles That Make Kids Think

Shapedoku–Level 3

Puzzle 1

1	**2**	**5**	3	4	**6**
6	4	1	2	**3**	5
4	5	3	6	**1**	2
3	**1**	2	**5**	6	4
5	6	4	1	2	**3**
2	3	6	**4**	5	1

Puzzle 2

6	2	**1**	3	4	5
5	1	4	6	**2**	3
1	**3**	6	2	5	**4**
4	5	3	**1**	6	**2**
2	**6**	**5**	4	3	1
3	4	2	**5**	1	**6**

Puzzle 3

5	**4**	3	6	2	**1**
3	**6**	2	1	4	**5**
4	1	5	**2**	**3**	6
6	2	**4**	**5**	1	3
2	5	1	**3**	**6**	4
1	3	6	4	5	**2**

Puzzle 4

6	1	4	2	3	**5**
5	**4**	2	1	6	3
4	**6**	**3**	5	**1**	2
1	5	**6**	**3**	2	4
3	**2**	1	4	5	6
2	3	5	6	**4**	1

Puzzle 5

4	2	1	5	3	6
6	**1**	3	4	5	2
3	5	**2**	6	4	1
2	4	5	**1**	6	3
1	6	4	3	2	**5**
5	**3**	6	**2**	1	**4**

Puzzle 6

6	**1**	2	5	4	**3**
4	3	5	**1**	2	6
5	4	1	**3**	**6**	**2**
3	2	**6**	4	**5**	1
1	6	**4**	2	3	5
2	**5**	3	6	1	4

Puzzle 7

4	3	**6**	1	2	**5**
5	1	4	**2**	6	3
2	6	**3**	5	1	**4**
6	5	1	**3**	**4**	2
3	4	2	**6**	5	**1**
1	**2**	5	4	3	6

Puzzle 8

4	1	5	**2**	6	3
5	3	**2**	1	4	6
3	2	6	4	1	**5**
2	**4**	3	6	**5**	**1**
1	**6**	4	5	**3**	2
6	5	1	**3**	2	4

Puzzle 9

5	**1**	2	4	6	**3**
3	2	**6**	1	**4**	5
6	3	**5**	**2**	1	4
4	**5**	1	6	**3**	2
1	4	3	5	2	**6**
2	6	**4**	3	5	1

Puzzle 10

3	6	**4**	1	5	2
5	4	2	6	3	**1**
4	2	3	**5**	1	**6**
1	**3**	6	**2**	4	5
6	5	**1**	4	**2**	3
2	1	**5**	3	**6**	4

Killer Sudoku–Level 1

Puzzle 1

6	2	1	5	3	4
3	5	4	1	2	6
4	1	2	3	6	5
5	6	3	4	1	2
1	4	6	2	5	3
2	3	5	6	4	1

Puzzle 2

6	1	3	4	5	2
4	2	5	6	1	3
1	6	2	5	3	4
3	5	4	1	2	6
5	3	6	2	4	1
2	4	1	3	6	5

Puzzle 3

3	2	5	6	4	1
6	4	1	2	3	5
1	5	6	4	2	3
4	3	2	1	5	6
2	1	3	5	6	4
5	6	4	3	1	2

Puzzle 4

4	2	1	5	3	6
6	5	3	2	4	1
1	4	5	3	6	2
2	3	6	4	1	5
3	6	2	1	5	4
5	1	4	6	2	3

Puzzle 5

4	5	6	1	2	3
3	1	2	4	5	6
6	4	1	5	3	2
5	2	3	6	1	4
1	3	4	2	6	5
2	6	5	3	4	1

Puzzle 6

2	1	6	4	3	5
4	5	3	1	2	6
3	4	5	2	6	1
6	2	1	3	5	4
1	6	2	5	4	3
5	3	4	6	1	2

Puzzle 7

5	2	3	4	1	6
1	6	4	5	2	3
4	5	6	2	3	1
3	1	2	6	5	4
6	3	5	1	4	2
2	4	1	3	6	5

Puzzle 8

3	2	5	4	1	6
1	4	6	5	3	2
2	3	4	6	5	1
6	5	1	2	4	3
4	6	3	1	2	5
5	1	2	3	6	4

Puzzle 9

3	6	2	4	5	1
5	4	1	2	3	6
2	3	6	5	1	4
4	1	5	6	2	3
1	2	4	3	6	5
6	5	3	1	4	2

Puzzle 10

6	1	2	3	5	4
5	4	3	6	1	2
1	3	5	4	2	6
4	2	6	1	3	5
3	5	4	2	6	1
2	6	1	5	4	3

Killer Sudoku-Level 2

Puzzle 1

2	6	5	8	7	4	1	3
1	7	4	3	6	5	8	2
3	1	6	5	8	7	2	4
7	2	8	4	5	3	6	1
8	5	7	2	4	1	3	6
4	3	1	6	2	8	7	5
6	4	3	7	1	2	5	8
5	8	2	1	3	6	4	7

Puzzle 2

5	3	8	4	2	7	6	1
2	7	1	6	8	3	5	4
1	8	7	5	3	2	4	6
3	4	6	2	7	8	1	5
6	1	3	7	5	4	8	2
4	2	5	8	1	6	3	7
8	6	2	1	4	5	7	3
7	5	4	3	6	1	2	8

Puzzle 3

5	6	7	1	2	8	3	4
4	3	8	2	6	5	7	1
7	2	6	5	1	3	4	8
3	1	4	8	5	2	6	7
8	5	2	4	7	6	1	3
1	7	3	6	8	4	5	2
2	4	5	7	3	1	8	6
6	8	1	3	4	7	2	5

Puzzle 4

1	8	3	4	7	2	6	5
5	7	6	2	4	3	1	8
6	2	8	1	3	5	4	7
4	5	7	3	6	1	8	2
8	6	1	5	2	7	3	4
2	3	4	7	1	8	5	6
7	1	5	6	8	4	2	3
3	4	2	8	5	6	7	1

Puzzle 5

7	1	5	4	6	8	3	2
6	2	8	3	5	7	4	1
3	7	2	5	8	4	1	6
4	8	1	6	7	2	5	3
1	5	6	8	4	3	2	7
2	3	4	7	1	6	8	5
5	4	7	2	3	1	6	8
8	6	3	1	2	5	7	4

Puzzle 6

7	1	4	2	8	5	3	6
5	8	6	3	1	2	7	4
3	5	7	8	4	1	6	2
4	6	2	1	7	8	5	3
1	3	8	6	2	7	4	5
2	7	5	4	6	3	8	1
8	4	1	5	3	6	2	7
6	2	3	7	5	4	1	8

Puzzle 7

1	8	5	6	3	2	4	7
4	3	7	2	5	6	1	8
8	4	6	3	1	5	7	2
7	1	2	5	4	3	8	6
3	6	4	1	8	7	2	5
2	5	8	7	6	4	3	1
6	2	3	8	7	1	5	4
5	7	1	4	2	8	6	3

Puzzle 8

5	7	1	6	3	2	8	4
3	2	8	4	7	6	5	1
4	3	7	1	5	8	2	6
2	5	6	8	4	7	1	3
7	8	4	5	1	3	6	2
1	6	3	2	8	5	4	7
6	4	5	7	2	1	3	8
8	1	2	3	6	4	7	5

Math and Logic Puzzles That Make Kids Think

Puzzle 9

5	6	2	3	7	8	1	4
7	4	8	1	3	6	2	5
4	5	7	2	1	3	6	8
3	1	6	8	4	5	7	2
2	7	4	5	6	1	8	3
1	8	3	6	5	2	4	7
8	3	1	7	2	4	5	6
6	2	5	4	8	7	3	1

Puzzle 10

3	4	2	8	1	6	7	5
7	5	6	1	3	2	4	8
2	3	8	6	7	4	5	1
4	7	1	5	2	3	8	6
8	1	3	2	5	7	6	4
5	6	7	4	8	1	2	3
1	8	4	7	6	5	3	2
6	2	5	3	4	8	1	7

Killer Sudoku–Level 3

Puzzle 1

3	5	1	7	8	6	2	9	4
6	2	9	5	3	4	8	7	1
8	7	4	1	2	9	6	5	3
5	3	7	2	9	8	1	4	6
1	8	6	3	4	7	9	2	5
4	9	2	6	5	1	7	3	8
2	4	8	9	6	3	5	1	7
7	6	5	4	1	2	3	8	9
9	1	3	8	7	5	4	6	2

Puzzle 2

7	8	3	5	4	9	2	1	6
5	1	4	3	2	6	7	8	9
9	2	6	7	1	8	3	4	5
3	5	7	4	8	1	6	9	2
4	9	8	2	6	5	1	7	3
2	6	1	9	3	7	4	5	8
6	4	9	8	7	3	5	2	1
8	3	2	1	5	4	9	6	7
1	7	5	6	9	2	8	3	4

Puzzle 3

7	5	2	6	4	3	1	9	8
1	8	4	2	5	9	6	3	7
9	6	3	1	8	7	4	2	5
2	9	6	4	3	8	7	5	1
4	1	7	9	2	5	3	8	6
5	3	8	7	6	1	2	4	9
8	2	9	3	7	6	5	1	4
6	4	5	8	1	2	9	7	3
3	7	1	5	9	4	8	6	2

Puzzle 4

9	8	1	5	7	4	6	3	2
7	2	5	1	6	3	9	4	8
4	3	6	8	2	9	7	5	1
5	4	8	9	1	7	2	6	3
3	1	2	4	8	6	5	9	7
6	7	9	2	3	5	8	1	4
2	9	3	6	4	8	1	7	5
8	5	7	3	9	1	4	2	6
1	6	4	7	5	2	3	8	9

Puzzle 5

1	9	6	5	2	7	4	8	3
2	5	8	6	3	4	1	7	9
3	7	4	9	8	1	6	5	2
7	1	5	8	4	3	9	2	6
8	6	9	1	5	2	3	4	7
4	3	2	7	9	6	8	1	5
5	4	7	3	6	8	2	9	1
9	2	3	4	1	5	7	6	8
6	8	1	2	7	9	5	3	4

Puzzle 6

8	6	7	3	2	5	4	1	9
4	1	9	7	6	8	5	3	2
5	3	2	1	4	9	7	8	6
7	4	8	9	3	6	1	2	5
3	9	5	4	1	2	8	6	7
6	2	1	8	5	7	9	4	3
1	5	6	2	7	4	3	9	8
9	7	4	6	8	3	2	5	1
2	8	3	5	9	1	6	7	4

Puzzle 7

9	5	6	4	2	3	8	7	1
2	3	4	1	7	8	9	5	6
1	7	8	9	5	6	2	3	4
3	1	7	6	4	2	5	8	9
5	4	2	7	8	9	6	1	3
8	6	9	3	1	5	7	4	2
4	8	5	2	6	1	3	9	7
7	2	3	8	9	4	1	6	5
6	9	1	5	3	7	4	2	8

Puzzle 8

4	2	7	8	5	3	9	6	1
8	9	5	4	6	1	3	2	7
3	6	1	9	2	7	8	5	4
7	4	8	1	3	6	5	9	2
2	1	3	5	4	9	6	7	8
6	5	9	2	7	8	1	4	3
1	8	6	7	9	2	4	3	5
5	3	2	6	8	4	7	1	9
9	7	4	3	1	5	2	8	6

Puzzle 9

2	1	8	4	7	6	9	5	3
6	3	7	2	5	9	1	8	4
5	9	4	1	3	8	6	7	2
8	5	2	6	1	7	3	4	9
9	6	1	8	4	3	7	2	5
4	7	3	9	2	5	8	1	6
1	8	9	5	6	4	2	3	7
3	4	6	7	8	2	5	9	1
7	2	5	3	9	1	4	6	8

Puzzle 10

3	9	2	1	7	5	8	4	6
7	4	6	3	2	8	1	9	5
1	8	5	9	4	6	7	2	3
9	2	4	6	1	7	5	3	8
6	3	8	4	5	9	2	7	1
5	7	1	8	3	2	9	6	4
2	5	3	7	8	4	6	1	9
4	6	7	5	9	1	3	8	2
8	1	9	2	6	3	4	5	7

Calcudoku–Level 1

Puzzle 1

1	5	2	3	4
3	4	5	2	1
2	1	3	4	5
4	2	1	5	3
5	3	4	1	2

Puzzle 2

5	1	4	3	2
4	2	3	1	5
2	3	1	5	4
3	5	2	4	1
1	4	5	2	3

Puzzle 3

1	5	2	3	4
3	4	5	2	1
2	1	3	4	5
4	2	1	5	3
5	3	4	1	2

Puzzle 4

5	4	1	3	2
1	2	5	4	3
4	5	3	2	1
2	3	4	1	5
3	1	2	5	4

Puzzle 5

3	1	5	4	2
4	2	1	5	3
5	3	4	2	1
2	5	3	1	4
1	4	2	3	5

Puzzle 6

2	1	3	4	5
4	5	1	3	2
3	2	4	5	1
5	3	2	1	4
1	4	5	2	3

Puzzle 7

5	2	3	4	1
1	3	5	2	4
2	1	4	5	3
3	4	2	1	5
4	5	1	3	2

Puzzle 8

3	4	1	5	2
5	2	4	1	3
1	3	5	2	4
2	1	3	4	5
4	5	2	3	1

Puzzle 9

2	5	4	3	1
5	1	3	2	4
4	3	5	1	2
3	2	1	4	5
1	4	2	5	3

Puzzle 10

1	4	5	3	2
4	2	3	1	5
5	3	4	2	1
3	1	2	5	4
2	5	1	4	3

Calcudoku–Level 2

Puzzle 1

2	1	3	5	6	4
3	5	4	6	1	2
5	4	6	2	3	1
4	3	5	1	2	6
6	2	1	3	4	5
1	6	2	4	5	3

Puzzle 2

2	4	5	3	1	6
6	3	4	1	5	2
1	2	6	4	3	5
3	1	2	5	6	4
5	6	1	2	4	3
4	5	3	6	2	1

Puzzle 3

1	5	2	6	3	4
4	3	6	2	1	5
6	2	4	3	5	1
3	4	1	5	2	6
2	1	5	4	6	3
5	6	3	1	4	2

Puzzle 4

6	4	2	1	3	5
2	3	1	5	4	6
4	2	5	3	6	1
1	5	6	4	2	3
5	6	3	2	1	4
3	1	4	6	5	2

Puzzle 5

4	6	3	1	2	5
1	2	5	6	4	3
6	4	1	5	3	2
2	5	4	3	6	1
3	1	6	2	5	4
5	3	2	4	1	6

Puzzle 6

6	3	2	5	4	1
4	1	3	6	5	2
5	2	4	1	3	6
2	6	5	3	1	4
1	5	6	4	2	3
3	4	1	2	6	5

Puzzle 7

6	5	4	2	1	3
4	2	3	6	5	1
2	4	1	5	3	6
1	6	5	3	2	4
5	3	6	1	4	2
3	1	2	4	6	5

Puzzle 8

3	5	1	4	2	6
6	4	5	2	1	3
2	3	6	5	4	1
4	2	3	1	6	5
1	6	2	3	5	4
5	1	4	6	3	2

Puzzle 9

2	3	6	4	1	5
5	4	3	1	6	2
1	2	5	3	4	6
4	1	2	6	5	3
6	5	1	2	3	4
3	6	4	5	2	1

Puzzle 10

5	4	1	2	3	6
1	3	2	6	4	5
4	1	6	3	5	2
2	6	5	4	1	3
6	5	3	1	2	4
3	2	4	5	6	1

Math and Logic Puzzles That Make Kids Think

Calcudoku–Level 3

Puzzle 1

6	8	7	9	3	4	5	2	1
3	7	2	6	1	9	8	4	5
9	4	3	1	5	7	6	8	2
4	9	5	8	7	2	3	1	6
5	3	1	4	2	8	9	6	7
1	6	9	3	4	5	2	7	8
7	2	4	5	8	6	1	3	9
2	5	8	7	6	1	4	9	3
8	1	6	2	9	3	7	5	4

Puzzle 2

2	3	6	8	5	1	4	7	9
8	5	3	6	7	2	1	9	4
1	2	8	9	4	6	3	5	7
5	1	2	7	3	8	9	4	6
7	8	1	4	9	3	2	6	5
9	7	5	1	6	4	8	2	3
4	9	7	3	8	5	6	1	2
6	4	9	2	1	7	5	3	8
3	6	4	5	2	9	7	8	1

Puzzle 3

2	3	9	5	1	4	7	6	8
5	1	3	9	6	2	4	8	7
4	2	5	8	7	9	3	1	6
1	4	2	6	3	5	8	7	9
6	5	4	7	8	3	2	9	1
8	6	1	4	9	7	5	2	3
7	8	6	3	5	1	9	4	2
9	7	8	2	4	6	1	3	5
3	9	7	1	2	8	6	5	4

Puzzle 4

1	4	6	8	7	5	9	2	3
7	2	5	4	6	1	3	9	8
2	6	4	3	9	8	5	1	7
3	7	1	9	8	6	2	4	5
9	1	3	6	5	2	7	8	4
8	9	7	5	2	3	4	6	1
6	3	2	7	1	4	8	5	9
4	5	8	1	3	9	6	7	2
5	8	9	2	4	7	1	3	6

Puzzle 5

9	1	6	2	8	7	4	5	3
2	8	1	6	5	9	7	3	4
7	9	2	3	4	6	1	8	5
8	7	9	5	1	2	3	4	6
5	2	7	4	3	1	9	6	8
3	5	8	7	6	4	2	9	1
4	3	5	1	2	8	6	7	9
6	4	3	9	7	5	8	1	2
1	6	4	8	9	3	5	2	7

Puzzle 6

9	2	7	6	1	3	8	5	4
8	5	1	2	4	9	3	6	7
7	8	6	9	5	2	1	4	3
3	7	8	4	9	6	5	2	1
2	4	3	1	7	5	9	8	6
6	3	5	8	2	1	4	7	9
1	6	4	7	3	8	2	9	5
4	1	9	5	8	7	6	3	2
5	9	2	3	6	4	7	1	8

Puzzle 7

8	6	1	3	7	9	4	5	2
3	7	6	1	5	8	9	2	4
9	8	3	2	4	1	6	7	5
7	9	8	5	6	3	2	4	1
5	3	9	4	2	6	8	1	7
2	5	7	9	1	4	3	8	6
4	2	5	6	3	7	1	9	8
1	4	2	8	9	5	7	6	3
6	1	4	7	8	2	5	3	9

Puzzle 8

3	4	6	8	2	7	1	5	9
5	6	3	1	4	8	9	7	2
7	5	8	3	1	9	6	2	4
8	1	9	5	6	4	2	3	7
1	2	5	9	7	6	3	4	8
4	3	7	6	9	2	8	1	5
9	7	1	2	8	5	4	6	3
2	8	4	7	3	1	5	9	6
6	9	2	4	5	3	7	8	1

Puzzle 9

5	9	8	3	7	6	1	4	2
2	7	3	1	5	9	4	6	8
8	2	6	4	1	3	9	7	5
6	8	7	9	2	5	3	1	4
1	6	4	2	3	8	5	9	7
9	1	2	7	6	4	8	5	3
7	4	9	5	8	1	2	3	6
3	5	1	6	4	2	7	8	9
4	3	5	8	9	7	6	2	1

Puzzle 10

2	7	5	8	3	9	1	4	6
8	3	7	5	4	2	9	6	1
9	2	8	6	1	5	7	3	4
3	9	2	4	7	8	6	1	5
4	8	9	1	6	7	2	5	3
6	4	3	9	5	1	8	2	7
1	6	4	7	8	3	5	9	2
5	1	6	2	9	4	3	7	8
7	5	1	3	2	6	4	8	9

About
the Author

Jeffrey Wanko is an associate professor at Miami University of Ohio where he teaches preservice and inservice mathematics teachers. He began solving and creating puzzles in elementary school and saw his first published puzzles in his middle school newspaper. He and his wife, Molly, live in Ohio with their three amazing and energetic children. Dr. Wanko views all of life as a puzzle and is constantly seeking solutions by making educated guesses and jotting notes in the margins of his work.

User's Guide
to
Walch Reproducible Books

As part of our general effort to provide educational materials which are as practical and economical as possible, we have designated this publication a "reproducible book." The designation means that purchase of the book includes purchase of the right to limited reproduction of all pages on which this symbol appears:

Here is the basic Walch policy: We grant to individual purchasers of this book the right to make sufficient copies of reproducible pages for use by all students of a single teacher. This permission is limited to a single teacher, and does not apply to entire schools or school systems, so institutions purchasing the book should pass the permission on to a single teacher. Copying of the book or its parts for resale is prohibited.

Any questions regarding this policy or requests to purchase further reproduction rights should be addressed to:

Permissions Editor
J. Weston Walch, Publisher
321 Valley Street • P. O. Box 658
Portland, Maine 04104-0658

1   2   3   4   5   6   7   8   9   10

ISBN 0-8251-3826-4

Copyright © 1984, 1998
J. Weston Walch, Publisher
P. O. Box 658 • Portland, Maine 04104-0658

Printed in the United States of America

CONTENTS

CREDITS

Dover Pictorial Archives

Pages 1, 5, 13, 21, 29, 37, 38, 45, 46, 53, 60, 71, 79,
87, 95, 103, 111, 117, 120, 121

Corbis-Bettmann

pages 126, 139

UPI/Corbis-Bettmann

page 146

Digital Stock CD

pages 159, 160

TO THE TEACHER

These plays were created for one overriding purpose: to more actively involve students in the study of United States History. They are not meant to be a gimmick, time filler, or purveyor of "history lite." They are a resource for the professional. It is the classroom teacher who can best decide how and when these plays should be used.

Each and every one of these plays has been thoroughly researched. All the main characters are historical and authentically portrayed. Only a few characters are fictional. They often serve as narrators to provide useful background information or to keep the story moving. In no way do these fictional characters compromise the historical accuracy and integrity of the work.

The dialogue of each character can best be described as "what might have been said."

Here are some general suggestions regarding how and when these plays can be employed. Teachers can use them to introduce a particular unit, conclude one, or use in the middle as a catalyst for discussion and further research. They can be simply "read" by the students or produced as an historical drama with appropriate costumes and scenery.

Here are some specific suggestions to consider (from my own personal experience).

1. Make a complete copy of the play for each student in your class.

2. Decide beforehand how the roles are to be assigned: one student reading the same part for the entire play, or splitting it with another student. This is a choice between continuity and expanded participation.

3. Avoid having students read their parts "cold." Give them ample opportunity to practice at home or in class. Otherwise, you invite embarrassment or a lesson that simply "bombs."

4. Have the students without speaking roles make scene signs or backgrounds.

5. If the play is to be produced, not just read, organize two full casts and have at least two performances. (Two casts cover absences on performance day.) Those without speaking roles can make scenery and costumes, and function as directors, prompters, etc.

6. Use the plays to encourage students to write their own plays. Emphasize the need for comprehensive and systematic research. Model for them dialogue that "flows" naturally, has substance, and is interesting to the reader/listener.

INTRODUCTION

With the exception of the first play (a spoof, with considerable authenticity) the plays can be divided into two broad categories: those with a prime focus on a noteworthy individual, and those focusing on a significant period in our history. While the dictum, "No man is an island," rings true in all societies, our nation's story is replete with bold, imaginative, and paradigm-smashing individuals. This selection of plays honors some of those men and women. It includes inventors, scientists, explorers, writers, humanitarians, missionaries, political activists, social crusaders, doctors, and Ben Franklin, who seems to fit all categories. Each has made a significant contribution to America's story.

Five of the plays (including "Jamestown Adventurers") focus primarily upon a significant period in our history. While individuals remain essential to the particular story, it is the collective experience of the characters that is of paramount importance. These works include stories about the Jamestown settlement, the creation of the Constitution, the 1930's Dust Bowl, the Little Rock, Arkansas, school integration crisis of the 1950's, and highlights of the post-World War II era.

Acknowledgments

This volume is dedicated to my mother, a retired teacher, who very early instilled in me a love of history and the English language. It is also dedicated to the late Peggy Haseltine, longtime librarian at San Juan Elementary School in San Juan Bautista, California. Peggy exemplified all that is best in our elementary school librarians: a lover of the printed word, friend and helper to all students and teachers, and an inspiration to budding authors young and old.

THE JAMESTOWN ADVENTURES (1607)

Characters (in order of appearance)

English Settlers		Native Americans
AEROGANT	NEWPORT	FOURGAWN
BLUSTER	Captain John SMITH	KONKLUSHUN
KHANARTIST	Rev. Robert HUNT	Chief POWHATAN
DEFAHSIT		POCAHONTAS (chief's daughter)

John Smith

Scene 1:
Chesapeake Bay, the New World, April 26, 1607

AEROGANT: Land! We've finally made it to the New World!

BLUSTER: I can't wait to get my hands on all that gold!

KHANARTIST: Whoa! Do you think it's just waiting there to be picked, like apples at a Safeway? The task involves getting your fat pinkies a little dirty.

DEFAHSIT: But not yours, of course. You'll sit back and watch us do all the digging and then try to swindle it all out of us. But we're not that stupid.

AEROGANT: Speak only for yourself! Now, regarding manual work—these sensitive and delicate hands have never been sullied or blistered by mundane tasks. But I am willing to employ them to garner gold.

KHANARTIST: Covered, of course, with your white "gentleman" gloves.

AEROGANT: Which can be removed to slap bad-mannered lowlifes like you with their grinning goat-feet faces!

(enter Smith and Newport)

NEWPORT:	Gentlemen, gentlemen, it appears we have entered a bay. I suggest we sail up the first large river we encounter so we will be sheltered from the sea.
DEFAHSIT:	Captain! We've been over five months at sea! Let's land immediately and go for the gold!
SMITH:	Gold, gold, gold. That's all you've been talking about since we left England! Must I remind you of the purpose of this expedition? We are here to establish a permanent English colony. Proceed, Mr. Newport.

Scene II:
Jamestown, Virginia, summer 1607

KHANARTIST:	This place is the absolute pits!
BLUSTER:	For once you're telling the truth. No gold and not a decent FM station in reach.
AEROGANT:	Nothing but blood-sucking mosquitoes.
DEFAHSIT:	And heat!
BLUSTER:	It's a crazy heat, too. It leaves you all wet.
AEROGANT:	The proper term is "high humidity," underling.
BLUSTER:	Tame your tongue, toad face, or I'll be forced to throw you into the river with your cousins!
AEROGANT:	You have the unmitigated gall to compare my aristocratic countenance with an amphibian's? Yours looks like a—

(enter Smith and Hunt)

HUNT:	Gentlemen, please communicate in a more sensitive and polite manner.
SMITH:	What's going on here? Why aren't you men working? You seem to have all the time in the world to argue and fight, but not a minute for weeding our fields. We need those crops! Our supplies are nearly exhausted!
AEROGANT:	Captain Smith! Let me remind you that we are English gentlemen, not peasants! This work is beneath our dignity.
SMITH:	I don't care if it's above, below, or in-between! Your dignity won't keep you from starving in this land! Now get to work!

(all but Smith and Hunt exit)

HUNT:	Captain Smith, may I suggest making another trading trip up the river? The people certainly gave us a lot for our goods.
SMITH:	True, true, true. I know another trip is necessary, but I don't like it. We're rapidly running out of things to trade, and I don't think they'll honor our credit cards. This colony must become self-sufficient!
HUNT:	But until then?
SMITH:	We'll just have to load up the canoe and see what happens with the locals.

FOURGAWN: Great Chief, in light of recent developments, I think you would concur that something must be done about these intruders from abroad, the snowfaces.

KONKLUSHUN: I wholeheartedly agree! We have become victims of their grossly unfair trade practices. We have provided them with good food and sound building materials—

FOURGAWN: In exchange for their cheap English knives and trinkets that even Mega Mall Discounts wouldn't sell!

KONKLUSHUN: Furthermore, they are indiscriminately polluting our pristine environment!

FOURGAWN: There is litter everywhere!

POWHATAN: What is your counsel, then?

KONKLUSHUN: Remove their leader, John Smith. Without him the English will certainly leave or perish.

FOURGAWN: They are all a bunch of lazy bums, except Smith.

POWHATAN: OK. Get Smith and bring him back to me. Do you think you need the Antelope Team for this job?

KONKLUSHUN: The A Team? No way—they're too sloppy for the likes of John Smith. We'll use the Bear Team.

POWHATAN: The B Team—a wise choice. That's a very clever group. Good hunting.

HUNT: Mr. Newport, have you seen our Captain Smith lately?

NEWPORT: No, I haven't. He's been tied up with business for quite some time.

HUNT: What kind of business?

NEWPORT: He's been kidnapped by the locals. Chief Powhatan, it appears, has our fearless leader tied up in knots.

HUNT: What! Surely we must do something immediately!

NEWPORT: There's only one sure way to get him out alive at this point: invite his captors to a pizza potluck.

HUNT: But we've already consumed all our pepperoni, and we used our mozzarella for fish bait! We need another plan.

NEWPORT: How about this, then. We'll sneak a guitar into their camp—

HUNT: And they'll become curious, and Captain Smth will offer to demonstrate if they'll untie him—

NEWPORT: And he'll be free! Won't he?

**Scene V: Chief Powhatan's home,
three days later**

FOURGAWN: Chief Powhatan, look what the English have snuck into our compound.

3 *20 Plays for U.S. History Classes*

KONKLUSHUN: I think it's called a guitar.

POWHATAN: Of course it is! I saw one played at a concert up North when I was in college. I wonder if John Smith can play it.

FOURGAWN: I'll go get him.

(exits and returns with Smith)

POWHATAN: John Smith, can you play this instrument?

SMITH: Ah, shucks, yeah.

POWHATAN: Excellent! Call the tribe to gather. We'll have a concert on the green forthwith! Untie Smith.

Scene VI: On the green, soon after

SMITH: Great Chief, what would you like to hear?

POWHATAN: Something natural, possibly with a forest theme; the sounds of beetles or stones rolling . . .

SMITH: Sorry, no can do—too subtle. Hard rock in the trees, yes, or the bees' sting of spring sounds—

POWHATAN: No, no, no, Smith. I'll have nothing of the sort. You are in deep, deep trouble if you cannot play what I request.

POCAHONTAS: Oh, Daddy! I love spring sting music. Please let him play.

POWHATAN: Let me think about it for a minute. Oh, all right. I'm doing this only because you're my dearest daughter. Smith, you may now

play the music like the bees' stings in spring.

POCAHONTAS: Spring sting, Daddy!

SMITH: Boorrrnnn in the U.S.A. . . .

POCAHONTAS: Ohhhhh, Daddy! Isn't he the boss!

POWHATAN: The boss? Absolutely and emphatically NOT! I'm the chief around here! Now, what on earth is he singing about? I thought John Smith was an Englishman.

SMITH: Boorrrnn in the U.S.A. . . .

POWHATAN: There he goes again! Enough!

POCAHONTAS: Oh, Daddy, he's only singing about us—our people! Isn't he wonderful!

POWHATAN: If you say so, my dear. I just don't understand these things.

POCAHONTAS: What about him, Daddy? Can he go free?

POWHATAN: Not just yet. He has to keep the concert going for awhile since there's such a large crowd. But just remember, Smith, don't try to get rich off my people with any silly T-shirt sales. And keep the encores brief. There is much work to be done tomorrow for the tribe.

SMITH: Thank you so much, Chief. Aren't you going to stay?

POWHATAN: No. I told you what style of music I enjoy. I'm going home to listen to my tapes of Vivaldi's *The Four Seasons*. Good night.

BENJAMIN FRANKLIN: A MAN FOR THE PEOPLE

Characters (in order of appearance)

SARAH Read, Deborah's mother

DEBORAH, Ben Franklin's wife

BEN Franklin

WILLIAM Parsons, NICHOLAS Scull, JOSEPH Breintnal, and ROBERT Grace, members of the Junto Club

THOMAS Bond, physician

BILLY Franklin, Ben and Deborah's son

Benjamin Franklin

Scene I: Market Street, Philadelphia, Pennsylvania, autumn 1723

SARAH: Deborah! Come quickly!

DEBORAH: What is it, Mother?

SARAH: The sorriest- and funniest-looking man ever to walk the streets of Philadelphia! And he looks to be about your age. I'll bet he's a runaway servant.

DEBORAH: Maybe he's a bread vendor. He has a huge loaf under each arm.

SARAH: Now, who would buy bread from such a dirty and untidy seventeen-year-old? Look! His pockets are stuffed with shirts and socks. The poor boy can't even afford a sack for his clothes!

DEBORAH: Mother, I think he's coming this way.

BEN: Excuse me, ladies. Can you please point me to the printing shop of a Mr. Bradford?

DEBORAH: Do you know the streets of Philadelphia?

BEN: No. This is my first visit to your fair city.

SARAH:	Where do you come from, young man?
BEN:	Boston.
SARAH:	By your appearance I would say you left that great city in quite a hurry. Are you a fugitive?
BEN:	I am not running away from any law I've broken, only a most unjust and unfair apprenticeship contract. It would have taken four more years to complete, four more years of no wages, four more years as a subject to the tyranny and bad temper of my master.
SARAH:	So you have come to Philadelphia to be free.
BEN:	Yes, and to create a new life.
SARAH:	Well, good luck to you, young man.
BEN:	Thank you. But whether I succeed or fail here, luck and good fortune will not be the ladders I will set my feet upon. My aim is to succeed through hard work and wise planning.
DEBORAH:	What is your name?
BEN:	Benjamin Franklin. And yours?
DEBORAH:	Miss Deborah Read. I'll show you where to find Mr. Bradford's shop.
BEN:	Thank you. You have been most kind and helpful. I hope we can meet again.

Scene II: Franklin home, Philadelphia, 1731

BEN:	Dear wife, I'm off to the Junto Club.
DEBORAH:	Can't you miss one meeting? It's so very cold tonight, and you have worked such a long, long day.
BEN:	I thank you for your concern for my bodily welfare and comfort. But I do not think it proper to be absent from an organization I myself fathered.
DEBORAH:	But all you seem to do with those men is talk, talk, talk.
BEN:	We are devoted to a free and unbridled inquiry into truth—philosophy, science, politics—
DEBORAH:	Well, to me it's still just a lot of wind blowing nowhere useful. But if you must go, you have my blessing. I know how much pleasure those meetings give you.

Scene III: The Junto Club, Philadelphia, soon after

WILLIAM:	Ben, glad you finally arrived.
BEN:	Thank you.
NICHOLAS:	If any man in Philadelphia has a good reason to be late for a meeting, it's Ben Franklin. Don't you ever stop working? When do you start your day, anyway?
BEN:	Five o'clock. Early to bed, early to rise makes a man healthy, wealthy, and wise!

JOSEPH: That's a catchy phrase, Ben.

BEN: Thank you. I've sort of made a hobby of collecting little pearls of wisdom, the kind anyone can understand and find worth emulating.

WILLIAM: Give us a couple more.

BEN: If you insist. The rotten apple spoils its companions. God helps them that help themselves. Never leave till tomorrow what you can do today. An empty bag cannot stand upright. A penny saved is a penny earned. Little strokes fell great oaks.

NICHOLAS: Well done, Ben. Any proverbs about the value of swimming and being a vegetarian?

BEN: Not yet. I'd rather not draw too much attention to my individual interests and habits.

NICHOLAS: Why not? You are one of the city's most successful young men. People could benefit greatly by your example. I suggest that you share your wise sayings in that newspaper of yours.

BEN: Thank you for that affirmation. Actually, I have planned on compiling these proverbs into something more permanent than a newspaper.

JOSEPH: And what might that be?

BEN: An almanac—an almanac of useful information for all our citizens, an almanac written in clear and plain English, an almanac with a good deal of humor to amuse the readers.

JOSEPH: What will you call your almanac?

BEN: *Poor Richard's Almanac.*

WILLIAM: Well, I think it's an excellent idea. There are so few good and useful books to be read in this city.

NICHOLAS: And nearly all of them have come from England at a very stiff price.

JOSEPH: Is it any wonder why the level of learning rises so slowly amongst the general population?

BEN: Gentlemen, gentlemen! There is a solution to this dilemma that will benefit all.

WILLIAM: Speak your mind, Ben.

BEN: Each of us possesses a small library. Why don't we pool all our books into one large library? We can then conveniently have an opportunity to read many more books than we can now.

NICHOLAS: Ben, you are onto something worthwhile here. All we would need to do is to set up some rules and regulations for borrowing the books. It's all so very simple.

BEN: Yes! And look how easily it could be expanded into a free public library for all the citizens of Philadelphia!

JOSEPH: Imagine what a library could do for this city! The quality of life would improve immeasurably!

BEN: Precisely! My dear wife thinks all we do here is talk, talk, talk. She has a point. I propose we use the

Junto Club to launch new ideas for improving Philadelphia.

NICHOLAS: A free public library is certainly a noble idea! But let us not forget that good ideas can be like flames—easily quenched by the waters of practical concerns. Building a library will take much more than talk amongst members of the Junto Club.

BEN: Nicholas is correct. But let's not be defeated by the challenge before us. Remember my maxim, "Little strokes fell great oaks." If we plan carefully and wisely and above all, follow through with our energies, we can bring this idea to life.

WILLIAM: What should be our first "little stroke"?

BEN: Bringing our idea to the whole community. I'll write an article about it in my next paper.

JOSEPH: That should certainly stir up some interest.

NICHOLAS: And if we can show that our Junto Library works, people will start believing a library servicing all Philadelphia can work, too.

BEN: Yes! Next meeting bring all your books here.

Scene IV: The Junto Club, Philadelphia, five years later (1736)

ROBERT: It's so good to have you back with us, Ben.

NICHOLAS: Your little boy's untimely death touched us all.

JOSEPH: If only there was a safer way to prevent smallpox.

WILLIAM: Some day science will give us such a wonderful gift.

BEN: Thank you, one and all for your many acts of kindness to the Franklin family during this time of great sadness.

ROBERT: Ben, your presence here tonight is an inspiration to us all.

BEN: Again, thank you. Though I have lost a dear child, I am more resolved than ever to help improve the lives of all the children of Philadelphia.

NICHOLAS: You've done so much already. So much useful and inspiring knowledge has been spread by your newspaper and almanac.

ROBERT: And the public library has been a huge success!

BEN: Which all of you helped to bring about. Lately I have been thinking along the lines of what Joseph just said—"If only there was a safer way."

JOSEPH: Surely you don't think this club can take on the challenge of preventing smallpox. We're a collection of craftsmen and mechanics, not scientists and doctors.

BEN: Of course. I was considering something quite different: a safer way to run our city. Men, stop for a moment and think what happens when a fire breaks out in Philadelphia. Is it fought with any plan or organization?

NICHOLAS:	No. It's pretty much a lot of yelling, running, spilling, and hoping.
BEN:	Hardly an efficient way to fight a fire, wouldn't you all agree?
ROBERT:	That's for certain. Ben, by the look on your face, something important is cooking in that brain of yours.
BEN:	What if we organized a permanent fire company, trained to fight any fire in the city quickly and efficiently?
WILLIAM:	I would certainly volunteer.
JOSEPH:	And I as well.
NICHOLAS:	I think we could recruit plenty of men to volunteer. All we need to do is get the word out.
ROBERT:	Ben, here is where your newspaper can build interest in an important community project.
BEN:	Of course. And while we're on the subject, there's a lot that can be done to prevent fires.
WILLIAM:	And it only takes a little common sense. I can't believe how carelessly people remove hot coals from their homes. It's a wonder we don't have more fires!
BEN:	Excellent point, William. I'll write an article on simple ways to ensure fire safety. As Poor Richard says, "An ounce of prevention is worth a pound of cure."
ROBERT:	I knew Poor Richard would join this discussion sooner or later.

Ben, what other safety measures do you have in mind?

BEN:	Our streets. How can we make them more safe, clean, and well lit?
NICHOLAS:	Those are issues and concerns far beyond our resources. I think we need to be more practical and realistic regarding which problems we can effectively deal with.
BEN:	Your point is well taken, Nicholas. So permit me to break down the problem into more digestible pieces. Men, what comes to your mind when I say *constable*?
JOSEPH:	A ragtag bunch of lowlife characters paid a few cents to walk the rounds by the men who should be doing the job!
WILLIAM:	And they cannot do the job because they're too busy drinking ale in some tavern.
NICHOLAS:	And that leaves our city largely unprotected because the substitutes spend most of their time sleeping!
BEN:	A most unfortunate situation for a growing city like Philadelphia. Here is what I propose: a trained and organized police force of men of honest and sober temperament, men all the citizens of Philadelphia can place their faith and trust in.
JOSEPH:	It's a fine idea, Ben, but it will cost lots of money. You can organize a fire department with volunteers, but not a police force. It would be hard to

convince people we need it because it means more taxes.

BEN: Of course. But if we can make the people see the need for such a police force and how it will benefit each citizen, I believe the people will be willing to pay for it.

ROBERT: I agree with Ben. Hard-working people are willing to part with their money if it goes for necessary and useful services. They hate waste and frivolous expenses.

JOSEPH: Ben, it looks like your newspaper won't lack for articles to print: a fire department, a police force— What else do you have in mind for improving out city?

BEN: Paving our streets! I realize that would be an expensive enterprise, but in the long run, it would be very rewarding to all the people. When it rained, people and carts would no longer be slowed down by water and mud. Commerce would increase, as would safety and comfort for walkers. I suggest we begin with one street, Market Street, to demonstrate the value and usefulness of solid pavement.

ROBERT: Excellent ideas, Ben—all very practical and possible. I suggest that we help Ben with some specific plans for his articles and then start stirring up interest in the community.

Scene V: The Franklin home, Philadelphia, 1740	

BEN: Thank you all for coming to my home. I realize having our Junto meeting here is a bit irregular, but there is something I wish to show you that is not easily moved.

ROBERT: We understand, Ben. We know you're always tinkering with something. What is it this time?

BEN: A stove. A stove that burns like no other in the colonies.

NICHOLAS: Why have you gone to the trouble of making a stove?

BEN: I'll answer that question by first asking one of my own. What has happened to the price of wood?

WILLIAM: It's gone straight through the roof!

BEN: Just like the heat from our heating stoves and fireplaces.

NICHOLAS: What are you talking about, Ben?

BEN: Most of the heat from the fuel we burn is lost up the chimney!

JOSEPH: And this contraption of yours works differently? How?

BEN: Come take a closer look. By means of this series of vents, the heat is circulated about so it radiates out, not up.

ROBERT: Do you mean that in the dead of winter a family doesn't have to hover close to the fire?

10   *20 Plays for U.S. History Classes*

BEN:	Move about the room and notice how the heat is spread equally throughout.
ROBERT:	Amazing! Ben, I'm certain you could sell thousands of these devices.
BEN:	I suppose so, but I would rather give that job to you since you have the iron foundry, Robert. I have some "other irons in the fire," as the saying goes.
NICHOLAS:	Like what?
BEN:	I've asked a friend of mine, Dr. Thomas Bond, to answer that question. He's the expert.
THOMAS:	Thank you so much for giving me this opportunity. I'll get right to the point. Philadelphia has no hospital. Is there any doubt that this city needs one?
WILLIAM:	No, of course not.
THOMAS:	So far, all my efforts to interest people in such a worthy project have failed. Then I reminded myself of the obvious: get Ben Franklin behind a good idea and it will become a reality.
BEN:	Please, Dr. Thomas, not me alone. All the members of the Junto Club are responsible. And once they hear what you have to say, I'm confident that Philadelphia will soon have its very first hospital. Gentlemen, I give you Dr. Bond.

Scene VI: Franklin home, Philadelphia, June 1752

DEBORAH:	Husband, I think this is a very silly idea. And you're certain to get drenched in the process. Just look at those clouds.
BEN:	Have no fear, my dear. It's just a little experiment. Billy, are you ready?
BILLY:	Yes, sir, but I am not too happy about getting all wet.
BEN:	But it's for a worthy cause: the advancement of science! Besides, it will be great fun!
BILLY:	If you say so.
BEN:	Do you have the Leyden Jar to capture the electricity?
BILLY:	Yes, father.
BEN:	Excellent! Well, I've got the kite, key, string, and ribbon. Onward! Follow me onto the noble path to truth and understanding!
DEBORAH:	Oh, don't be so dramatic! A man of your age flying a kite in a thunderstorm! If your friends see you they'll think you've gone mad!
BEN:	My friends know better. Besides, I'll let Billy get the kite up in the air. We'll be home soon.
	(a few hours later)
DEBORAH:	Just look at the both of you! Did you fall into the creek?
BILLY:	Mother! We did it!
DEBORAH:	Did what?

BILLY: I got the kite real high in the sky. And when the lightning struck, it traveled down the string to the key father was holding!

DEBORAH: It's a wonder he wasn't struck dead. What does all this kite flying and lightning prove?

BILLY: That lightning is electricity! Father also says it proves that electricity is caused by friction.

DEBORAH: Hmmm. Billy, you know your father is a practical man. There has to be some way he's going to use this knowledge.

BILLY: There is. Father told me that people can now protect their houses and buildings from lightning by putting a metal rod on the rooftops. And you connect the rod down into the ground.

So in a lightning storm, the lightning will hit the rod and then go down into the ground.

DEBORAH: Well, if such a rod can prevent fires and people from being hit by lightning, it's a good idea. And I'm sure your father will tell everyone about it in the newspaper.

BEN: Of course. And I also plan to write up my experiment for scientists around the world. Some day science will harness the power of electricity and change our lives forever.

DEBORAH: Hmmm. Speaking of changing— you two kite-flying scientists best change those wet clothes before you both end up in the hospital!

PHILLIS WHEATLEY, AFRICAN-AMERICAN POET, 1753-1784

Characters (in order of appearance)

SUSANNAH Wheatley, wife of John	John HANCOCK, influential Boston citizen
JOHN Wheatley, Boston tailor	PHILLIS Wheatley, poet born a slave
DEERG, slave trader	COUNTESS (of Huntington), English socialite
AUNT SUKEY, slave in Wheatley household	NATHANIEL Wheatley, Susannah and John's son
MARY Wheatley, Susannah and John's daughter	John PETERS, African-American soldier/ messenger
BIGUTT, Boston citizen	SOLDIER (Massachusetts militia)

Phillis Wheatley

Scene I: Wheatley home, Boston, Massachusetts, 1761

SUSANNAH: John, where are you going in such a hurry?

JOHN: To the harbor. A slave ship just arrived.

SUSANNAH: Now, why should that stir you up so?

JOHN: We could use another pair of hands with all the household chores.

SUSANNAH: We already have Aunt Sukey.

JOHN: True, but she's getting on in years and slowing down. Besides, I think some company would be good for her spirits. Would you like to help pick someone out?

SUSANNAH: No. I cannot bear the sight of those poor souls chained up and

then moved about like cattle. I trust your judgment in this matter.

Scene II: Boston Harbor, soon after

JOHN: Sir, can you please direct me to where the auction is to be held?

DEERG: It's all over and done.

JOHN: You mean all were sold?

DEERG: No. A few are left. If you're interested, follow me.

JOHN: I am. This young girl here—Why is she chained?

DEERG: To keep her from running away, of course!

JOHN: But she's so little and young!

DEERG: That's right. No more than seven or eight by the looks of those missing front teeth.

JOHN: Can she talk? She seems absolutely terrified.

DEERG: Of course she can talk, but no words you or I could understand. They don't speak much English where she came from.

JOHN: What about her family? Did they come with her? Where are they now?

DEERG: This girl is all by herself. In this business I don't keep track of family connections. Besides, most of them were broken off back in Africa.

JOHN: Tell me more about your "business."

DEERG: It's pretty simple. I sail to the west coast of Africa, put in at a slave trading port, get as many slaves as I can on board, chain them so they don't jump off, and sail west.

JOHN: You really don't mean they're chained for the whole journey across the ocean?

DEERG: Of course they are! The more slaves I deliver, the more profit I earn, understand?

JOHN: Will this amount pay for this girl?

DEERG: Plus another shilling for my time explaining things.

JOHN: Done! Come with me sweet little one. Don't worry. Everything is going to be all right now.

Scene III: Wheatley home, Boston, a week later

SUSANNAH: Aunt Sukey, how is our little Phillis getting along?

AUNT SUKEY: Much better than when Master John brought her home. There was so much fear and suffering in those eyes. I know that look. I know that look.

SUSANNAH: Has she spoken to you?

AUNT SUKEY: No words I can understand. I've tried to teach her some English, but I'm so busy with the chores.

SUSANNAH:	Of course. I understand. The twins and I will take care of her education.
AUNT SUKEY:	Mistress Susannah, this is one sweet child. I think Phillis and I will become very close friends. Thank you for bringing her to us.

Scene IV: Wheatley home, Boston, a few months later

SUSANNAH:	Mary, how is Phillis progressing with her lessons?
MARY:	Mother, you might not believe what I am going to say, but I think Phillis is a genius.
SUSANNAH:	Genius? What makes you say that?
MARY:	Everything I teach her she masters immediately.
SUSANNAH:	Mary, you must remember young children are like parrots. It's easy for them to repeat what adults say. Understanding what you say, now that's a different matter entirely.
MARY:	Mother! She can already read! From the Bible! Long and difficult passages! And she seems to understand what she reads.
SUSANNAH:	What does your brother, Nathaniel, say about her?
MARY:	He's teaching her science and Latin!
SUSANNAH:	Well, if she truly is a genius, I want a hand in her education. I'll fill her mind with great literature.

MARY:	Mother, we are all blessed by having Phillis.
SUSANNAH:	I know. Aunt Sukey has been a different person ever since she arrived.
MARY:	Just like little Phillis. When she first came to us she was shivering with cold and shaking with fear. Now she's a happy child.
SUSANNAH:	Aunt Sukey is mostly responsible for that. She's become like a second mother to Phillis.

Scene V: Wheatley Tailoring Shop, Boston, 1766

JOHN:	Yes, sir, can I help you?
BIGUTT:	A neighbor said you did good and honest work.
JOHN:	Integrity is the cornerstone of my business. Now, do you need something made or mended?
BIGUTT:	Neither. I have come to question and challenge your notion on integrity. I think you are a liar and a hypocrite and above all a great deceiver.
JOHN:	If there is some flaw or defect in my work, I will gladly make amends and refunds.
BIGUTT:	This has nothing to do with coats or pants, but poetry.
JOHN:	Kindly explain yourself, sir. I have no idea what you are talking about.
BIGUTT:	There are numerous poems circulating around Boston with

your slave girl's name as author. I've seen them, and they are of considerable quality and skill.

JOHN: So, what's your purpose in coming here?

BIGUTT: To have you end this shameful deceit! These are all counterfeit poems. First of all, no slave is supposed to read or write. And second, even if they do learn, none is capable of such writing as these poems. You or someone in your family wrote these lines.

JOHN: You are mistaken. Even though Phillis is only thirteen years old, she did in fact write these poems, all by herself.

BIGUTT: Dark-skinned people do not have the mind for such things. They are, in truth, only fit for manual work, like cutting wood and carrying water.

JOHN: I am telling you the truth. Phillis can read both English and Latin and even knows science.

BIGUTT: You are a liar, Mr. Wheatley. You are spreading shameful lies, and I mean to tell all Boston the truth about this deception. There are many others who already agree with me, I might add.

JOHN: Is that so? How about a test, a public demonstration of Phillis's knowledge, skills, and capabilities?

BIGUTT: You are trying to silence the truth with a clumsy and grotesque bluff.

JOHN: Then call my bluff, sir.

BIGUTT: Done!

JOHN: Just make sure you are there and that your eyes and ears and mind are fully open! Good day!

Scene VI: Governor Hutchinson's house, Boston, a few weeks later

HANCOCK: Distinguished citizens of Boston, thank you for coming to this unusual event. As most of you know, various poems, all well received and admired, are circulating around the city claiming Phillis Wheatley, a thirteen-year-old slave, is the author. Some citizens have doubted her ownership, stating, in effect, that a young black woman is not capable of such a literary achievement. We are gathered here tonight to determine if Phillis possesses sufficient learning and ability to write such poems. Our goal, like that of an impartial jury, is to render a just verdict based on evidence and not on rumor or prejudice. We shall now begin. Phillis, please recite the Twenty-Third Psalm.

PHILLIS: "The Lord is my Shepherd, I shall not want . . ."

HANCOCK: Excellent. Now I am going to pick a passage of scripture at random and ask you to read it. Please read from First Corinthians, chapter 13, verses 4 and 5.

PHILLIS: "Charity suffereth long, and is kind; charity envieth not; charity vaunteth not itself, is not puffed up, doth not behave itself unseemly, seeketh not her own,

HANCOCK: Perfectly done. Now I am going to ask you to read in Latin a passage from the *Aeneid* by the Roman poet Virgil.

(Phillis reads the selection flawlessly.)

Thank you, Phillis. You are a very brave and learned young woman. I think I speak for all in attendance here this evening. There is no doubt in my mind that you are capable of writing such wonderful poetry. I wish you all the best in your life and in your writing career. You are indeed a rare and gifted talent.

Scene VII: The Countess of Huntington's home, London, England, 1773

COUNTESS: Ladies and gentlemen, thank you for coming to this reception for one of the Colonies' rising literary stars. I present Miss Phillis Wheatley of Boston, Massachusetts, who will honor us with a reading from her recently published book entitled *Poems on Various Subjects, Religious and Moral.*

PHILLIS: Thank you. I am deeply moved by your presence here this evening. Allow me, please, to tell you a little about myself. I was born in Africa, taken from my family while still a child, bound in chains, and sent by ship to Boston. There God's gracious hand of protection brought me to a kind and loving family, the Wheatleys. Few slaves were as fortunate as I, however. Blessed and happy as my life with the Wheatleys has been, the painful memories of being taken from my family in Africa have never been erased. This poem is based on those memories:

"Should you, my lord, while you
        pursue my song
Wonder from whence my love of
        FREEDOM sprung,
Whence flow these wishes for the
        common good,
By feeling hearts alone best
        understood,
I, young in life, by seeming
        cruel fate
Was snatched from Africa's
        fancied happy seat:
What pangs excruciating must
        molest,
What sorrows labour in my
        parent's breast?
Steeled was the soul and by no
        misery moved
That from a father seized his
        babe beloved
Such, such my case. And can I
        then but pray
Others may never feel tyranny's
        sway?"

(great applause)

COUNTESS: Phillis, my dear, you have taken our hearts.

PHILLIS: Thank you, Countess, for all your support and encouragement. Without your help my poems would have never been published here in England.

COUNTESS: You are too modest, my dear. Would you please answer some

	questions about your work? You have a very interested audience.	PHILLIS:	The Stamp Act was especially hated. It seemed the people had to pay for a stamp on everything they bought.
PHILLIS:	I would be most happy to.		
COUNTESS:	What are some of the major sources of your themes and ideas?	NATHANIEL:	Don't forget how the Crown tried to force us to quarter troops in our own homes. People in Boston fought like terriers to prevent that.
PHILLIS:	My own experiences, of course. And the Scriptures.		
COUNTESS:	And your writing style?	COUNTESS:	And I can certainly understand why. At least Parliament had the good sense to repeal those acts.
PHILLIS:	I believe your poets Thomas Gray and Alexander Pope have most influenced me in this area.		
		NATHANIEL:	But that hasn't erased the lingering bitterness and resentment.
COUNTESS:	How much longer will we have the pleasure of your company in England?	COUNTESS:	That's a pity. Why is that?
		PHILLIS:	Just a few years ago in Boston, British troops fired on a crowd and killed five people.
PHILLIS:	I am not certain. Nathaniel, my travel guardian, has received word that his mother is very ill.		
		COUNTESS:	The colonists were throwing snowballs at them, weren't they?
NATHANIEL:	We are to leave for home on the next available ship.		
		NATHANIEL:	True, but that is no justification for shooting and killing unarmed civilians.
COUNTESS:	How unfortunate—just like the present state of affairs between England the Colonies. I just hope and pray cool heads and good sense will prevail.		
		PHILLIS:	I don't think the memory of that massacre in Boston will ever go away.
NATHANIEL:	I share your sentiments, Countess, as do most people in the Colonies. But that has not stilled their growing anger and impatience with your government.	COUNTESS:	I hope you are mistaken and that that incident will be the last of any bloodshed.
		PHILLIS:	So do we all. But the British government must respect how determined the colonists are to safeguard their freedoms. They will not back down. Of this I am certain.
COUNTESS:	I understand—all those irritating taxes the king imposed on you— so high-handed and unfair.		

Scene VIII: Militia Encampment, Boston, July 1775

PETERS: Messenger from General Washington! Messenger from General Washington!

SOLDIER: Who is it for? Our commanding officer is away.

PETERS: A Miss Phillis Wheatley of this detachment.

SOLDIER: Hmmmm. What business would the general have with Nurse Phillis? I'll take you to her quarters.

(shortly thereafter)

PETERS: Are you the Miss Phillis Wheatley who wrote a poem to General Washington?

PHILLIS: I am.

PETERS: I have been ordered to communicate his response: General Washington was deeply honored and moved by your poem and wishes to meet with you personally.

PHILLIS: How kind and thoughtful of him. I would like that very much. Please inform General Washington that I will meet with him at his convenience. Thank you.

Epilogue

Phillis Wheatley did meet with General Washington. Unfortunately, her years thereafter were filled with great sorrow and personal tragedy. Her husband's business failed, and he was put into a debtor's prison. All of Phillis's children died young. However, she composed one of her most memorable poems "Liberty and Peace" in 1781 when the American Revolutionary War ended. She died in poverty in 1784, just as her poems were about to be published in America. Her name and work were lost to history until 1834, when Margaretta Odell re-established Phillis Wheatley's reputation as a fine poet.

JUNÍPERO SERRA

CHARACTERS (in order of appearance)

CAPTAIN, ship captain

Junípero SERRA, Franciscan priest

Francisco PALOU, Franciscan priest

PEDRO, priest

VELASCO, Franciscan leader

MONICA and CATALINA, wealthy aristocrats

JUAN, Indian convert and aid to Serra

Father Junípero Serra

Scene I: Aboard ship, the Mediterranean Sea, April 1749

CAPTAIN: So, if it isn't the priests from the backward island of Majorca. Out for a stroll on my deck? Be careful you don't trip over your ridiculous robes.

SERRA: A pleasant day to you, Captain.

CAPTAIN: Of course, if you do fall and hit your heads, maybe some good sense will result.

PALOU: Yes, a very good day to you, Captain.

CAPTAIN: What's this? Trying to sweeten me up?

SERRA: Captain, we wish you no ill will. For some unknown reason you do to us. We are sorry for this. We will try hard not to aggravate you in any way.

CAPTAIN: So, it's the old turn-the-other-cheek tactic, eh?

PALOU: That is what our Lord has taught.

SERRA: And we are His obedient servants. Why are you so angry with us?

CAPTAIN: Because you're both priests! Always telling people what to do, what to think, what to believe. I suppose you're off to some far-off place to do that now.

20 Plays for U.S. History Classes

PALOU:	We are going to the New World to spread the Catholic faith and help the native peoples.
CAPTAIN:	I knew it! And what gives you the right? You should leave those people—what do they call them? Indians, I think—alone. If they need any missionaries, it should be Protestants, not Catholics!
SERRA:	Our intent is not to argue theology with you, sir. It would be pointless and cause bad feelings. Our goal is to serve our Lord, not to engage in debates.
CAPTAIN:	Get out of my sight before I personally throw both of you overboard!

Scene II: Vera Cruz, Mexico, December 6, 1749

PALOU:	Father Serra, please forgive me, but I am too weak from the fever to accompany you.
SERRA:	It was a very difficult voyage for us all. One hundred days at sea with little water or food! But God has spared me from your sickness.
PALOU:	But you are still tired and weak. Why do you insist on walking all the way to Mexico City?
SERRA:	Could I call myself a Franciscan and not walk all the way?
PALOU:	But it's 270 English miles! You must cross blazing deserts, steamy jungles, and then climb up rugged mountains. You could be attacked by wild animals!
SERRA:	The journey will prepare me for life in the New World.
PALOU:	Or cause your premature death. Please wait for the caravan, my brother.
SERRA:	God will protect me. Francisco, get well. I will see you in Mexico City.
PALOU:	How strange life can be. When we began our journey, I was the strong and healthy priest and you were weak and frail. Now I must be carried while you walk the whole way.
SERRA:	Adiós.

Scene III: Between Vera Cruz and Mexico City, mid-December 1749

PEDRO:	Father Serra! What happened to your leg? It's all swollen. We must get you to a doctor immediately!
SERRA:	Something bit me during my sleep. I fear I made the wound worse by scratching it.
PEDRO:	Can you walk?
SERRA:	Of course I can.
PEDRO:	But you are limping badly. Let me carry you.
SERRA:	Pedro, dear brother, if I allow you to carry me, neither of us will finish the journey.

Scene IV: College of Fernando, Mexico City, January 1, 1750

VELASCO: Father Serra! We had given you up for dead!

SERRA: God has provided.

VELASCO: Welcome to the college. I am the Father Guardian.

SERRA: Thank you. Has Father Palou arrived safely?

VELASCO: Yes. He's resting.

SERRA: Good. I am ready to begin my duties.

VELASCO: Rest will be your first task. You had quite a trip, according to Brother Pedro. I see you are still limping.

SERRA: It is of no concern. To what tribe will I be assigned?

VELASCO: Let's not rush things, Father Serra. First, you will receive some specialized training here at the college. During this time you will be responsible for some preaching at the great cathedral. Most of your parishioners will be from the aristocracy.

SERRA: But I came thousands of miles to serve the native peoples, the poor and needy.

VELASCO: Father Serra, remember your vow of obedience. These people have heard of your coming and are very excited. They feel especially honored to have such a renowned scholar and preacher as you hold services for them.

I trust you will not disappoint them.

Scene V: Church service, Mexico City, March 1750

(Father Serra preaching)

SERRA: The New Testament lesson for today is from St. Paul's letter to the Romans, chapter 12, verse 16: "Live in harmony with one another. Do not be proud, but be willing to associate with people of low position. Do not be conceited."

MONICA: Catalina, that's the first time I ever saw you pay attention to the Scripture reading.

CATALINA: I am very curious to hear what the scholarly priest from Spain will say about it.

MONICA: Hmmm. Maybe I will listen to him as well.

SERRA: Dear brothers and sisters, do not think that because you adorn your clothes and bodies with diamonds and gold you are better than your servants who bring you chocolate during the service. They, too, are God's children, and so are the native peoples here in Mexico. You must not abuse or take advantage of them. Instead, reach out to them with hands of respect and generosity.

CATALINA: These are hard words for rich people like ourselves.

MONICA: He's just a priest. We do not need to do what he says. Besides,

caring for others is his job, not ours.

CATALINA: You may think that, Monica, but I cannot ignore what Father Serra has said. He speaks from the heart.

Scene VI: College of San Fernando, Mexico City, April 1750

VELASCO: Father Serra, you are remarkable. When I heard about your sermons I thought you would empty every church you entered. Instead it seems you've developed something of a following amongst many of the rich. They appreciate your honesty, integrity, and eloquence.

SERRA: Does that mean I am to remain here? My heart is with the poor and the needy, not those corrupted by wealth.

VELASCO: I understand. That's why I'm asking you to take charge over all the missions in the Sierra Gorda. Father Palou will assist you. But I must warn you, it will be an almost impossible challenge. Will you go?

SERRA: Yes. Tell me about the challenge.

VELASCO: The climate there is horrible: hot and humid. The land is very poor and the Indians indifferent to our presence. Nearly all the priests we have sent there died. The buildings are falling apart from neglect.

SERRA: How soon can Brother Palou and I begin?

Scene VII: July 1767 (seventeen years later)

VELASCO: Father Serra, you and Father Palou have worked a miracle in the Sierra Gorda! You have brought the missions back to life! And you have taught the Indians so many useful skills! Farming, building, weaving—

SERRA: Give credit to God and Father Palou.

VELASCO: You are too modest. These past few years, how many miles have you traveled?

PALOU: Over 2,000, I've calculated. All by walking.

VELASCO: Father Serra, does your leg still trouble you?

SERRA: How could I have done all that walking if it did?

VELASCO: Father Palou, give me a straight answer about Father Serra's leg.

PALOU: He still walks with a limp. I know it pains him at times, but he never complains. He just keeps going.

SERRA: Do you have a new assignment for me and Father Palou?

VELASCO: Among your many gifts, it appears you can read minds. Yes, there is a new challenge for you: the Franciscans will be in charge of all missions in lower California. And that means you, Father Serra. Father Palou will be your assistant.

SERRA: But those missions were built and operated by the Jesuits. They were very successful, I've been told. Why the change?

VELASCO: The reasons are very complicated and very political. Orders from the king.

SERRA: This does not seem to be a great challenge. The Jesuits built a very solid foundation in lower California.

VELASCO: But that foundation is crumbling fast. As soon as the Jesuit priests were forced to leave, Spanish soldiers were left in charge of the missions.

PALOU: That would be expected until new priests arrived. What problems would that cause?

VELASCO: Many! The troops looted the missions and terrorized the Indians. There was no one to control them. Father Serra, you are the only person who can bring back order and stability to those missions.

SERRA: I will obey your commands.

VELASCO: You do not look so eager as when you left to resurrect the Sierra Gorda missions seventeen years ago. Is that because of your health?

SERRA: No. I am fifty-four years old. It seems I have spent most of my life here repairing old missions. I was hoping for once in my life to have the chance to build something new. It seems I will not have that opportunity.

VELASCO: But you will!

SERRA: But you just said—

VELASCO: I did not tell you the rest of your assignment. The new king is very alarmed by the growing Russian and English presence to the north. You are to build a chain of missions in Alta California— upper California. The reasons are obvious.

SERRA: For the king, yes. But I operate in the spiritual realm, not the political. My only goals are to spread the Catholic faith and improve the lives of the native peoples.

VELASCO: Of course.

PALOU: Alta California? Isn't that where Vizcaino explored nearly 170 years ago?

VELASCO: Yes, and found a very strategic bay the king wants Spain to reclaim and occupy. Unfortunately, no one has found it since Vizcaino.

PALOU: Wasn't it called Monterey Bay— the bay near the King's Mountain?

VELASCO: Yes. The Crown is sending Portola to find it once again. Then you, Father Serra, are to build a mission there.

SERRA: I trust we will be allowed to build many missions in Alta California and not just in Monterey.

VELASCO: That will depend on many factors, such as how much support you receive from the viceroy.

SERRA:	Supplies, you mean.
VELASCO:	Of course. You will also need the cooperation of the military commander and of the native peoples and your own energy and ingenuity. Remember, Alta California is a long, long way from Mexico City and civilization.
SERRA:	Thank you so much for giving me this opportunity. It is a dream come true.

Scene VIII: Carmel Mission, Carmel, Alta California, August 1784

JUAN:	Father Serra, do not get up. You must rest.
SERRA:	There is so much work to be done.
JUAN:	Yes, but you have just completed a long journey—all the way from San Diego.
SERRA:	I had to see the nine missions, my very own children. Juan, do you remember when we both journeyed all the way to Mexico City together?
JUAN:	Yes. That was when the military commanders would not let you build any new missions. You went right to the viceroy himself to get them to change.
SERRA:	That was very exciting. Now, I fear my end is near.
JUAN:	Please don't talk like that, Father Serra. You just need to rest.

SERRA:	Juan, you have been so faithful to me and the work here. Would you please ask Father Palou to come to me?

(Juan exits, Father Palou enters)

PALOU:	You wish to see me, Father?
SERRA:	Yes. Thank you for coming. My heart is heavy. I feel I have not lived up to my calling here in Alta California.
PALOU:	Nonsense! Look at all the missions you have built between here and San Diego, and all the people you have baptized into the Faith, and all the ways you have helped the native peoples to have better lives.
SERRA:	But there were so many problems with the military commanders. They wanted me to stop planting new missions. And how badly they treated the Indians—so many hard feelings and misunderstandings.
PALOU:	But that was their sin, not yours. You treated the Indians with gentleness and compassion.
SERRA:	I always looked upon them as God's children, and mine. I never wanted to hurt any of them.
PALOU:	Father Serra, you need to rest now.
SERRA:	Father Palou, do you remember the sea captain who abused us so long ago?

PALOU: Yes. He was a very angry and bitter man.

SERRA: Remember how he said we priests had no right to come to the New World to change the Indians?

PALOU: I remember. We did not come to enrich ourselves or to misuse the native peoples. We came in a spirit of love and peace.

SERRA: Yes. I am very tired. I am going to rest now.

PALOU: Rest well, dear friend. Rest well.

(Father Serra died a few days later)

ELI WHITNEY AND THE BIRTH OF THE MACHINE AGE

Characters (in order of appearance)

ELIZABETH, Eli Whitney's sister	PHINEAS Miller, Whitney's business partner
ELI Whitney	APPERTOON and GATES, Georgia cotton growers
JOSIAH Stebbins, friend of Eli Whitney	DIEMAKER and LATHEMAN, factory mechanics
CATHERINE Greene, plantation owner	

Eli Whitney

Scene I: Whitney Farm, Westborough, Massachusetts, 1779

ELIZABETH: Eli! Why aren't you doing your chores?

ELI: Because I'm busy making something.

ELIZABETH: You're always doing that instead of your chores. Stepmother said you were supposed to fetch some wood.

ELI: I'll get it later.

ELIZABETH: She's going to be real mad again.

ELI: Not when she sees this.

ELIZABETH: Eli, are you making a knife?

ELI: That's right. To replace the one she broke from her fancy English set. Here, take a look.

ELIZABETH: It's—it's just like it. How did you do it? Father doesn't have any knife-making tools in his shop.

ELI: I know. I went and made them myself.

ELIZABETH: What? How?

ELI: Father does have a lathe and other useful tools.

ELIZABETH: Hmmm. Eli, you would be content to spend all day and all night in some workshop making things, wouldn't you?

ELI:	Yes, sister. But I would like to attend college first. My mind needs more education and stimulation.	JOSIAH:	Will Mrs. Greene be accompanying you?
		ELI:	Yes, and her children. They have a home in Rhode Island.

Scene II: Yale College, New Haven, Connecticut, late September 1792

JOSIAH: Eli, old friend, why the glum look? You just graduated. You should feel on top of the world. What happened?

ELI: The teaching job in New York didn't work out.

JOSIAH: So? You didn't want it in the first place, remember? You want to be a lawyer. That's your chosen star.

ELI: Right now it's a star hidden behind a mountain—of debts. I needed that job in New York before I could go on with my legal studies.

JOSIAH: What are you going to do, then?

ELI: President Stiles arranged a tutoring position for me in South Carolina.

JOSIAH: South Carolina? The climate is beastly there.

ELI: I know, but for the present it's all I can count on.

JOSIAH: What are your travel arrangements?

ELI: I'm to sail to New York and meet a gentleman from Connecticut, Phineas Miller, who is employed by Mrs. Catherine Greene in Georgia. He is to assist me in the voyage to Savannah.

JOSIAH: Is this Mrs. Greene the widow of George Washington's quartermaster general in the Revolutionary War?

ELI: Yes.

JOSIAH: Then you'll be in the company of quite a woman. During that terrible winter at Valley Forge, she was the model of courage and endurance and an inspiration to her husband and his fellow officers.

ELI: Hmmm. Maybe she can help me overcome my fear of sailing. You know how easily I get seasick.

Scene III: Greene Plantation, Mulberry Grove, Georgia, late October 1792

CATHERINE: You wish a word with me, Eli?

ELI: Yes, Mrs. Greene. It concerns my staying here.

CATHERINE: Eli, you need not be so formal. Call me Catherine. Now, what's the matter?

ELI: Ever since that position in South Carolina didn't work out, I have been your guest. You have been so kind to me. But I feel I must return home and to useful employment.

CATHERINE: So it's your Yankee Puritan conscience that's upsetting you. You haven't been idle. The frame

	you made to hold my needlework is absolutely ingenious, and so practical!
ELI:	Any of your workers could have easily made one.
CATHERINE:	Possibly, but only your mind could have conceived its design.
ELI:	You are very kind, but I must be getting along.
CATHERINE:	So, it's a challenge you're looking for.

(enter Phineas Miller)

PHINEAS:	Oh, hello, Eli.
CATHERINE:	Phineas, you have arrived at a most opportune time. Eli thinks he should return home and find a job. Don't you think we could better employ his mechanical talents here in the South? Tell him about our "cotton problem."
ELI:	What problem? I've seen it growing everywhere here.
PHINEAS:	But there is no market for it.
ELI:	What? English textile factories are desperately short of cotton. They'll pay anything to get it.
PHINEAS:	Clean cotton, Eli, clean cotton. The cotton you've seen growing like a weed is upland cotton. It's full of small green seeds. It takes forever and a day to clean, which is very costly—too costly to be profitable.
ELI:	Is it cleaned by hand?
PHINEAS:	Of course.

ELI:	If there were a machine that could clean this upland cotton, growers could make significant profits.
CATHERINE:	Yes, and bring economic revival to the whole South.
PHINEAS:	Eli, the South hasn't recovered from the war like the North has. It's poor and desperate. Cotton could change that. It could mean thousands of jobs, planting and picking.
ELI:	You mean for slaves?
CATHERINE:	Yes. Right now there isn't much for them to do. Owning slaves is very costly.
ELI:	So you want me to create a machine that can easily clean large quantities of this upland cotton. Very well, I accept the challenge. All I ask is a secluded and well-equipped workshop— and, of course, some of that cotton.

Scene IV: Workshop, Greene Plantation, Mulberry Grove, Georgia, March 1793

CATHERINE:	Eli, can we have a look?
ELI:	Come right in.
PHINEAS:	The clogging problem—have you found a solution yet?
ELI:	You mean when the fibers get caught on the teeth and keep rolling around and around on the cylinder?

PHINEAS:	Yes. Have you made any adjustments to your cotton engine?
ELI:	I have. I've inserted a second and smaller roller here. Take a look for yourselves.
PHINEAS:	You mean the one with the bristles? What does it do?
ELI:	I've set it to revolve faster than the main roller, but in the opposite direction. Look what happens.
CATHERINE:	It sweeps the cleaned cotton from the teeth! No more clogging! Eli, you've done it!
PHINEAS:	This engine should be patented immediately!
CATHERINE:	How about a small demonstration here first?
PHINEAS:	That could be risky. Someone might steal Eli's invention.
CATHERINE:	Nonsense. My neighbors are all honorable people. Besides, a great idea like this needs some publicity to create a market.
ELI:	I'll trust your judgement, Catherine.
CATHERINE:	Thank you. Leave me to make all the arrangements.
	(Catherine exits)
PHINEAS:	Eli, how fast can you make one of these cotton gins?
ELI:	What are you driving at?
PHINEAS:	The future! Imagine the impact a hundred machines like this would have on the entire South! Cotton would become king!
ELI:	A hundred machines? I couldn't make them here. But in Connecticut, yes. There are plenty of skilled mechanics there. It would mean building a complete factory. But I don't have that kind of money.
PHINEAS:	What if you had a partner who could raise the capital?
ELI:	In that case, it could be done.
PHINEAS:	Let's talk.

Scene V: Greene Plantation, April 1793

CATHERINE:	Thank you one and all for coming. Eli—
	(Eli demonstrates his cotton gin)
APPERTOON:	It would take one of my slave crews weeks to clean that much upland cotton.
GATES:	How can we purchase one of your cotton gins?
PHINEAS:	We're not exactly going to sell them outright. For the use of each one, Mr. Whitney and I will receive a percentage of all the cotton cleaned.
APPERTOON:	Precisely what percentage?
PHINEAS:	For every five pounds of cotton we process, we guarantee you one clean pound.
GATES:	And you keep the remainder?
PHINEAS:	Yes.

GATES:	Five pounds normally yields one and two-thirds pounds clean.
APPERTOON:	You'll get a 40 percent profit!
PHINEAS:	Gentlemen, gentlemen—everyone will profit!

(Gates takes Appertoon aside)

GATES:	I've got an idea. Let's see if we can sneak one of our best mechanics into Whitney's workshop and study this cotton gin. It's ingenious, but not that complicated.
APPERTOON:	I agree. Why should these two Yankees get so rich on a little box? We're the ones who supply the cotton!
GATES:	You know what else this invention means?
APPERTOON:	We'll all be needing lots more slaves to plant and pick.

Scene VI: Home of Eli's sister, Westborough, Massachusetts, April 1798

ELIZABETH:	Dear brother, what are you going to do now?
ELI:	Forget about making any more cotton gins, that's what.
ELIZABETH:	Just because your factory burned down? You can start over.
ELI:	With what money? Do you realize how much I've spent on legal bills? And every cent going to protect my patent rights. What good has it done me?
ELIZABETH:	Sooner or later you will get what is rightfully yours. All those people who made copies of your cotton gin will pay.
ELI:	No, that isn't going to happen. There are too many imitations scattered about the South. I'm going into business with people who are unconcerned about my zero credit rating.
ELIZABETH:	And who might these people be?
ELI:	Leaders of our federal government.
ELIZABETH:	Making what?
ELI:	Thousands of new muskets, all delivered in record time.
ELIZABETH:	What's the emergency? Our country is not at war.
ELI:	We might be soon with France. Relations with the French are very fragile right now. The government needs a well-stocked arsenal, and I can give them one.
ELIZABETH:	How can you make guns so quickly? Where are you going to find so many skilled gunsmiths?
ELI:	I'm not going to need that many. I'm going to make new machines that will make the gun parts.
ELIZABETH:	Can you really make such machines?
ELI:	Yes.
ELIZABETH:	Then every individual part will be uniform.

ELI:	Precisely! The same size and shape.
ELIZABETH:	The parts will be interchangeable. If one part needs to be repaired, you will only have to fix or replace it rather than make a whole new musket.
ELI:	Elizabeth, you are most perceptive.
ELIZABETH:	Eli, if you can assemble muskets that way, you could certainly do the same with knives, sewing needles, even shoes. You could change all industry in the United States!
ELI:	I'm sure others in New England have similar ideas. But you are correct. Industry will change dramatically in the next few years. With reliable milling machines we will be able to mass produce just about anything.

Scene VII: Simeon North's gun factory, Middletown, Connecticut, 1816

DIEMAKER:	What did you think of Mr. North's big demonstration? It seems like those federal government armory boys' eyes grew bigger than wild pumpkins.
LATHEMAN:	Well, the factory's mass production system with interchangeable parts impresses most visitors.
DIEMAKER:	I heard Mr. North himself is going to the big armory at Harper's Ferry to show them how it's all done. Won't that be something to see.

LATHEMAN:	Nah. That's small potatoes compared to what old Eli Whitney did back in 1801.
DIEMAKER:	What on earth are you talking about?
LATHEMAN:	I was working for him then in New Haven. We had this big contract to make muskets for the government. But we were having lots of problems, and the army was getting restless. They were threatening to cancel the entire order.
DIEMAKER:	So what happened?
LATHEMAN:	Eli and I raced down to Washington with a box of gun parts. Next thing I knew he had a room full of government bigwigs for a demonstration. Right in front of John Adams, Thomas Jefferson, and others, he put together a musket from those parts. He even let them do it! They were so convinced he could make the muskets, they gave him more money!
DIEMAKER:	Are you trying to tell me that Eli Whitney was the first man to use mass production with interchangeable parts?
LATHEMAN:	Say, you're smarter than I thought.
DIEMAKER:	Let me educate you on something. Mr. Whitney's contract with the government didn't say anything about muskets with interchangeable parts. Simeon North's pistol contract does! He started it all. And besides, his factory here was the first to use a filing jig and milling machines!

LATHEMAN: Eli Whitney started it all!

DIEMAKER: It's no use trying to convince you. I say North and you say Whitney.

LATHEMAN: Well, there's one thing we can agree on—machines will be doing most of the manufacturing from now on.

THE U.S. CONSTITUTION

Characters (in order of appearance)

James MADISON, Virginia delegate, major contributor

Alexander HAMILTON, New York delegate

MARTHA, wife of George Washington

George WASHINGTON, president of the Constitutional Convention

Robert MORRIS, James WILSON, Gouverneur MORRIS, Pennsylvania delegates

Edmund RANDOLF, Virginia governor

William PATERSON, New Jersey delegate

Roger SHERMAN, Connecticut delegate

Charles PINCKNEY, South Carolina delegate

George MASON, Virginia delegate

Benjamin FRANKLIN, Pennsylvania delegate

Alexander Hamilton

Scene I: Tavern, Annapolis, Maryland, September 1786

MADISON: Alexander, are you thinking what I'm thinking?

HAMILTON: That this convention is a failure? Most certainly.

MADISON: Of our thirteen states, only five are represented here. Without a majority, nothing of substance can be accomplished.

HAMILTON: Congress will have to call another one; otherwise this fragile young nation of ours will not survive.

MADISON: I share your pessimism. The fundamental reality is that the government of our Articles of Confederation is too weak and ineffective.

James Madison

HAMILTON:	I agree. It can't even stop Pennsylvania and Maryland from being at each other's throats over a simple matter like oyster fishing rights in Chesapeake Bay!
MADISON:	A strong national government could step in and mediate such disputes and keep peace and order.
HAMILTON:	Order, you say? We certainly need more of that when it comes to our money system. Right now it's absolute chaos with each state having its own currency.
MADISON:	And commercial, credit, and tax laws! Do you realize that Virginia goods sold in New York are taxed in Pennsylvania if they pass through that state? It's like the medieval toll system.

HAMILTON:	It's no wonder prices are so high, our economy so sluggish, and so many people in debt. Why can't people see the need for a strong national government?
MADISON:	I think because so many have bitter memories of the last one we had: the British Crown. People fear losing their liberties and being taxed too much.
HAMILTON:	How can we raise a strong army and navy to protect us unless we have a national government with the power to tax? What happens to our liberties if we are invaded? And furthermore, only a strong national government can finance the building projects that will make this nation great and prosperous.
MADISON:	I have an idea. Let's write a proposal to this Annapolis convention, asking it to contact Congress and call a new convention. And this time we'll make sure it has the power and authority to fix this mess!

Scene II: Mount Vernon, Virginia, April 1787

MARTHA:	A rider just brought this letter from Montpelier.
WASHINGTON:	Must be from James Madison. Martha, please read it to me. My eyes are a bit strained from the sun.
MARTHA:	Let me get you a cool drink first. You've been working very hard today.

WASHINGTON: Thank you.

MARTHA: It reads, "In light of recent events in Massachusetts, would you please reconsider attending next month's convention in Philadelphia?" The words "SHAY'S REBELLION" are boldly printed. What does that mean?

WASHINGTON: Don't you remember a few months back when some poor farmers in Massachusetts feared losing all their possessions to their creditors?

MARTHA: Now I remember. They tried to prevent the courts from convening to take their farms. Didn't they take up arms as well?

WASHINGTON: They certainly did. Anarchy threatened the whole region.

MARTHA: What's this convention Madison is referring to?

WASHINGTON: A meeting to change the Articles of Confederation so that anarchy like Shay's Rebellion doesn't spread.

MARTHA: Why is he asking you to reconsider attending?

WASHINGTON: Because I told him I wouldn't attend. I'm a planter, not a politician. You know all the responsibilities I have here.

MARTHA: I certainly do. But if you think I spent all those days and nights freezing at Valley Forge to later see this country fall apart, you've forgotten what kind of a woman you married!

WASHINGTON: I understand, Martha.

MARTHA: He ends the letter with the words "Remember Cincinnatus." Do you know what that means?

WASHINGTON: I do. Cincinnatus was a Roman general and statesman of long, long ago. When the Roman Republic was threatened by invaders, the government sent messengers to his farm. They found him plowing his fields.

MARTHA: Hmmm. Very interesting. What did he do?

WASHINGTON: He put down his plow, organized the troops, and defeated the enemy.

MARTHA: And saved Rome. Here's a postscript: "Ben Franklin will attend the convention."

WASHINGTON: And so shall I.

Scene III: City Tavern, Philadelphia, Pennsylvania, May 14, 1787

R. MORRIS: The Virginians want a private meeting with us.

WILSON: That's fine with me. Maybe we can accomplish something. The formal meeting certainly didn't.

G. MORRIS: How could it? Not enough delegates have arrived. I certainly hope this convention doesn't end like the one in Annapolis last year.

WILSON: I don't think it will. Washington's coming this time. Right now he's visiting with Ben Franklin.

G. MORRIS: That's most encouraging.

(enter Madison and Randolf)

MADISON: Thank you, Pennsylvania delegation, for obliging us. You know our Governor, Edmund Randolf—

R. MORRIS: Yes. Follow me. I've arranged a place for us to talk. Now, James, what's on your mind?

MADISON: Facing facts. We all know this convention was called to amend the Articles of Confederation, but that would be like blowing air into a dead horse.

WILSON: Are you suggesting we find a new horse?

MADISON: Precisely! We must start all over, with a new plan for a national government. Otherwise, this nation could disintegrate.

WILSON: I must say I agree with your assessment, James. But I'm concerned about how the other delegates will respond. This is not what they came here to do. Even people like your Patrick Henry have attacked this convention before it's begun!

RANDOLF: We know, we know. He keeps telling people, "I smell a rat."

G. MORRIS: With all due respect to the patriotism of Patrick Henry, he's a bit behind the times. We need a national government with real authority and power—now! One that can levy taxes.

WILSON: I agree, but creating a sound plan for a new government will take many months. I'm worried that the delegates will walk out.

MADISON: The Virginia delegation has anticipated that fear, Mr. Wilson. That's why we've come with a plan already in place. It's organized, fair, logical, and above all, a solution to our present lack of a strong central government.

R. MORRIS: I like the idea of not starting from scratch. But will the other delegates think they've been set up? That this is the "rat" Patrick Henry warned about?

RANDOLF: We've anticipated that fear as well.

WILSON: What's your medicine?

MADISON: As soon as the convention begins, make George Washington the presiding officer.

G. MORRIS: Brilliant! No one commands more respect and attention than he.

RANDOLF: Secondly, we make all the proceedings secret until we've come up with a new constitution.

WILSON: That will certainly encourage people to speak freely.

R. MORRIS: But that would require us to close all windows and doors. Do you Virginians realize how hot and uncomfortable Philadelphia can be this time of year?

MADISON: Virginia is no different. It's a price we must pay.

G. MORRIS: Gentlemen, I believe we are about to create something so grand and noble that future

generations will not soon forget the fruits of our labors.

Scene IV: Pennsylvania State House, Philadelphia, June 9, 1787

WASHINGTON: According to the rules of this convention, all matters can be reopened until settled by a majority vote. The chair recognizes Mr. Paterson of New Jersey.

PATERSON: We have debated the Virginia Plan for numerous sessions without reaching a consensus. The reason is obvious: it clearly favors the large states at the expense of the smaller ones. Furthermore, the strong national government it proposes is a certain threat to the rights of ordinary citizens.

WASHINGTON: Do you have a motion, Mr. Paterson?

PATERSON: No, Mr. President, I have a new proposal—the New Jersey Plan. I've asked my fellow delegates to distribute copies.

WILSON: This is nothing more than the Articles of Confederation rebaked! We can't abide by something already proven to be a failure—a disaster, if you will!

PATERSON: And the small states refuse to abide by a form of government in which they have no voice!

WILSON: No voice! If we don't accept the Virginia Plan, there will be anarchy! Then the voices heard will only be those of lawless mobs! Use your head, man!

PATERSON: You're a pompous idiot!

WASHINGTON: Gentlemen, let us recess to cool our passions.

Scene V: June 9, 1787

SHERMAN: Mr. President, the Connecticut delegation offers a plan to break this logjam.

WASHINGTON: Proceed, Mr. Sherman.

SHERMAN: We propose a legislature of two houses. The lower house, representing local interests, would be apportioned by population. In the upper house, representing state interests, each state would possess an equal voting power of two, and only two, members.

WASHINGTON: Thank you, Mr. Sherman, for presenting this compromise. It is worthy of thoughtful consideration. The chair recognizes Mr. Pinckney of South Carolina.

PINCKNEY: Regarding a state's number of representatives in the lower house, how will that figure be determined?

SHERMAN: As I stated, by the population of the individual state.

PINCKNEY: Nearly half the people of South Carolina are slaves. Will they be counted?

SHERMAN: Do you count them as citizens, Mr. Pinckney?

PINCKNEY: Don't get high and mighty with me, Mr. Sherman. Are women represented in this convention?

WASHINGTON: Mr. Pinckney, please make your point.

PINCKNEY:	If our slaves aren't counted, southern states will be underrepresented in the lower house. Some provision must be made, or all of us will leave this convention.
WASHINGTON:	At this time I will use my prerogative as president to appoint a committee to address these matters.

Scene VI: September 12, 1787

WASHINGTON:	The chair expresses its deep appreciation to the committee that has prepared a final draft of the new constitution. Gouverneur Morris, I especially laud your strong and lucid prose. Your beginning words, "We the People," are most compelling. Mr. Mason of Virginia, you wish to speak?
MASON:	I do, sir.
WASHINGTON:	I trust it does not involve amending or revising the document before us.
MASON:	I'm afraid so, Mr. President.
WASHINGTON:	Proceed.
MASON:	How can this convention of delegates accept a document that begins "We the People" when the document contains no provisions for protecting the rights and liberties of individual citizens?
WILSON:	What are you talking about? We have a system of checks and balances to make sure none of the three branches of government is given unreasonable power.
MASON:	Unreasonable power, you say? Look at the entire document, gentlemen. Written into Article VI is the clause stating that the Constitution is the supreme law of the land. Gentlemen, that is unreasonable power! If this document is not amended to include a citizen's bill of rights, I will not sign it.
WASHINGTON:	The chair recognizes Benjamin Franklin of Pennsylvania.
FRANKLIN:	How much longer will we argue and quibble? Is this constitution perfect? No. I disagree most strenuously that it permits the continuation of slavery. But all of us here have made compromises. All of us have specific reservations about its content. But I doubt we can expect to write a better one. I say we sign it now and place our faith in Almighty Providence and the good sense of our citizens to make it succeed.

Scene VII: September 17, 1787

WASHINGTON:	The motion for adoption is carried. I invite all delegates to sign this Constitution at this time.
FRANKLIN:	James, do you see that sun on Washington's chair?
MADISON:	Yes.
FRANKLIN:	I've stared at it all through this long, hot summer. A short time

ago I thought it was setting. Now I see it rising.

(delegates proceed to sign)

WASHINGTON: According to the rules of this convention, each state will call a popular convention for the purpose of ratifying this Constitution. When nine have ratified it, the Constitution will take effect and become the law of these United States. I invite all the delegates to retire with me to the City Tavern.

R. MORRIS: James, do you think we can get those nine states?

MADISON: There will be some formidable opposition, especially from the likes of older patriots like John Hancock, Patrick Henry, and Sam Adams. But Hamilton, Jay, and I have a plan to neutralize them.

R. MORRIS: And what might that be?

MADISON: Influence public opinion to support ratification through a series of newspaper articles. We've already lined up some New York publishers.

R. MORRIS: What will the articles say?

MADISON: They'll mainly be concerned with explaining the Constitution so people won't fear it.

R. MORRIS: If you plan to write many articles, it would be wise to have an interesting title. People remember things better that way.

MADISON: How about "The Federalist Papers"?

R. MORRIS: Good. What are you going to say to the people who insist on a bill of rights for the common citizen?

MADISON: That it should be the first item of business of the new Congress to write one.

R. MORRIS: James, I admire your forward thinking. But in the end, I think the most persuasive factor in getting this Constitution ratified will be the support of Washington and Franklin.

MADISON: I couldn't agree with you more, Robert. And I think people will look at Article II about the election of the president and see George Washington.

Scene VIII: Mt. Vernon, Virginia, April 1789

WASHINGTON: Who was that man racing madly up to the house? He nearly ran me over.

MARTHA: A messenger from New York.

WASHINGTON: Must be from the new Congress. What's the message?

MARTHA: You have been unanimously elected the first president of the United States.

WASHINGTON: I was afraid of that.

MARTHA: Why? Do you realize what a great honor this is?

WASHINGTON: Yes, and what a great responsibility it is.

MARTHA: But you've always been more than equal to any task.

WASHINGTON: This one is different. What am I supposed to do? Being the first, I have no model to follow.

MARTHA: That's why the Congress chose you, my dear. You, George Washington, are to chart the course for all future presidents to follow.

WASHINGTON: What does it say about the inauguration?

MARTHA: It will take place April 30, at the New York City Federal Building.

WASHINGTON: That doesn't give me much time to organize things around here. I'm worried about Mt. Vernon's finances.

MARTHA: You leave that to me until I join you in New York. Your job now is to take care of running this young country.

SACAGAWEA AND THE LEWIS AND CLARK EXPEDITION

Characters (in order of appearance)

Thomas JEFFERSON, president of the United States

Meriwether LEWIS, coleader of the expedition

William CLARK, coleader of the expedition

Ben YORK, African-American member of the expedition

George DREWYER, Indian sign language expert and expedition member

Toussaint CHARBONNEAU, French trader/ guide

SACAGAWEA, Shoshone guide

CAMEAHWAIT, Shoshone chief and brother to Sacagawea

Meriwether Lewis

Scene I: The White House, Washington, D.C., April 1802

JEFFERSON: Meriwether, you're rather keen on challenges, correct?

LEWIS: Yes. What do you have in mind, Mr. President?

JEFFERSON: Sending out a group to explore the vast territory between the Mississippi River and the Pacific Ocean.

LEWIS: Now, that would interest me! I'll volunteer.

JEFFERSON: I thought you would. You will be the expedition leader. Well, what do you think?

LEWIS: I assume it would mainly involve mapping the area.

William Clark

JEFFERSON: Yes, but much, much more. I want a comprehensive and detailed account of all the people, flora, and fauna in that region. I also want to learn if the Pacific can easily be reached by water. There will be untold obstacles: mountains, roaring rivers, bitter cold and heat, dangerous animals, and suspicious Indians.

LEWIS: Have you forgotten the political obstacles? They can be the most formidable of all.

JEFFERSON: You are referring to the fact that this area does not belong to the United States.

LEWIS: Exactly. Doesn't Spain claim sovereignty over most of it?

JEFFERSON: That's what most governments think. But I've learned that the Spanish have secretly ceded it to France.

LEWIS: What! Let me think for a moment. Doesn't Emperor Napoleon have thousands of his best troops in Haiti?

JEFFERSON: He certainly does! France is very worried about a growing native rebellion there.

LEWIS: Hmmm. Haiti is a lot closer to us than France. What's to stop Napoleon from moving those troops to Louisiana and threatening our nation's interests? Our people will sooner or later be pushing past the Mississippi River. There could be bloodshed if they confront a foreign army like the French.

JEFFERSON: Meriwether, you are most astute! That's why I've developed a plan to prevent such a thing from happening.

LEWIS: Certainly not a military one.

JEFFERSON: No. That would be a disaster. I aim to buy the whole Louisiana Territory from France.

LEWIS: Are you joking, Mr. President?

JEFFERSON: Not in the least. I'm putting James Monroe to work on it right away, all in complete secrecy, of course. He'll soon be sailing to France to make an offer.

LEWIS: Should I wait until Monroe brings back title to this land before I set out?

JEFFERSON: No. Get your group organized right away, forty to fifty at the

	most. I'm confident you'll pick the right people.
LEWIS:	For such a task I would like to have a coleader.
JEFFERSON:	Very wise. Anyone in mind?
LEWIS:	A good friend, William Clark. He's ideal for such an expedition: fearless, resourceful, tenacious, and gifted with a special personality trait.
JEFFERSON:	And what might that trait be?
LEWIS:	All kinds of people are drawn to him. Even strangers quickly like and trust him.
JEFFERSON:	Then he's the perfect man to be your coleader. You'll need someone like Clark to make it through all the different tribal lands. I don't want this expedition to have to shoot its way to the Pacific.
LEWIS:	Of course.
JEFFERSON:	It might be awhile before I give you the official word to go. But in the mean time, start organizing the supplies and men you'll need. I hope and pray you find some friendly Indians along the way. Otherwise, you might be forced to turn back before reaching the Pacific.

Scene II: On the Missouri River (near present-day Sioux City, Iowa) mid-August 1804

LEWIS:	William, you have done an outstanding job of forming this group. All the drunks and trou-

	blemakers that showed up at Camp Wood near St. Louis have been weeded out. Well done!
CLARK:	Thank you. This group has already proved its mettle with all the heat, bugs, thunderstorms, and back-breaking paddling it has endured this far.
LEWIS:	Well, we've a long, long way to go. Winter comes early this far north, so we'll have to build safe quarters soon, most likely in Mandan Indian Territory. Any budding morale problems?
CLARK:	I'm worried about how the men will react to Indians.

(enter York)

YORK:	Captain Clark, Captain Lewis, I have sad news. Sergeant Floyd is dead.
LEWIS:	Poor fellow. He was a good man. I wonder how the others will take this.
CLARK:	They know you treated Sergeant Floyd with every medicine we had.
LEWIS:	I think something in his stomach just burst open and filled his body with poisons.
CLARK:	I'll organize a burial detail.

Scene III: Fort Mandan (North Dakota), December 1804

DREWYER:	Captain Lewis, Captain Clark, there's a Frenchman outside who says he can help us.

LEWIS: Bring him in, please.

(enter Charbonneau and Sacagawea)

CHARBONNEAU: Chief Sheheke tells me you are trying to reach the big water in the West.

LEWIS: Yes. Our great chief in the East has sent us to find a way to the Pacific Ocean. Have you been there?

CHARBONNEAU: No. But I have traveled all the way to the big mountains. I can guide you there—if you pay me.

CLARK: What is your name, and who is this woman with you?

CHARBONNEAU: I am Toussaint Charbonneau. This is Sacagawea, my wife.

CLARK: Why is she shaking?

CHARBONNEAU: She has never seen a black man before. And your dog is as big as a buffalo.

CLARK: You mean my man, Ben York? Tell your wife he's the kindest man she'll ever meet. Though he's stronger than an ox, he wouldn't hurt anyone.

LEWIS: And tell her my Newfoundland, Scannon, is very friendly. He keeps wild animals from our camps.

CHARBONNEAU: Are we hired?

LEWIS: What do you mean, *we*? Your wife looks like she'll be having a baby soon.

CHARBONNEAU: Sacagawea is very strong—she'll carry the baby on her back when you leave in the spring. Saca-gawea is Shoshone. You must pass through her people's land. Sacagawea can help get you through.

LEWIS: Charbonneau, we wish to speak with your wife—alone.

CHARBONNEAU: She does not speak your tongue.

LEWIS: Drewyer knows Indian sign language.

CHARBONNEAU: I'll leave, then. But if Sacagawea does not go with you, I won't either.

(Charbonneau exits)

CLARK: George, ask her if she really wants to go with us, even if this means carrying her baby.

(pause while Drewyer and Sacagawea sign)

DREWYER: She wants very much to go—to see her people again, to see new places.

LEWIS: Ask her why she is so far from her people.

CLARK: And how she became Charbon-neau's wife. *(pause)*

DREWYER: The Minnetarees kidnapped her when she was a young girl and made her a slave. When Char-bonneau told the chief he wanted her for his wife, the chief made him play a game of chance against two other men. Charbon-neau won the game and the girl.

LEWIS: Well, William, what do you think?

CLARK: I don't trust this Charbonneau one bit. But I like this girl. I think

she could be more useful to us than just getting us through Shoshone Territory.

LEWIS: I agree. It seems her husband only wants to use us—and her. I would much prefer communicating with Sacagawea directly.

CLARK: I'll teach her English. By next spring I'll have "Janey" speaking like Dolly Madison!

DREWYER: Her name is Sacagawea. That means Bird Woman.

CLARK: I know, I know. But she reminds me of a Janey I once knew, and that is what I'll call her.

Scene IV: Along the Missouri River, West of Fort Mandan, April 1805

YORK: Captain Clark! Look what I've found for dinner!

SACAGAWEA: No! No! Must not eat! Make you very sick, maybe die.

YORK: But, but it looks just like—

CLARK: Ben, I think we'd be wise to follow Janey's advice. She knows what plants are poisonous out here. She's already saved us from some wild animals and nervous Indians.

YORK: I know, Captain Clark. You're right about Janey. It's just that these greens looked so tempting and I'm sick of the same old food.

Scene V: Along the Missouri River (in Montana), May 1805

LEWIS: It's certainly pleasant to get out of the boat for awhile, except for these rattlesnakes. Janey has been a big, big help to us. She's held up very well.

CLARK: She's a very determined woman. I also think she enjoys our company.

LEWIS: I must confess I was very anxious about her being along when we left Fort Mandan. But she's certainly proved her worth, especially when we've encountered suspicious Indians.

CLARK: The men admire and cherish her. She's really helped the group's morale.

LEWIS: Without a doubt, she brings out the best in the men.

CLARK: It's as if her endurance of all the trip's hardships without complaint or hesitation inspires them to do no less.

LEWIS: William! Look in the river! The white pirogue's in trouble!

CLARK: What is Charbonneau doing! He's supposed to be at the helm!

LEWIS: It's going to capsize for sure!

CLARK: Oh, no! All my equipment! Our medicines and gunpowder!

LEWIS: Sacagawea is jumping into the water with her baby! I think she just grabbed your precious wooden box!

(*Sacagawea and baby make it safely to shore*)

CLARK: Janey! Are you and the baby all right?

SACAGAWEA: We are fine, Captain Clark. Here is your box. I know it is very important.

CLARK: My journal! And my little compass! You saved them both! Oh, Janey, thank you, thank you. You are so brave.

Scene VI: At Three Forks of Missouri River (near Continental Divide), August 1805

LEWIS: Look at those mountains! We'll never make it through them without horses.

CLARK: Look at Janey! She's carrying on like she's found gold!

LEWIS: Let's have a talk with her.

CLARK: Janey, what are you all excited about?

SACAGAWEA: We are in Shoshone land! This is where I was taken by the Minnetarees long ago.

LEWIS: Do you think anyone will remember you? Can you get your people to trade for horses?

SACAGAWEA: I do not know if anyone remembers me here. Horses? I do not know if the Shoshone have any to trade. They are a poor people; they need many horses to survive. But I will ask them to help us get some.

LEWIS: We won't be able to go on without some. Captain Clark, I have a plan. Make a temporary camp here while I try to make contact with the Shoshone chief.

(*a week later*)

CAMEAHWAIT: Where is the black man and the Shoshone woman you promised to show me?

LEWIS: They will be here soon.

CAMEAHWAIT: If they do not come I cannot trust your words. I will give you no help then.

(*Sacagawea and York appear*)

LEWIS: This is Mr. York.

CAMEAHWAIT: Let me rub his face. You speak the truth! His black skin is not from paint. Now I'll speak to the woman in our language.

LEWIS: George! What is happening?

DREWYER: The chief is Sacagawea's brother! He never thought he would ever see her again. He is very pleased.

LEWIS: Sacagawea, ask your brother if he will trade for horses.

SACAGAWEA: He says his tribe has no horses to spare but that he will trade for some because I am with you.

CLARK: You mean, Janey, you are going to go with us all the way to the Pacific Ocean? What about your people?

SACAGAWEA: I will return to them. Nothing will stop me and my son from going with you all the way to the big water. Nothing.

LEWIS:	That's the spirit we need, especially at this point. William, the most difficult part of the trip is before us: crossing the Rockies, finding the Columbia River, building boats and sailing down it. With Sacagawea along, our chances of making it are greatly improved.		LEWIS:	Cup an ear with your hand—there's your answer.

LEWIS: That's the spirit we need, especially at this point. William, the most difficult part of the trip is before us: crossing the Rockies, finding the Columbia River, building boats and sailing down it. With Sacagawea along, our chances of making it are greatly improved.

CLARK: Agreed. We couldn't have made it this far without her. Now that we'll have some horses, the men will be more eager to press on.

Scene VII: Pacific Ocean (Oregon), November 18, 1805

SACAGAWEA: Captain Clark, what is that big sound?

CLARK: I don't know. I can't see anything in this fog. Captain Lewis! Are you there?

LEWIS: Right over here. What took your group so long? We've been here for four days.

CLARK: How much further?

LEWIS: Cup an ear with your hand—there's your answer.

CLARK: But it sounds like the great falls. You mean we have to go around this one, too?

LEWIS: Listen again. That's the roar of the Pacific Ocean!

CLARK: Are you certain?

LEWIS: I saw it with my very own eyes yesterday when the fog lifted. It's an unbelievable sight!

CLARK: Meriwether! We've done it! We've spanned the North American continent! I didn't think we could do it.

LEWIS: It took all of us. And in all honesty, I don't think we would have made it this far without Sacagawea. She deserves most of the glory.

CLARK: She's an amazing person—simply amazing.

LEWIS: The kind that comes along maybe once in a hundred years.

SEQUOYAH AND THE NINETEENTH-CENTURY EASTERN INDIANS

Characters (in order of appearance)

OLD KALUNA, Cherokee Wise Man	BRAVE II
SEQUOYAH, developer of Cherokee writing system	REPORTER I
UTIYA, Sequoyah's first wife	Henry CLAY, U.S. senator
John ROSS, Cherokee tribal leader	REPORTER II
BRAVE I	

Sequoyah

Scene I: Outside a Cherokee Village, Tuskegee, Tennessee, around 1785

OLD KALUNA: Sequoyah, how old are you now?

SEQUOYAH: Fifteen years.

OLD KALUNA: That is an age when you should be with other young braves playing their games. Why do you wander about the woods all alone and with such a sad, sad face?

SEQUOYAH: I have many burdens.

OLD KALUNA: Are you sad because you have no father? Many braves like you have never known their fathers.

SEQUOYAH: I am not sad about that, only curious.

OLD KALUNA: Curiosity is a good thing, but it should not keep you away from the other braves. Why don't you join them in their games?

SEQUOYAH: Because they all make fun of me, and the losing side blames me for their defeats.

OLD KALUNA: Your limp makes you run slower than the others?

SEQUOYAH: Yes, and I am not as strong either.

OLD KALUNA:	My son, do not feel sorry because you lack the speed and strength of the other braves. Such things are like grass—they will soon wither. Instead, seek the strength that will never weaken or grow tired.
SEQUOYAH:	Where can I find such strength?
OLD KALUNA:	You will not find it in your feet or your arms but in your heart and mind.
SEQUOYAH:	What do you mean?
OLD KALUNA:	In your heart you will find courage, courage to swim through the swift waters that block the path to your dreams. And in your mind you will find wisdom and the secret power of the white man.
SEQUOYAH:	Why do I need to learn his secret?
OLD KALUNA:	Because it is the power to keep our people strong and united. Without it, the white man will take away our land, our culture, and our dignity.
SEQUOYAH:	The Cherokee can shoot guns like the white man. Am I to seek a gun more powerful than his?
OLD KALUNA:	That is not the power you should seek. It will only lead to sorrow and death. The white man's secret power comes from something else.
SEQUOYAH:	Old Kaluna, please tell me what it is.
OLD KALUNA:	When you find it, you will know.

Scene II: Sequoyah's home, near Willstown, Alabama, 1814

UTIYA:	Husband! What is wrong with you?
SEQUOYAH:	What do you mean?
UTIYA:	What has happened to the man I married long ago? That man always kept our house and garden in perfect condition. Today, you will not tend to the weeds or fix the leaky roof!
SEQUOYAH:	I have been very busy.
UTIYA:	Busy? Once you were the finest blacksmith and silversmith in the whole area. White people came from far away to ask you to fix something or to buy your beautiful work. Now your tools rust while you make strange figures on the ground and bark of trees. Did fighting in the white man's war sicken your spirit and mind?
SEQUOYAH:	No. I have been very busy thinking.
UTIYA:	I wish you would stop it and get back to some useful work! If you ask me, fighting with General Andrew Jackson against the British caused a great change in you.
SEQUOYAH:	You are right. When I was a soldier I would observe the white man while he rested. From his bag he would take out "talking leaves." They would tell him stories to amuse him or news from his home that would comfort him. We Indians could only sit and watch.

UTIYA:	Talking leaves? What nonsense! If you do not fix our roof we'll soon have leaves and raindrops invading our home!
SEQUOYAH:	Don't you understand? Our people need their own "talking leaves" so we can send messages like the white man. They will keep the Cherokee Nation together, united and strong.
UTIYA:	So that's what all your markings on bark and in the dirt have been about. What do you plan to do?
SEQUOYAH:	Go off into the woods with Ah-yoka and make "talking leaves" for the Cherokee.
UTIYA:	Why must you take our little daughter? Do you want her to get sick in the head like you?
SEQUOYAH:	She will be my student. If I can teach a little girl to understand the Cherokee "talking leaves," then the secret power of the white man will be ours, too.

Scene III: Capital, Eastern Cherokee Nation (Georgia), 1823

ROSS:	So, the dreamer has returned to the East. What news do you bring from our people in the West?
SEQUOYAH:	Many, many messages.
ROSS:	Your head must be very, very full.
SEQUOYAH:	I have written them down so I didn't need to memorize them.
ROSS:	Hmmm. Very well. May I read them? Did you know, Sequoyah, that while I was a student at Dart-

	mouth College in New Hampshire, I mastered English, French, Spanish, Latin, and Greek?

(Sequoyah hands Ross a letter)

SEQUOYAH:	Is something the matter with the distinguished chairman of the Cherokee Tribal Council?
ROSS:	This is no language I know. What is it?
SEQUOYAH:	Cherokee. I have been working many years to perfect a written form.
ROSS:	I don't believe this! It has taken hundreds of years to create a written language like English. You can't do such a thing alone.
SEQUOYAH:	I did.
ROSS:	Let me examine it more carefully. Hmmm. It seems to have too many characters to be practical.
SEQUOYAH:	Are you asking why it is not like the English system with twenty-six letters?
ROSS:	Precisely.
SEQUOYAH:	Our language cannot be poured into such a mold. Some of the white missionaries tried but failed. My system works.
ROSS:	What exactly is your system?
SEQUOYAH:	It is not an alphabet of single letters like English. Rather, it is a syllabary of eighty-six characters. I have included six open, continuous sounds—

ROSS:	In English they are called *vowels*.
SEQUOYAH:	And twelve dividing sounds—
ROSS:	*Consonants* would be the English equivalent, I believe.
SEQUOYAH:	And some combinations.
ROSS:	Hmmm. It still seems far too complicated. You might as well keep it to yourself. There is no practical application for our people. It would be simpler to teach them Greek.
SEQUOYAH:	A child can easily master it.
ROSS:	Sequoyah, are you mocking me?
SEQUOYAH:	No. I am only asking you to give me a chance to prove my system works. My ten-year-old daughter is with me. She has learned my system.
ROSS:	You are a very bold and determined man, Sequoyah. You have also traveled a great distance carrying this strange dream of yours. Though I do not believe in your dream, I will be open-minded and honor your request. I will gather the council for a demonstration.

(a short time later)

BRAVE I:	How will the test be conducted?
ROSS:	Sequoyah will be far away from us. I will dictate some words to his daughter. She will change them into symbols on the paper. Then we will send for Sequoyah and ask him to speak the symbols. We will decide how near his words are to mine.

(the demonstration takes place)

BRAVE II:	They used magic and trickery.
BRAVE I:	I agree. The father and daughter have a secret way of passing words.
BRAVE II:	John Ross, you have wasted the council's time.
ROSS:	Wait, please. Let's reverse the test. Someone take the girl away. We will dictate a message to Sequoya and then see if his daughter can read his words.
BRAVE I:	Very well. We will sit for this demonstration.
BRAVE II:	If she can speak what we told Sequoyah, I will be convinced that this is not trickery.
BRAVE I:	Yes, especially if Sequoyah is not with her.

(the second demonstration takes place)

ROSS:	Thank you, Ah-yoka. You can go get your father now and bring him before us.

(Sequoyah re-enters)

ROSS:	Sequoyah, I am sorry I doubted you the way I did. We are convinced!
BRAVE II:	Can you teach our sons and daughters to do what Ah-yoka has done?
BRAVE I:	How I long to send messages to my brothers and sisters in the western nation! Will I be able to do that now?

SEQUOYAH:	Yes! To both of your questions, yes!
ROSS:	If we can spread the knowledge of Sequoyah's system to our people, then someday the Cherokee will have newspapers and books like the white man!
BRAVE II:	This will keep our nation united even though great distances separate us.
ROSS:	This is truly a great power you have discovered, Sequoyah, a power that can be a great blessing to our people.

Scene IV: Outside the U.S. Senate, Washington, D.C., February 14, 1835

REPORTER I:	Senator Clay, would you please answer some questions for the press about the speech you just gave?
CLAY:	I'm not sure I have any energy left, but fire away.
REPORTER II:	Your speech describing the plight of the Cherokee Indians brought tears to the eyes of your fellow senators. Can you comment further?
CLAY:	I am glad they were so moved. I simply spoke the truth. Now, if I can only get our government to move in a more just and fair direction regarding its treatment of the Indians.
REPORTER I:	Senator, would you please be more specific?
CLAY:	Every treaty made with the Indians has been to the white man's advantage. Treaties that were fair were broken by the white man. All because of greed!
REPORTER II:	Are you referring to what happened to the Cherokee a few years ago in Georgia?
CLAY:	Most definitely. As soon as gold was discovered there in 1829, the white man rushed in and began forcing the Cherokee to move. Violence, threats, and laws clearly unconstitutional have been the means to carry out this thievery. Thievery, that's what it is—the white man stealing from the Indians.
REPORTER I:	Aren't you being rather extreme, Senator? White people represent a superior civilization and therefore deserve those lands.
CLAY:	Hogwash! Absolute hogwash! You would be wise to compare the Cherokee culture with that of those barbaric illiterates who have taken over their ancient lands!
REPORTER I:	Senator, how can you make such an outlandish claim?
CLAY:	Because it's the truth! Thanks to Sequoyah, the Cherokee have a written language, and many of them can read it. Did you know the Cherokee have newspapers and even a Bible written in their own language? And those white gold hunters down in Georgia can't even read or write their own names! Now, which culture is more deserving of that land?
REPORTER II:	Senator, do you foresee the government changing its Indian

	policy? In other words, is there any hope for the Eastern Indians?
CLAY:	I am not optimistic. Do you recall when the chief justice of the U.S. Supreme Court, the eminent John Marshall, ruled on the Cherokee's behalf regarding a land dispute in Georgia?
REPORTER I:	Yes. President Andrew Jackson said, "The Chief Justice has made his decision, now let him enforce it."
CLAY:	When the president of the United States ignores the law, where can the Indians turn for justice? That is why I am pessimistic about the future of the Eastern Indians.
REPORTER II:	What do you think will be the government's long-term policy for them?
CLAY:	Removal, forced if necessary, to lands far to the west and far away from any white settlers.
REPORTER I:	Realistically speaking, wouldn't that be a wise policy? The offer of land in the West is certainly better than the prospect of dying in a war in the East. At least the Indians will be safe and have the chance to keep their nation alive.
CLAY:	That seems to be President Jackson's thinking, and I utterly and completely disagree with it! Safe, you say? Can you imagine the sufferings and hardships of such a journey west? Through mile after mile of harsh and unknown land? Thousands would die. Safe, you say? Getting there would surely be a trail of endless tears.

Epilogue

Thousands of Eastern Indians did indeed travel a "Trail of Tears" to the west to what became known as Oklahoma. When Oklahoma became a state in 1907, the first statue honoring it in our nation's capital was a likeness of Sequoyah. Previously, Sequoia National Park in California was established in 1890 to honor him.

THE WHITMANS AND THE MOVEMENT WEST

Characters (in order of appearance)

JONES, a New York farmer

Dr. Marcus WHITMAN

PRENTISS, father of Narcissa

Reverend Samuel PARKER, missionary and adventurer

NARCISSA, Marcus Whitman's wife

Jim BRIDGER, legendary frontier trader, trapper, and scout

Nathaniel WYETH, frontier adventurer

John McLOUGHLIN, Hudson's Bay Company leader

ELIZA Spalding, missionary teacher, wife of Henry

Jason LEE, Methodist missionary in Willamette Valley

Henry SPALDING, missionary leader

Horace GREELEY, New York newspaper magnate

REPORTER

EAST, EVANS, STONE, BANKS, members of caravan traveling on the Oregon Trail

GRANT, trader

Jesse APPLEGATE, caravan leader

MESSENGER

Act I

Scene I: Farmhouse, Western New York State, September 1834

JONES: Mighty obliged to you, Dr. Whitman, for coming so far in the middle of the night.

WHITMAN: All part of being a country doctor, Clarence. You have a strong and healthy new daughter, and your Mary is doing just fine.

JONES: And how are you doing, Doc?

WHITMAN: Like I said, just doing my job.

JONES: I mean your spirit, Doc. It seems way down. Did you get some bad news?

WHITMAN: You are very perceptive, Clarence. Yes, I did. The Board of Foreign Missions turned down my application.

JONES: Sorry to hear that. Where did you want to serve?

WHITMAN: Out West—Oregon Territory, maybe.

JONES: Can't go much further than that. Why would you want to go where there's only savages, wild animals, and greedy trappers?

WHITMAN: Because I could be useful out there.

JONES: But look how useful you were tonight, Doc!

Westward Movement

WHITMAN:	A midwife could have done just as well. I guess I'm just restless and bored here.
JONES:	Well, Doc, I hope you find what you're looking for.

Scene II: Church meeting, Angelica, New York, November 1834

PRENTISS:	Reverend Parker, we thank you for coming all this way to describe the great needs out West. How can we best respond?
PARKER:	With your prayers and financial support and dedicated, able-bodied men to build and operate missions for the Indians.
NARCISSA:	What about dedicated and able-bodied women? I'm an experi-

enced teacher. I want to go out there to serve God.

PRENTISS:	That's utter nonsense, Narcissa. Reverend Parker, please remind my head-strong and dreamy-eyed daughter of the hardships and of why no white woman has ever crossed the Rocky Mountains.
PARKER:	Well, that's a fact. Hmmmm. Would your husband be so willing and determined?
PRENTISS:	Narcissa is not married.
PARKER:	What? How can that possibly be?
PRENTISS:	She's what folks call "unconventional."
NARCISSA:	Reverend Parker, I am pleading with you. Please help me find a

 20 Plays for U.S. History Classes

PARKER: way. I want to go out there and serve.

PARKER: The board doesn't welcome applications from unmarried women, especially to places where there isn't much civilization. I'm sorry.

NARCISSA: Please, please try to do something. I'm not afraid of any of those hardships you described.

Scene III: Parker Home, Ithaca, New York, January 1835

PARKER: Marcus, I am so pleased that the board reconsidered.

WHITMAN: Not nearly so pleased as I! I guess they turned me down the first time because I was a little sick. But look at me now, fit and ready to move. Say, we don't have much time to catch that fur caravan leaving St. Louis. When will it start?

PARKER: As soon as the spring grass is ready for the animals. Say, Marcus, now old are you?

WHITMAN: Thirty-two.

PARKER: Ever been interested in marrying?

WHITMAN: I suppose so. But right now I'm only interested in catching that caravan heading West.

PARKER: How could I persuade you to first catch a future bride?

WHITMAN: She would have to be a very special woman.

PARKER: The one I have in mind is! She's both beautiful and smart.

WHITMAN: But if I were to marry I would want someone willing and able to share all the hardships and challenges of the West.

PARKER: Marcus, that's where she wants to go! And she has the determination to serve God under the most difficult conditions. You interested?

WHITMAN: What's her name? Where does she live?

PARKER: Miss Narcissa Prentiss of Angelica.

WHITMAN: What do you propose that I do?

PARKER: Go there and start courting her!

WHITMAN: Just like that? That's about as subtle as a buffalo stampede. She'll be sure to shy away.

PARKER: Not if marrying you will be her only chance to get to Oregon. The board won't accept her application unless there's a "Mrs." before her name.

WHITMAN: Sounds like I would be more of a ticket to travel than a husband. Where's the romance?

PARKER: You'll have plenty of time to win her heart along the trail. Now, just go to her!

| WHITMAN: | I'll think about it. Sounds crazy, even dangerous to me. I'll see you in St. Louis this spring. |

Scene IV: Fur caravan camp (near present-day Omaha, Nebraska), May 1835

PARKER:	So, Dr. Whitman, when is the wedding date?
WHITMAN:	It's pretty complicated. The board has to accept her application as "Mrs. Whitman," and, of course, I have to return from this scouting mission.
PARKER:	Well, we're still a long way off from doing any of that. Meanwhile, I have some very important work to do here. I aim to preach to these men.
WHITMAN:	Reverend Parker, we're not in some polite and hospitable church back home. These mountain men despise such talk. It makes them uncomfortable.
PARKER:	All the more reason they should hear the truth. Gather around, men. I have something very important to say!
WHITMAN:	I hope you know what you're getting into.
PARKER:	Men of the fur caravan, take heed! You who think you are traveling beyond the pale of the law and have license to mistreat the Indians, BEWARE! God will punish all who loot, rape, and murder! Have nothing to do with such evil! Instead, I call upon you to be kind, gentle, understanding,

and fair to these dear children of your Heavenly Father.

| WHITMAN: | Reverend Parker, protect yourself! They've all got eggs! |

(Whitman comes to rescue Parker; crowd pelts them)

Scene V: Fur rendezvous, valley of the Green River, August 1835

BRIDGER:	Doc, I can't thank you enough for removing that dang arrowhead from my back. My, must be three inches long!
WHITMAN:	You were a perfect patient, and very brave, Mr. Bridger.
BRIDGER:	That's the way you got to be out here, Doc. This ain't no place for whiners—you just have to push through the hard times. Seems like I heard tell you've already done a lot of that on this trip.
WHITMAN:	The reverend and I were not exactly welcome company. Most of the men thought we would spoil their evil pleasures and tell how they treated the Indians.
BRIDGER:	The caravan captain told me you saved most of their hides when cholera hit.
WHITMAN:	I only did my job.
BRIDGER:	Sounds like you're no greenhorn anymore. You really know how to survive out here. Where are you heading?
WHITMAN:	I was going further to Oregon, but Reverend Parker wants me to return to New York. He's going

20 Plays for U.S. History Classes

	on to scout for possible mission sites.
BRIDGER:	New York? What for?
WHITMAN:	A wife, maybe. Supplies, more missionaries.
BRIDGER:	Doc, I've been moving about these parts for many years, and no white woman ever crossed the Rockies. She'd have to be quite a woman! Good luck to you!

Act II

Scene I: Fur rendezvous, valley of the Green River, August 1836

WYETH:	So this is the woman from New York I've been hearing so much about! Mrs. Whitman, I'm Nathaniel Wyeth, and I'm so pleased to meet you!
NARCISSA:	Thank you. The pleasure is mine.
WYETH:	I can't believe how fit and healthy you look after such a long journey. Do you realize you're the first white woman to get this far?
NARCISSA:	Mrs. Spalding made the trip as well. It's just that she's been rather sick—too sick to leave the wagon.
WYETH:	Your husband told me you rode a horse the whole way.
NARCISSA:	Wagon sitters eat dust all day and don't see much.
WYETH:	My, you have learned the ways of the trail. But tell me, do you fully

	realize what your presence here means?
NARCISSA:	Certainly. We're just that much closer to our destination.
WYETH:	Of course, but it's much more than that. Just look at the ragged men about you. Before your and Mrs. Spalding's arrival, this was the West: men, only men, desperate, half-civilized creatures forever roaming about. You, and the women who will surely follow now, mean civilization. Something permanent—raising families and building communities. Mrs. Whitman, your presence and spirit have changed a lot of these men's thinking. You just may have started a new malady of the mind.
NARCISSA:	What on earth are you talking about, Mr. Wyeth?
WYETH:	A fever—Oregon fever.

Scene II: Fort Vancouver, Oregon Territory, September 1836

MCLOUGHLIN:	Mrs. Whitman, Mrs. Spalding, I congratulate you both on your heroic journey. I trust you are comfortable with your lodgings.
ELIZA:	Yes. You have been very kind and generous, Mr. McLoughlin. After all those weeks bumping along the hot and dusty trail and then that wild ride down the Columbia River, your fort is heaven.
MCLOUGHLIN:	I hope you also enjoy our food.
NARCISSA:	For weeks we have had nothing but flyblown buffalo jerky. You

have set before us a gourmet's feast.

MCLOUGHLIN: Well, you can thank my employer, the Hudson's Bay Company, for that. I never tire of sharing its bounty. Speaking of sharing, Mr. Lee of the Methodist mission in the Willamette Valley will be joining us.

(Lee enters)

Oh, here he is now. Pull up a chair, Jason.

LEE: Thank you. Dr. and Mrs. Whitman, Rev. and Mrs. Spalding, welcome to Oregon Territory. I congratulate you on your overland feat. Most of our workers have come by ship.

WHITMAN: And how is your work proceeding in the Willamette Valley?

LEE: Slowly, very slowly. The plain truth is that we need more people like you folks—real families, dedicated to settling and building communities. But I don't think that will happen very soon.

SPALDING: And why is that?

LEE: Too much uncertainty. Getting here, the Indians, whose country this is. Now, Mr. McLoughlin has been most hospitable to us Americans. But don't forget that Hudson's Bay Company is British, and I don't think the British are too pleased with the prospects of lots of Americans settling under their noses.

SPALDING: What do you think about that, Mr. McLoughlin?

MCLOUGHLIN: Washington, D.C., is a lot closer to us than London, England. And because these good women have successfully made the overland journey, Oregon will never be quite the same. For better or worse, you people are the vanguard of an irresistible force.

LEE: Well, that's quite a pronouncement. To change the subject, have you decided on your mission sites?

NARCISSA: Marcus and I will be located amongst the Cayuse, about twenty miles from Fort Walla Walla.

LEE: Be careful; they're a rather difficult lot, very proud and not much open to our ways. Good luck.

SPALDING: Mr. Lee, please. As a man of God, you certainly know that luck has no role in such an endeavor! Now, as far as Eliza and I are concerned, we are to build our station amongst the Nez Perce at Lapwai.

MCLOUGHLIN: That's about three days ride to the northeast of the Whitmans' site.

LEE: Hmmm. It seems the two couples are more eager to work apart than together.

WHITMAN: We've had our differences along the way, but we're all dedicated to our calling.

Act III

Scene I: Whitman Mission at Waiilatpu, September 1842

SPALDING: Marcus, this is terrible news! Why would the board even consider closing our two stations?

NARCISSA: If only they could see what we have accomplished at Waiilatpu: fenced pastures, acres of grain and potatoes, a mill, workshop, and buttery; a school, hospital, and free hotel. It's not right!

ELIZA: It seems the board has made its decision because of past misunderstandings between us. I suppose they just don't know we've patched things up. If only we could show them how much progress we've made with the Indians at Lapwai.

WHITMAN: Then we must get word to the board without further delay and change their minds! I'm leaving in three days.

SPALDING: Marcus! Get a hold of yourself! Winter is coming on. You can't risk crossing the Rockies this time of year.

WHITMAN: What? Just sit back and watch everything we've built here sold off to the Hudson's Bay Company? I don't give up that easily. Besides, there is serious talk of a huge caravan of settlers heading this way next spring. I want to make sure it gets through. Let's face facts—only settlers will give our work any real future.

Scene II: Newspaper office, New York City, March 1843

GREELEY: So you're the man who beat the odds and traveled through the Rockies in the dead of winter.

WHITMAN: Mr. Greeley, that's what living out West prepares a man to do. I've felt cold and heat, eaten dust and bugs, squared off with bad-tempered mountain men and suspicious Indians, fought wild animals and isolation, even lost my three-year-old daughter to drowning. But I've also experienced freedom and opportunity you wouldn't think possible, seen sunsets, mountains, and rivers so beautiful you shiver. That's where this nation's future lies if the U.S. government ever gets serious about it.

GREELEY: And you're certain of that, despite all the dangers and hardships along the way?

WHITMAN: Yes, along with a thousand other folk forming a caravan for Oregon next month or so. And they aren't your typical fur caravan adventurers and lowlifes, either. I'll be joining up with them to help them to help as best I can.

GREELEY: Well, good luck to you, Dr. Whitman.

WHITMAN: Thank you for your time, Mr. Greeley.

GREELEY:	Thank you, Dr. Whitman. You've given me an idea for a line I might put in my newspaper.
WHITMAN:	And what would that be?
GREELEY:	"Go West, young man, go West."

Scene III: Independence, Missouri, May 1843

REPORTER:	Excuse me, excuse me. I'm a reporter from the local newspaper. Would you please tell me why you are joining this caravan to Oregon?
EAST:	Free land's out there, mister.
REPORTER:	But cheap land has just opened up in Iowa and Wisconsin. And you don't have to go 2,000 miles to get it.
EAST:	It's still $1.25 an acre.
EVANS:	There are no good roads in Wisconsin or Iowa to ship your goods to market. Out in Oregon you can do it easy by water— there are lots of rivers and streams.
STONE:	And there's easy selling to the Russians and people on those islands.
EVANS:	Sandwich Islands. Hawaii, they call it. Very important trading and supply station.
REPORTER:	How about you, ma'am? Looks like you have some pretty young children to take on such a journey. Aren't you a bit nervous?

BANKS:	Of course I am, but we'll make it. Besides, we're going West because people out there respect you if you work with your hands.
REPORTER:	I'm sorry, but I don't understand.
BANKS:	We're from a part of Missouri where they're bringing in slaves. We don't like that, and my husband doesn't care to be put down all the time by those slavers just because he works so hard with his hands, like slaves do.
REPORTER:	Well, good luck to all of you. I hope you find what you're all looking for.

Scene IV: Fort Hall (eastern Idaho), late August 1843

GRANT:	Folks, I hope you haven't all been fooled into thinking you can bring those wagons any further. I'm sorry, but this is the end of the trail for them.
EVANS:	Whitman! You tricked us! Always pushing, always prodding us like cattle with your "Travel! Travel! Travel!"
STONE:	And to think what we've been through trying to get them across every stream and rushing river! I almost drowned three times!
WHITMAN:	They'll make it, I tell you! All of them! Back in '36 I brought a wagon as far as Fort Boise.
GRANT:	But, Doc, that was just a little feller.
EVANS:	If we can't take our wagons any further, we won't have anything

to build with except our hands! Whitman, I could string you up for deceiving us all!

EAST: Hold on! Have you forgotten how far the doctor has already brought us? That's over a hundred wagons and a thousand folks, plus my new one the doctor delivered yesterday. If he thinks our wagons can make it, I say let's keep following him. My family is going to.

APPLEGATE: Mr. East makes good sense. As leader of this caravan I say we continue on, *with* our wagons.

Scene V: Valley of the Grande Ronde (eastern Oregon), early fall 1843

EAST: Looks like we've got a visitor, and he's riding mighty fast.

MESSENGER: Doctor Whitman! Doctor Whitman! The Spaldings are very sick. They need you right away!

APPLEGATE: He can't leave us now. There are more mountains ahead of us, and winter will soon be here.

WHITMAN: Mr. Applegate, you've trusted my judgment and experience to bring you and the wagons this far. Trust me again. Stickus will lead you all safely to the Columbia River.

EVANS: But he's an Indian!

WHITMAN: Have you forgotten that it was the Indian maiden Sacagawea who guided Lewis and Clark all the way to the Oregon coast? Stickus is no less capable, as he has shown for much of this trip.

He will get you through. And if you need any food, supplies, or just a place to rest, he'll bring you to the mission at Waiilatpu. I hope to see you there.

Act IV

Scene I: Whitman Mission at Waiilatpu, November 27, 1847

NARCISSA: Well, look who's coming—Henry Spalding leading a wagon train.

SPALDING: Hello! I brought the grain you asked for—and my daughter to start school.

NARCISSA: She'll be a welcome addition.

WHITMAN: Henry, I can't thank you enough for this grain. We certainly can use it, what with all the hungry settlers passing by and the Indians being too sick to hunt.

SPALDING: These have been very trying times for all of us, but especially for you and Narcissa. Your message reminded me of Job's troubles from the Bible. Both of you seem to have suffered as much as he.

NARCISSA: We've had measles, dysentery, and what not. All of us have been hit very hard, but none worse than the Cayuse. Marcus has been working night and day trying to help, but they keep on dying.

WHITMAN: Most of the white people here get over the measles, but not the Indians. They don't seem to be able to fight it off.

NARCISSA:	And that has caused some of them to think we're responsible, that we're trying to destroy them.
SPALDING:	How are those seven Sager orphans you took in from the caravan?
NARCISSA:	Three of them are very sick.
WHITMAN:	Henry, there's an Indian lodge about thirty miles from here. The people there are pleading me to come. Would you mind accompanying me?
SPALDING:	But how can you leave at a time like this?
WHITMAN:	Narcissa is very capable. She'll get along just as well without me. But those Indians won't. I need to leave right away.

Scene II: Umatilla Valley, that evening

SPALDING:	Sure is peaceful, just riding along out here.
WHITMAN:	I wish I could feel that way, Henry.
SPALDING:	What are you talking about, Marcus?
WHITMAN:	I know we've had our differences, and I haven't ever really confided in you, but Henry, I feel like my life here has been a failure.
SPALDING:	How can you say such a thing? Failure? Look at all the settlers you've helped get to Oregon. Look at what you've built at Waiilatpu.
WHITMAN:	But we were never able to build the most important thing.
SPALDING:	Meaning?
WHITMAN:	A bridge—a bridge of trust and goodwill between the mission and the Indians. You and Eliza seem to have done that at Lapwai.
SPALDING:	Maybe, but we've worked with different tribes, different personalities and attitudes.
WHITMAN:	I suppose it all boils down to personalities: mine and Narcissa's. You can't blame the Indians.
SPALDING:	Don't be so hard on yourself, Marcus.
WHITMAN:	I'm just telling you the truth, that's all. You know me, always working, doctoring, traveling, always too busy to sit down and talk, or as the Indians say, "parley" with them.
SPALDING:	That's their way. To parley is to show respect. Protocol is very important to the Indians, just like it is in Washington, D.C., with the diplomats.
WHITMAN:	Do you think all the settlers coming west care a hoot about protocol? Folks who survive the Oregon Trail aren't apt to give anyone respect who just talks. It's doing things that matters out here.
SPALDING:	How does Narcissa get along with the Indians?

WHITMAN: Oh, they like her pretty voice and all, but when she got upset with the squaws for sitting in her kitchen night and day, they thought her uppity and unfriendly.

SPALDING: Our cultures have different views of privacy.

WHITMAN: But what really seemed to build a wall between us was the friendly and helpful way we treated the passing settlers. The Indians thought each additional settler meant more of their land would be taken away.

SPALDING: I can understand how they might think that. Over 4,000 came this year, and the white man's diseases are certainly reducing the Indian population.

WHITMAN: Narcissa and I have done everything in our power to help the Indians. I guess we just didn't understand each other.

SPALDING: It's never been and never will be an easy task.

WHITMAN: Regardless of what we say or do, or what the Indians say or do, there's no stopping the flood of settlers now.

SPALDING: I know. I heard one settler say it was the United States' destiny—"Manifest Destiny," as he put it, to populate the continent from the Atlantic to the Pacific.

Epilogue

On November 29, 1847, a band of Cayuse attacked the mission at Waiilatpu, killing Marcus and Narcissa Whitman, the Sager boys, and nine others. Fifty were held hostage. In early 1848, news of the tragedy and petitions to Congress from Oregon settlers were taken to Washington, D.C., by Joseph Meek, a friend of the Whitmans. In August of 1848, Congress created the Oregon Territory, the first formal territorial government west of the Rockies.

CYRUS MCCORMICK AND THE REAPER

Characters (in order of appearance)

JOHN McCown, blacksmith	JO Anderson, African-American shop helper to Cyrus
MARY McCormick, Cyrus's mother	LEANDER and WILLIAM McCormick, Cyrus's brothers
ROBERT McCormick, Cyrus's father	JOHN B. McCormick, Cyrus's cousin
CYRUS McCormick, inventor of the mechanical reaper	JANE Bowman and EMILY McAlpin, writers for a church-women's paper

Cyrus McCormick

Scene I: McCormick home, Walnut Grove Farm, Virginia, 1824

JOHN: I appreciate you folks inviting me to dinner.

MARY: It's the least we can do, John McCown. My Robert says you always find time to do the work he can't do.

JOHN: Just doing my job—I'm a simple country blacksmith. Mmmm. There's nothing to compare with the smell of fresh bread coming from the oven.

MARY: Well, I think everything's ready. Robert?

ROBERT: For the bounty of Your gracious provisions, we give Thee thanks. Amen.

JOHN: Mrs. McCormick, if you could sell your bread you would make a million dollars.

MARY: You're so kind, Mr. McCown.

ROBERT: John's right, but it isn't the size or number of ovens that's stopping her, if you know what I mean.

JOHN: I do. Every farmer in the country has come to me asking for a tool to make harvesting easier and faster.

ROBERT: The way it is now, a man can harvest only enough grain to

feed his own family and a few animals.

MARY: It seems farmers have been reaping wheat the same way the Israelites in the Bible did long, long ago.

JOHN: That's why most folks are farmers; they're forced to. People keep coming to my shop asking me to build them a mechanical reaper. But I'm no inventor.

MARY: Robert has been working on something like that for nearly eight years now.

JOHN: Any luck yet?

ROBERT: No. But my boy, Cyrus, made today something that works.

JOHN: What's that, Cyrus?

CYRUS: It's nothing new, Mr. McCown. It's a cradle I can use, more to my size so I can keep up with the men.

JOHN: Well, cradles are a little faster than sickles, but not much. How much can you cut in one day?

CYRUS: Nearly the same as the men: two acres.

JOHN: And it's a long, hard day at that. Well, Robert, I wish you luck with your invention. Get it to work properly and you'll change farming forever.

Scene II: McCormick Farm Shop, Walnut Grove Farm, Virginia, May 1831

ROBERT: That's it. I quit. Fifteen years working on a reaper and nothing to show for it.

CYRUS: Father, can I use the shop?

ROBERT: What are you going to make?

CYRUS: A reaper.

ROBERT: Son, didn't you hear me? I spent fifteen years trying to make one. What makes you think you won't be wasting your time?

CYRUS: I have some different ideas that I want to try out. And Jo has agreed to help me.

ROBERT: Well, Jo is very clever with mechanical things.

CYRUS: Can I use the shop?

ROBERT: Yes, you can. You're twenty-two now, and that's old enough to make your own decisions. Just make sure you and Jo don't get behind on your chores.

(exit Robert)

CYRUS: Well, Jo, are you ready to get started?

JO: I sure am. How much time are you thinking about giving to making this reaper?

CYRUS: Certainly not as long as my father. A few months.

JO: That's not very much time, unless you have your ideas all lined up like ducks in a row.

CYRUS: I think I have, Jo. I've studied all of father's machines, and his ideas were all wrong.

JO: That's exactly the way I saw it. I just didn't think it was my place to correct Mr. McCormick.

CYRUS: Tell me what you saw.

JO: Well, your father thought a reaping machine should be pushed, not pulled. But it's like a rope—you can't push one in a straight line.

CYRUS: What else was wrong with his machine?

JO: You have to have something to make the wheat stand up tall and straight. Otherwise it won't cut right.

CYRUS: Yes. And how should a machine try to cut?

JO: Not the way he had it set up, with the blade staying put. That's why his machines were always getting clogged up.

CYRUS: How should the blade move?

JO: Like a saw. Back and forth, but real fast.

CYRUS: Jo! Do you realize we have been thinking similar thoughts? We might be able to make a working reaper by mid-summer!

JO: That would be grand! We could have a demonstration.

CYRUS: I think we have everything we need in the shop, except the tools for making the blade. It has to be like a saw—serrated, they call it, and set just right so it can move in a reciprocal motion.

JO: I bet Mr. McCown could make it for us.

CYRUS: Of course! I'll see him first thing tomorrow.

Scene III: Uncut field, near Steele's Tavern, Virginia, July 1831

JO: Oh, my! I never thought this many people would come.

MARY: Cyrus, we believe in you! Good luck!

ROBERT: Looks like a few of the local boys don't have faith, Mary. It seems they brought their cradles and sickles to mock our boy.

MARY: Pay them no heed, Cyrus. Their aching backs and arms will someday thank you.

JOHN: Ladies and gentlemen! You are about to witness a demonstration of a mechanical reaper, the creation of Cyrus Hall McCormick with the assistance of his Negro servant, Jo Anderson.

CYRUS: Jo! Walk alongside and make sure you rake the cut grain off the platform.

(fifteen minutes later)

MARY:	Have you ever seen such a beautiful sight!
ROBERT:	Look. Some of the boys are putting down their cradles to get a closer look.
MARY:	Maybe this is the day farmers start putting them down forever and letting reapers do the hard work.

Scene IV: McCormick workshop, Walnut Grove Farm, Virginia, 1847

LEANDER:	So, what's this meeting all about? Is big brother going to talk about his trip West?
WILLIAM:	If he does, I hope he doesn't talk too long. We have a lot of orders to fill.
CYRUS:	Gather around, everyone, I have some very important news. We're going to move the whole operation to Chicago.
LEANDER:	Chicago? Way out West?
WILLIAM:	I've read the weather is miserable there. Why Chicago?
CYRUS:	There are many very sound and practical reasons for the move.
LEANDER:	Please spell them out, because we like it here; it's home.
CYRUS:	How many reapers can we manufacture in our shop?
WILLIAM:	A couple a month.
CYRUS:	Is it hard to sell them?
LEANDER:	Of course not, you know that. We can't keep up with the demand. That's why you've licensed other companies to make reapers.
CYRUS:	And though they use our design, do their reapers stand up as well as the ones we make here?
WILLIAM:	They never have. You yourself, Cyrus, have criticized them for using cheap materials and for shoddy workmanship. But that's their problem, not ours.
CYRUS:	I disagree. Every poor-quality reaper reduces the confidence farmers have in all new farm machinery. And that attitude makes our business all the more difficult.
LEANDER:	How can you change that?
CYRUS:	By creating a huge factory where thousands of new reapers can be manufactured. By having such a plant, we can control quality.
JOHN B.:	You've made your point, cousin. But why not build such a factory here instead of Chicago?
CYRUS:	Do you know where this nation's breadbasket will soon be? The prairies. Chicago is right on the edge of what will someday be a huge ocean of grain feeding this growing country. I've seen it for myself.
LEANDER:	Well, if that sea of wheat ever comes to be, we'll need that huge new factory.
CYRUS:	Yes. But to keep it humming, every factory must be constantly fed the necessary raw materials.

	Chicago is right on Lake Michigan, easily reached by ships, barges, wagons, and someday railroads.
WILLIAM:	Railroads? Your vision has stretched beyond belief. There are only a few railroads around.
CYRUS:	But that will change! Once the prairies start producing acres and acres of wheat, the railroads will come. Why? Because there will always be a market for wheat in this world, as long as it can be reaped! Of course, that's where we come in.
JOHN B.:	I'm convinced. Build this factory in Chicago and have your brothers run it because they are so mechanical. But where does that leave me? Where do I fit into these big new plans?
CYRUS:	Sales and marketing, John B, sales and marketing.
JOHN B.:	What exactly do you mean, Cyrus? You make the best reapers in the world. Why, they practically sell themselves!
CYRUS:	To paraphrase the apostle Paul: "How shall they believe if they have not heard; how shall they hear if a preacher is not sent?"
JOHN B.:	Well, cousin, you know the Good Book much better than I do, but what is the connection?
CYRUS:	Many farmers don't know about our reaper. We have to educate them. And that means advertising and salesmen meeting them face to face.
JOHN B.:	I see. Anything else?
CYRUS:	Yes. Give them a money-back guarantee if they are not completely satisfied with their purchase.
LEANDER:	That means the factory must make machines that will be very durable.
CYRUS:	And if they do break down, we have the means to service and repair them promptly.
JOHN B.:	All these things will certainly help sell our reapers.
CYRUS:	Yes, but there is one ingredient missing: making it easy for farmers to buy.
JOHN B.:	Are you talking about credit?
CYRUS:	Yes. By offering liberal credit terms, we will sell more reapers than we could ever imagine.
WILLIAM:	Well, I guess everything's settled, except for one thing.
LEANDER:	Hasn't this meeting gone on long enough? What is it?
WILLIAM:	You and I, Leander, will be in charge of production in Chicago, and cousin John will have sales and marketing. Cyrus, what will you be doing?
CYRUS:	I want to be involved in everything for awhile. Once everything is going smoothly, I want to spend my time doing just one job: improving our machines. Well, this meeting is adjourned. Let's get packing.

JOHN B.: Cyrus, take a look at this.

CYRUS: Since when do you read the *London Times*, John?

JOHN B.: One of our new machinists from England, Ken Jackson, gave it to me. He thought you should read this item.

CYRUS: "Announcing an international exhibition in London next year for displaying the works of industry of all nations." Yes.

JOHN B.: Is that all you can say? Cyrus, this is our great opportunity to show the whole world your reaper!

CYRUS: Hmmm. How many machines have we sold since we came to Chicago?

JOHN B.: Around 3,000. Why do you ask?

CYRUS: I just wanted to know if we had enough money to pay for the trip. We'll have to assemble the reaper there.

JOHN B.: You worry about the reaper and I'll make all the traveling arrangements.

Scene VI: Mid-May 1851

WILLIAM: Did you get the newspaper?

JOHN B.: Yes, yes, but I'm afraid the first reaction from the English press is not very favorable.

WILLIAM: Well, what did they say?

JOHN B.: According to the May 1 edition of the *London Times*, "Cyrus McCormick's Virginia Reaper is . . . an extravagant Yankee contrivance . . . huge, unwieldy, unsightly, and incomprehensible."

WILLIAM: Just because our reaper isn't pretty to English eyes doesn't mean it won't work. Just wait until Cyrus gives them a demonstration, and they'll change their tune.

Scene VII: August 1851

JOHN B.: William! William! You were right! Our reaper won the exhibition's highest award! Cyrus's demonstration completely won over the judges, and the crowd.

WILLIAM: Let me read it. "At the July 21 trial . . . the McCormick reaper moved smoothly through the English wheat . . . cutting it well, despite the rain and soggy stocks. The judges calculated twenty acres could be cut in one day with the machine."

JOHN B.: Read where it says the crowd gave Cyrus four cheers!

WILLIAM: Look at this: "The *Times* first judgment of the McCormick reaper was grossly premature. The machine from America was worth more to England than the entire cost of the international exhibition."

JOHN B.: That's the kind of advertising I like!

CYRUS: Good morning, ladies. You are from the Presbyterian Women's Society Magazine, I believe.

JANE: I'm Jane Bowman, and this is Emily McAlpin.

CYRUS: I am pleased to meet you both. I assume you have come regarding a contribution.

JANE: No, though we are thankful for your generosity to various church causes, especially educational ones.

EMILY: We would like to do a feature article on you, Mr. McCormick.

CYRUS: Why me? I'm just a man who runs a factory.

JANE: Well, it seems the French Academy of Sciences offers a different description.

EMILY: They have just elected you to membership, which is a most rare and distinguished honor, especially for an American.

JANE: In the words of the French Academy, "Cyrus McCormick has done more for agriculture than any other living man."

CYRUS: I am not worthy of such praise. If I had not succeeded in building my reaper in 1831, someone else would have eventually done it.

JANE: You are too modest, Mr. McCormick.

EMILY: What is your response to the comment that Secretary of War Stanton made to President Lincoln regarding your reaper?

CYRUS: What was it? That was a long time ago.

EMILY: That without your reaper, the North would not have won the war.

JANE: Your reaper made more food available as well as troops for the Union army.

CYRUS: I do not like war. Again, this is an exaggeration. Besides, many years ago I once employed Mr. Stanton and Mr. Lincoln as my lawyers in a patent dispute.

EMILY: Would you agree that your invention changed the destiny of the United States?

CYRUS: There you go again. Yes, the reaper made abundant harvests possible and freed thousands from the drudgery of farm work.

JANE: So they could help build our cities and work in new factories and become doctors and teachers.

EMILY: Speaking of cities, some newspaper people we have talked with claim you deserve much of the credit for the growth and greatness of Chicago.

CYRUS: I'm just an honest, God-fearing man who makes machines for farmers—that's all. Where do people get these ideas about me and my importance?

JANE: From the plain fact that after the disastrous fire of 1871, you did not abandon Chicago. Instead, you stayed and built an even greater factory here.

EMILY: And your commitment inspired countless others.

CYRUS: Ladies, you embarrass me. I'm an old-fashioned Scotch Presbyterian. We all know who truly deserves this praise.

JANE: Thank you for your time, Mr. McCormick.

EMILY: And what your life has meant for all of us.

HARRIET BEECHER STOWE

Characters (in order of appearance)

AUNT H (Harriet Foote), Harriet Beecher Stowe's aunt

HARRIET Beecher Stowe, writer

SAMUEL Foote, Harriet's uncle, a businessman

SALMON Chase, lifelong friend of Harriet Beecher Stowe; antislavery lawyer from Cincinnati; later a U.S. senator, Secretary of Treasury, Chief Justice of the Supreme Court

CALVIN Stowe, biblical scholar and professor, Harriet's husband

ELIZA Buck, former slave, cook for the Stowes

MRS. E.B. (Edward Beecher), antislavery advocate

EDWARD Beecher, minister, antislavery advocate, brother of Harriet

FREDERICK Douglass, former slave, renowned abolitionist leader, speaker, and writer

WILLIAM Lloyd Garrison, renowned white abolitionist leader, speaker, and writer

HENRY Ward Beecher, renowned minister, antislavery spokesman, and brother of Harriet

Abraham LINCOLN, sixteenth president of the United States

Harriet Beecher Stowe

Scene I: Grandmother's home, Nut Plains, Connecticut, 1815

AUNT H: Children, children, it's time for your lessons.

HARRIET: Aunt Harriet, when you teach us, why can't Dinah and Harry sit with me?

AUNT H: Now Hattie, you mustn't concern yourself with such things. After all, you are only four years old.

HARRIET: Is it because they have dark skins? Papa teaches that we are all God's children: red, yellow, black, brown, and white.

AUNT H: Your father is an esteemed preacher—oh, I shouldn't be talking on like this—but he forgets that each person belongs to a different station in life.

	Dinah and Harry were born to be in the servant class.
HARRIET:	Why? Papa says everyone should be free to choose what they want to be. Today I want Harry and Dinah to sit with us for tea. I'll be the servant.
AUNT H:	Now Hattie, that would not be proper.

Scene II: Semi-Colon Literary Club, Cincinnati, Ohio, 1833

SAMUEL:	Hattie, my dear niece, I would like you to meet one of Cincinnati's most brilliant young lawyers, Mr. Salmon Chase.
HARRIET:	I am delighted to make your acquaintance, Mr. Chase.
SALMON:	The pleasure is mine, Miss Beecher. Your uncle tells me that along with your busy teaching schedule you write stories.
SAMUEL:	Some of them have been published in magazines.
SALMON:	Tell me what these stories are about.
HARRIET:	Oh, they're mainly sketches of village life in New England. I spent my first twenty-one years there.
SALMON:	It would please me greatly to read some of them.
SAMUEL:	Next time I see you, Salmon, I'll bring a few.
SALMON:	Miss Beecher, if I may be so bold, have you ever written anything about the abominable system of slavery?
SAMUEL:	Hattie, Salmon is one of the city's leading crusaders against slavery; he's very active in the underground railroad.
HARRIET:	To answer your question, Mr. Chase, no, I have not. I write only from personal experience.
SALMON:	What are your thoughts on slavery, then?
HARRIET:	It's a great injustice, an evil. As a Christian, it violates every virtue I cherish and everything the Gospel stands for.
SALMON:	I wish the churches in the South shared that perspective. It seems they have numbed their sense that slavery is sinful with the devil's perfume of economic necessity.
HARRIET:	I'm not sure I understand you, Mr. Chase.
SALMON:	As long as the debate over slavery is confined to the worlds of politics and business, slavery will grow like a cancer. Why? Because politics is about compromise, and business is about profits. Only when this nation's moral conscience is shaken out of its lethargy will slavery end.
HARRIET:	Are you suggesting that a writer can shake the nation's conscience?
SALMON:	The Bible says, "The pen is mightier than the sword." Miss Beecher, if you have the skill to write about the New England you

know so well from living there, then learn about the slavery system that exists only a few miles from here! Go see it for yourself. Smell, touch, and hear it. Then write!

HARRIET: Your challenge has touched my heart, Mr. Chase. Are you familiar with I Peter, Chapter 4 in the New Testament?

SALMON: It does not come quickly to mind.

HARRIET: The writer proclaims that a righteous person fighting evil does God's will, and though persecution may follow, that person is blessed.

SAMUEL: Hattie, I have contacts across the river in Kentucky, people who own a large plantation. I can arrange for you to stay with them for a few days.

HARRIET: Thank you, Uncle Samuel. I'm ready to go right now.

Scene III: Stowe home, Cincinnati, Ohio, 1845

CALVIN: Hattie, dear, I know how limited our budget is. But raising five children, running this household, and writing your articles all require too much time and energy. You need a helper.

HARRIET: But, but—

CALVIN: I insist. Remember eight years ago when the twins were born? You were so overwhelmed with work I had to send you off to your brother's. You were close to a complete physical breakdown.

HARRIET: The rest did me much good, I recall.

CALVIN: Besides, having someone help you is only right. Your writing brings more money into this household than my salary as a professor does. Eliza is waiting for you in the kitchen.

(Calvin exits, Harriet goes into the kitchen)

HARRIET: You must be Eliza. I'm so glad to meet you. Please call me Hattie like everyone else.

ELIZA: I'm pleased to meet you. Miss Hattie, what should I do about this table? This is a mountain of clean clothes—and all these papers—where should I put them?

HARRIET: That's my writing. We can leave the table for later. I need some help peeling these potatoes.

ELIZA: Yes, Miss Hattie.

HARRIET: Eliza, where do you come from?

ELIZA: Louisiana—New Orleans and places near there.

HARRIET: How did you get to Cincinnati?

ELIZA: The Underground railroad.

HARRIET: Eliza, may I ask you about your life in Louisiana?

ELIZA: Certainly, Miss Hattie, if you don't mind me not looking your way on account of those potatoes.

HARRIET:	Don't worry about that. I visited a plantation once, across the Ohio River. I'm curious if the plantations in Louisiana are like the one I saw in Kentucky.
ELIZA:	What do you mean, Miss Hattie?
HARRIET:	How the slaves were treated by their masters. The plantation owner I visited treated his slaves kindly, though he made them perform for me like pets. That made me very uncomfortable.
ELIZA:	It wasn't like that way down in Louisiana. The masters and bosses were always beating the men for any old reason. Sometimes the men would pass out and nearly die from the whippings. It was awful, Miss Hattie, awful.
HARRIET:	And the women? How were you treated, Eliza?
ELIZA:	It's painful to talk about.
HARRIET:	Please—
ELIZA:	They took all my children away from me. Sold them at the auction in New Orleans.
HARRIET:	And their father—your husband?
ELIZA:	I had no husband. The master was my children's father. He'd come in the middle of the night and force himself on me.
HARRIET:	Are all slave women treated like that?
ELIZA:	Most of them, I think. We had no one to protect us, Miss Hattie.

	Even the more kindly masters, if they got drunk, would violate us.
HARRIET:	I'm sorry.

Scene IV: Home of Rev. Edward Beecher, Boston, Massachusetts, early spring 1851

MRS. E.B.:	Well, Hattie, have you finally taken up my challenge?
HARRIET:	With a vengeance!
EDWARD:	What challenge? I'd say my sister has had plenty of challenges in her forty years on this earth: raising six children, losing a child, surviving cholera, and keeping her family from the poorhouse with her writings.
MRS. E.B.:	About a year ago I asked Hattie to write something the whole country would read—a novel that would show in dramatic human terms what an accursed thing slavery is.
EDWARD:	Well, sister, what has come of it?
HARRIET:	The first chapter has been sent to the publisher. It's going to be serialized weekly in the *National Era*.
MRS. E.B.:	That's how they publish Charles Dickens in England. Do you know yet how the story is going to turn out?
HARRIET:	In my mind, yes. I have to get back to Maine to put all my notes together. The whole project should take about a year.

EDWARD: I assume the story is based on your experiences in Kentucky and your conversations with Eliza.

HARRIET: Yes, and my correspondence with Frederick Douglass. He's been a big help.

EDWARD: Well, he's an amazing and gifted person. He taught himself five foreign languages!

MRS. E.B.: And became the most gifted speaker against slavery in the whole United States, I might add. Hattie, have you chosen a title for your story?

HARRIET: Yes—*Uncle Tom's Cabin.*

Scene V: Offices of the abolitionist paper *North Star, Rochester, New York, summer 1852*

FREDERICK: William, good to see you again. What brings you to Rochester? Certainly not this dreadful heat!

WILLIAM: The hottest story in America, that's what brings me.

FREDERICK: Meaning the book, of course.

WILLIAM: Over fifty thousand already sold! The publisher can't print copies fast enough.

FREDERICK: Well, any heart that isn't gripped by *Uncle Tom's Cabin* is made of ice. In all of literature, are there any more memorable characters than Little Eva, Topsy, and Tom?

WILLIAM: I agree, and so does much of America. And don't forget Simon Legree.

FREDERICK: Yes, the very personification of evil and brutality.

WILLIAM: For the northerner who has never been to the South, Harriet Beecher Stowe has made Simon Legree the face of every slave-owner and master. That's power.

FREDERICK: And contrast Simon with Tom, the very epitome of goodness. Tom risks his life to rescue a white child—

WILLIAM: And in the end is beaten to death by the drunken Legree. No wonder this book has created such a stir.

FREDERICK: It's like all the speeches you and I have made against slavery are but candles in the wind compared with the bonfire Mrs. Stowe has lit.

WILLIAM: I'm not sure about that, Frederick. But I will say that her book has dramatically altered the whole debate over slavery, especially in the North.

FREDERICK: I know. The book will certainly give birth to a moral crusade to abolish slavery once and for all. And you know what risks that crusade entails.

WILLIAM: More bloodshed—maybe even civil war, I fear.

Scene VI: Home of Rev. Henry Ward Beecher, Brooklyn, New York, June 1861

HENRY: Hattie, I know you don't like discussing politics, but there is

	an issue that requires your attention.
HARRIET:	And what might that be, brother?
EDWARD:	We both know the war is not going well for the Union. If Great Britain goes ahead and recognizes the Confederacy, things could get even worse.
HARRIET:	The British would never do that! Don't you remember how they reacted to *Uncle Tom's Cabin*? It nearly outsold Dickens's most popular works there.
EDWARD:	How ironic that you should mention Charles Dickens. Do you realize that he's publicly supported the independence of the Confederate states? And there are many other influential members of the British social and commercial elite who agree with him!
HARRIET:	Why do you bring such news to me? What could I possibly do?
EDWARD:	After your visit to Great Britain in 1853, over a half-million British women signed a letter to you expressing their opposition to slavery.
HARRIET:	Yes. The "Affectionate and Christian Address from the Women of Great Britain." It's one of my most cherished possessions, all twenty-six volumes.
EDWARD:	Have you ever made a public reply to it?
HARRIET:	I don't understand. What would be the point?

EDWARD:	Those signatures are like a deep reservoir of support. Now is the time to draw from it—to open its floodgates to move public opinion in Britain away from recognizing the Confederacy. All it would take is a public reply from you.
HARRIET:	It's not that simple, Edward, and I'll tell you why. How committed is President Lincoln to the complete emancipation of all four million slaves? Since the war began, he's been silent on the issue. Therefore, how could I in good conscience ask my friends in Britain to support the Union when Mr. Lincoln's stand on slavery is in doubt?
HENRY:	Then you should go see him yourself! Hattie, we cannot allow Great Britain to recognize the Confederacy!
HARRIET:	I respect you completely, brother, and so I will try to see President Lincoln.
HENRY:	And?
HARRIET:	If he convinces me he's working towards full emancipation, then I'll write that reply—in the *Atlantic* magazine, where I have friends and supporters.

Scene VII: The White House, Washington, D.C., late November 1862

LINCOLN:	So you are the little lady whose book made the big war! I am so glad to meet you at last, Mrs. Stowe.

HARRIET:	Thank you, Mr. President. I pray for you every day.
LINCOLN:	Thank you. I can't get enough prayers with the job I have to do. So, what brings you to Washington?
HARRIET:	To visit with my son, who's in the Union Army. And I was invited to a Thanksgiving dinner for a thousand former slaves.
LINCOLN:	Oh, yes, I heard about that. But you haven't told me why you've come to the White House.
HARRIET:	To understand your position on slavery, Mr. President.
LINCOLN:	Well, I don't know if there is anything more to be said. Are you familiar with the Emancipation Proclamation, which I've ordered to take effect January 1, 1863?
HARRIET:	I am, and I'm troubled that it only mentions the Confederate states. What about slavery in the border states—Kentucky, Tennessee, Missouri, and Maryland?
LINCOLN:	Their omission has to do with hardheaded practical politics— holding them to the Union side.
HARRIET:	Mr. President, political expediency has never given this Christian any comfort or solace.

LINCOLN:	Would it give you any comfort to know that I have private assurances from the legislatures of those states that they too will enact emancipation? And that if they do not, in due time I will issue an executive order forcing them to?
HARRIET:	Yes.
LINCOLN:	And furthermore, Mrs. Stowe, once this horrible war is over, I am fully confident that there will be an amendment to the U.S. Constitution forever abolishing slavery. Trust me, it will come to pass.
HARRIET:	Thank you, Mr. President. Now, I have a very important letter to write.
LINCOLN:	To whom, may I ask?
HARRIET:	To the women of Great Britain, urging them to support the Union cause.
LINCOLN:	Mrs. Stowe, if such a letter helps prevent the British government from recognizing the Confederate states, you will have performed another great and noble public service, and you will once again deserve the heartfelt appreciation of millions. Thank you.

ALEXANDER GRAHAM BELL

Characters (in order of appearance)

ELIZA Bell, Aleck's mother

MELVILLE Bell, Aleck's brother

MR. BELL (Alexander), Aleck's father

ALECK (Alexander Graham Bell)

THOMAS Sanders, financial backer and father of one of Aleck's students

GARDINER Hubbard, financial backer, father of one of Aleck's students, and his future father-in-law

WATSON, Thomas, Aleck's assistant

MABEL Hubbard, later Bell, one of Aleck's deaf students, later his fiancée and wife

WILLIAM Hubbard, nephew of Gardiner Hubbard

DOM PEDRO, emperor of Brazil

Sir William THOMSON, later Lord Kelvin, distinguished English scientist

Alexander Graham Bell

Scene I: Bell home, Edinburgh, Scotland, 1863

ELIZA: Boys, your father wishes to see you in his study.

MELVILLE: Yes, Mother.

(Mr. Bell's study)

MR. BELL: Boys, I've just witnessed something most interesting—a machine from Germany that makes human sounds.

MELVILLE: You mean like a real person's voice?

MR. BELL: Not really. It was a rather crude device. I'm convinced you two could make a better one.

ALECK: Is this a challenge, Father?

MR. BELL: Most certainly! Aleck, just because you are but sixteen and your brother eighteen, no two young men in all of Scotland know more about the mechanics of human speech.

MELVILLE: We've had the finest speech teachers in all of Great Britain: you and grandfather!

MR. BELL: Well, boys, are you up to the task?

MELVILLE: We'll give it our best. Aleck, you make the head, mouth, and tongue. Since I'm a wee bit more skilled with tools, I'll make the larynx and vocal cords.

ALECK: Can I help it if I'm so clumsy with my hands?

MR. BELL: Melville! Where are you running off to?

MELVILLE: The butcher's shop for a lamb's larynx to study.

MR. BELL: Good thinking! And, good luck to both of you!

(a few weeks later)

"Mama! Mama! Mama!"

ELIZA: Alexander, I know I'm going deaf, but I could swear I just heard a baby crying. It must be one of the neighbors' children. Please be a dear and take a look.

(enter Melville)

MELVILLE: No need to worry, Mother. It was only our talking machine.

MR. BELL: Well done, boys! Well done!

Scene II: Bell home, Edinburgh, Scotland, 1870

ELIZA: What did the doctor say?

MR. BELL: Aleck has tuberculosis.

ELIZA: We must do something! First little Edward, then Melville. I won't see Aleck follow them to the grave!

MR. BELL: A more healthy climate might be the answer. I have some good contacts in Canada.

ELIZA: What about your work?

MR. BELL: There are many deaf people in North America, too. If I can teach my visible speech system here, I can do it there as well.

Scene III: Bell family home, Brantford, Ontario, Canada, 1871

ELIZA: How was Boston, my good husband?

MR. BELL: Invigorating as always. It reminds me of Edinburgh: so many well-educated and talented people. The city is bursting with creative energy.

ELIZA: Speaking of bursting with energy—I think our Aleck has fully recovered.

MR. BELL: Whooping all over the house with his Mohawk dancing, I suppose.

ELIZA: Yes. You know he spends a great deal of time with his Indian friends. He's even mastered their

language. And furthermore, he's helping some of the deaf ones learn how to speak. He has them watch and study his mouth and lips, your "visible speech" system.

MR. BELL: Hmmm. Speaking of teaching, while I was in Boston I secured a position for Aleck there. Where is he?

ELIZA: In his room tinkering with tuning forks. He never seems to stop studying sounds.

MR. BELL: Well, that's an interesting activity, but it's time Aleck made his way in the world. After all, he's twenty-four and a gifted teacher already.

Scene IV: Boston School for the Deaf, Boston, Massachusetts, 1874

ALECK: Mr. Sanders, what a pleasant surprise. Please come in and have a seat.

THOMAS: Thank you. I see you're busy making something, so I'll just stay a minute.

ALECK: Please, stay as long as you like. I'm only tinkering.

THOMAS: I just wanted to personally express my gratitude for what you have done for our little George.

ALECK: He's a delightful boy, Mr. Sanders, and such a willing and capable student.

THOMAS: When we learned he was born deaf, we never expected him to

speak. You have changed all that, Mr. Bell, and we are eternally grateful to you. Say, what are you tinkering with? It looks rather interesting.

ALECK: I'm trying to invent something—a telegraph that can send more than one message at a time.

(enter Mr. Hubbard)

GARDINER: Sorry to intrude. I've just come by to extend a dinner invitation to Mr. Bell.

ALECK: Why, thank you. It's always a great pleasure to dine at the Hubbard home.

GARDINER: We appreciate so much what you have done for our Mabel. I never thought we would be able to understand her speech after she lost her hearing as a child.

THOMAS: Gardiner, take a look at what Mr. Bell is working on. It might have a promising future.

GARDINER: What is it?

ALECK: Not much at this point, I'm afraid. I'm trying to construct a device that will send many messages over a telegraph wire simultaneously.

GARDINER: A multiple telegraph? Is that really possible?

ALECK: Yes.

THOMAS: Well, you've worked a miracle with my son, so I believe you, Mr. Bell. What do you need to make it?

ALECK:	Time, materials, and an assistant skilled in making things and well versed in electricity. I'm rather clumsy with my hands.
GARDINER:	Such an invention would be worth a fortune! Tell me how much money you'll need and I'll back you.
THOMAS:	And so will I!
ALECK:	Are you serious?
THOMAS:	Most certainly!
ALECK:	Then let's form a partnership here and now!
GARDINER:	Excellent idea! Now, regarding an assistant, I'm sure you would find someone suitable at Williams Electric Shop. We'll pay his wages.

Scene V: Williams Electric Shop, Boston, Massachusetts, a few days later

WATSON:	Can I be of any help?
ALECK:	I hope so. I'm working on a device for improving the telegraph. I purchased this item here last week. I'm afraid it's just not right.
WATSON:	Yes, so I see. I'm very sorry. I'm the one responsible, so I'll fix it at no charge.
ALECK:	Why, thank you. I appreciate your honesty and integrity, Mr.—?

WATSON:	Watson. Thomas Watson.
ALECK:	Mr. Watson, would you mind showing me some other things in the shop you have made?
WATSON:	Not at all. Follow me.
ALECK:	You have a great deal of talent, Mr. Watson. What schools have you attended?
WATSON:	None, sir. I've taught myself, by and large.
ALECK:	Hmmm. Allow me to introduce myself. My name is Alexander Graham Bell and I teach deaf children to speak.
WATSON:	I'm pleased to meet you, Mr. Bell.
ALECK:	Would you consider coming to work with me? You would be given a good wage if your work was satisfactory.
WATSON:	Helping to teach deaf children? Not me, Mr. Bell.
ALECK:	No, no. I'm so sorry for the misunderstanding. I want you to assist me in my workshop, not in my classroom.
WATSON:	Are you trying to invent something?
ALECK:	Yes.
WATSON:	That has always been my dream, Mr. Bell. I will gladly come to work with you.

Scene VI: Bell's attic workshop, Boston, Massachusetts, June 2, 1875

ALECK: How long have we been working on the multiple telegraph?

WATSON: I've stopped thinking about the long days and nights.

ALECK: It's like an endless stream of adjustments.

WATSON: Each one more delicate than the one before.

ALECK: I suggest we take a little break.

WATSON: That's a good idea. We don't seem to be accomplishing anything anyway.

ALECK: That's the frustrating part. Sometimes it's useful to think about other things for awhile and then come back with a new perspective.

WATSON: That makes sense.

ALECK: Good. Did I ever mention the invention I dreamed up in Canada last summer?

WATSON: I'm not sure. What was it?

ALECK: A device that could transmit speech electrically.

WATSON: You mean a real human voice and not just dots and dashes like the telegraph?

ALECK: Yes, an actual human voice.

WATSON: What's the biggest challenge to making it?

ALECK: How to make a current of electricity vary in intensity precisely as air varies in density during the production of a sound.

WATSON: Oh, my! That's a mouthful! I don't think I can be of much help figuring that out. If you don't mind, I think I'll go back to adjusting those transmitting springs.

ALECK: Go right ahead. I'll be in the other room tuning the different transmitters.

(Aleck exits to another room sixty feet away)

WATSON: Oh, oh. This one looks stuck. I better pluck it free.

(Aleck comes running to Watson)

ALECK: Watson! I heard a "ping" at the other end of this connection! What did you do?

WATSON: I—I'm not sure. Wait! Now I see! When I snapped the spring the circuit remained unbroken.

ALECK: And you created a current of electricity that varied in intensity precisely as the air varied in density within hearing distance of the spring. Watson! You did it! Don't change a thing!

WATSON: Tell me in simple English what happened.

ALECK: You made sound travel electrically!

WATSON: What does this mean for our work with the multiple telegraph?

ALECK:	Oh, forget about that! We're going to make a device that will transmit a human voice electrically! Let me roughly sketch what I want you to make.
WATSON:	Hmmm. A lambskin diaphragm—opposite a magnet in a transmitter—running a connecting wire through sulfuric acid—causing a receiving membrane to vibrate.
ALECK:	Well, can you make it?
WATSON:	With enough time, yes.
ALECK:	Excellent! Speaking of time, I'd best be getting a patent before someone else comes up with a similar idea.

Scene VII: Bell's workshop, 5 Exeter Street, Boston, Massachusetts, March 10, 1876

WATSON:	How close do you think we are?
ALECK:	I really don't know. We could be at the edge of the forest or right in the middle of it. I've made hundreds of adjustments to this transmitter, and I still can't get it right.
WATSON:	Is there anything I can do?
ALECK:	No, thank you. You'd better go back to your work.
WATSON:	I'll be in the other room if you need me.
	(a few minutes later)
ALECK:	Mr. Watson, come here. I want you!

(Watson comes running into the room)

WATSON:	I could hear you! I could hear you! Your voice was loud and clear over the connection! The telephone works!

Scene VIII: Hubbard home, Boston, Massachusetts, June 18, 1876

MABEL:	Aleck, I want you to go to Philadelphia. You must demonstrate your telephone at the Centennial Exhibition.
ALECK:	But, Mabel, dearest, it's the end of the term. I have so many exams to grade.
MABEL:	They can wait! Never again will you have such an opportunity to show the world your great invention.
ALECK:	But—but I'm not sure it will work outside my workshop. Things could go badly.
MABEL:	Then make it work!
ALECK:	But even if it does, who will take the telephone seriously? Even your father thinks it's no more than a toy.
MABEL:	You'll never know what people will think unless you go there!
ALECK:	Your father is disappointed in me for not perfecting the multiple telegraph yet. He says he won't allow me to marry you until I have a steady income.
MABEL:	Disappointed? Alexander Graham Bell, if you don't go

to Philadelphia with your tele-phone, you will have the most disappointed fiancée in history! And don't worry about a steady income! Your telephone will certainly take care of that! Now get packing!

Scene IX: Centennial Exposition, Philadelphia, Pennsylvania, Sunday, June 25, 1876

WILLIAM: It sure is hot, Mr. Bell.

ALECK: That it is, Willie. Too hot, I'm afraid, for the judges to bother seeing my telephone.

WILLIAM: What if we moved everything away from this dark corner and into the center of the hall? Then they would surely see it.

ALECK: I'm afraid that's not allowed. This is the place I've been assigned. Besides, I think the heat has driven them off to cooler places.

WILLIAM: Don't give up hope, Mr. Bell.

ALECK: I knew it was a waste of time coming here. I think I'll just pack everything up and get the next train back to Boston.

(Emperor Dom Pedro and judges enter the hall)

DOM PEDRO: That gentleman in the corner— he looks so familiar. Does anyone know him?

THOMSON: I will inquire.

(shortly after)

DOM PEDRO: Yes?

THOMSON: The gentleman's name is Alex-ander Graham Bell. He's demon-strating a device called the telephone.

DOM PEDRO: Alexander Graham Bell! Wonderful! I know him. I must speak with him.

(the entire entourage moves towards Bell's exhibit)

WILLIAM: Mr. Bell, stop packing! A big crowd is coming this way!

DOM PEDRO: Professor Bell, how good to see you again. And, how are all your students at the school for the deaf progressing?

ALECK: Very well, thank you. Emperor Dom Pedro, this is a great honor and privilege to see you again.

DOM PEDRO: The pleasure is mine, Professor Bell. Now, what is this invention of yours?

ALECK: The telephone. It transmits human speech electrically.

DOM PEDRO: Over a wire? How far can it do this?

ALECK: Allow me to demonstrate. I will go to the other side of the hall. That is about 500 feet away. Hold this up to your ear and I will speak to you.

(Bell goes to the other side of the hall)

"To be, or not to be: that is the question."

DOM PEDRO: It talks! I can hear every word! Mr. Thomson, listen!

THOMSON: Amazing! I can hear every word clearly. This could be the greatest invention of the age! It will change the whole world!

DOM PEDRO: Gentlemen, I realize you had not planned on judging any more exhibits, but in light of this demonstration, I believe

Mr. Bell's telephone deserves consideration.

THOMSON: Most definitely! As a scientist I believe it is without question the most important invention on display. It is worthy of the grand prize!

CLARA BARTON, HEROINE OF HOPE

Characters (in order of appearance)

SARAH Barton, Clara's mother	HENRY Wilson, Massachusetts senator
CLARA Barton	JAMES Dunn, Union Army doctor
STEPHEN Barton, Clara's father	FRED, Freight Depot Manager
CHARLES Mason, superintendent of U.S. Patent Office	MICHAEL Holmgren, American Red Cross official
SALLY Vassall, Clara's older sister	JIMMY and JOHNNY, teamsters

Clara Barton

Scene I: Barton home, North Oxford, Massachusetts, 1828

SARAH: Clara, my child, why do you look so upset?

CLARA: Some of the village girls wouldn't stop teasing me.

STEPHEN: What did they say?

CLARA: That I'm a tomboy and all I'm good for are climbing trees, playing baseball, and riding bareback.

STEPHEN: Hmmm. Sounds to me like they're jealous. Not many other six-year-olds can do those things like you.

CLARA: They said I should only do girl things so I'll grow up to be a proper lady.

SARAH: Don't you fret about that, Clara. I'll teach you how to run a sound household.

STEPHEN: Clara, my dear, don't ever let anyone hold you back by telling you what you should or shouldn't do. And remember, you have the mind and spirit to be anything you want.

Scene II: 1833

SARAH: Clara, your brother is not improving.

STEPHEN: The blow to his head is much more serious than the doctors first thought. He was fortunate he didn't break his neck when he fell off the barn roof.

SARAH: Nothing seems to help David's fever. He keeps calling for you.

CLARA: I'll stay with him. I'll try to nurse him back to health.

STEPHEN: It could be for a very long time.

CLARA: That doesn't matter. I love my big brother.

STEPHEN: It's a big, big job for an eleven-year-old, but I know you can do it.

CLARA: I'll do my best and never give up hope for David.

Scene III: 1835

SARAH: The doctor says David has fully recovered and can go back to a normal life.

STEPHEN: Clara, my dear, you sacrificed two years of your life to bring back our David. We can never thank you enough.

CLARA: Father, I only did what had to be done for the good of someone in great need, just as you always taught us to do.

STEPHEN: I am so proud of you. Always remember, Clara, giving of yourself to help others, like you did for David, is the greatest and most noble thing you can do in your life.

Scene IV: Patent Office, Washington, D.C., 1855

CHARLES: So, Miss Barton, you wish to work as a copyist? What was your most recent employment?

CLARA: I was a schoolteacher in New Jersey.

CHARLES: Anything unusual about that experience?

CLARA: I opened and operated the first free school in Bordentown.

CHARLES: Hmmm. Most interesting. What were your students like?

CLARA: They were mainly poor children roaming the streets because they could not afford school.

CHARLES: Until you opened yours. That must have taken a great deal of time and effort. Why did you do it?

CLARA: All children deserve a proper education. These children weren't getting any. I saw a need and set about filling it.

CHARLES: Was the school a success?

CLARA: I started with only a handful of students. Eventually nearly 600 were enrolled.

CHARLES:	You must be a very resourceful individual, Miss Barton. Tell me, why did you leave such a successful venture?
CLARA:	Once the school grew to 600 students, the board thought that only a man could administer it.
CHARLES:	Miss Barton, I trust you are not under the impression that such attitudes towards women do not exist here in Washington, D.C. In fact, I can't think of any woman presently working for the federal government except for maids and building cleaners.
CLARA:	Mr. Mason, I can do the job.
CHARLES:	I'm sure you can. Believe it or not, I fully support vocational opportunities for women. Unfortunately, the same cannot be said for most men in the federal government.
CLARA:	And the job?
CHARLES:	I'll support you, but don't expect a warm reception from your co-workers. They can be very rude and insensitive, especially if your work is superior. Report tomorrow at 9:00 A.M.

Scene V: Clara Barton's apartment, Washington, D.C., late April 1861

SALLY:	Who is your interior decorator? Is "military warehouse" the new style?
CLARA:	Very funny, sister.
SALLY:	What are you ever going to do with all this food, soap, and blan-

	kets? There's enough for a full regiment!
CLARA:	The Massachusetts Sixth, to be exact.
SALLY:	What are you talking about, Clara? Are you working for the Patent Office or the War Department?
CLARA:	I'm still at the Patent Office, but as we both know, Washington is the new temporary home for thousands of young men, many of whom were my students!
SALLY:	And how does that concern you?
CLARA:	The War Department has not shown itself to be the most organized or generous host to these troops. The boys are sleeping wherever they can and are not being fed properly but are expected to go out and fight for the Union in a few days! They're mostly boys! And they're tired, hungry, homesick, and bored, not to mention scared.
SALLY:	How did you get all these supplies?
CLARA:	I've been very busy writing letters, especially to newspapers back in Massachusetts. I've asked the editors to print my urgent request for supplies. You wouldn't believe the response: books, blankets, food, all from mothers, sweethearts, sisters, aunts, and wives of the Massachusetts Sixth.
SALLY:	You must need help distributing all this.

CLARA:	I certainly do. This war could last a lot longer than people think, maybe three or four years.
SALLY:	Well, you can count on my help and the help of some of my friends in Washington. I'll see to that.

Scene VI: Office of Senator Wilson, Washington D.C., July 1862

HENRY:	Clara Barton, on behalf of the people of Massachusetts, I extend my utmost appreciation for what you are doing for our boys. Everywhere I go in the city, people praise your humanitarian work in securing vital supplies, nursing and comforting the wounded, and enlisting others to help. You are a most remarkable person, and we are all in your debt.
CLARA:	Thank you, Senator Wilson.
HENRY:	How can I help?
CLARA:	Get the army to grant me the necessary passes so I can do my work on the battlefield.
HENRY:	That's a rather tall order, I'm afraid. No woman has ever been allowed near the fighting, for obvious reasons.
CLARA:	And the reasons for me going to the battlefront are also obvious! Hundreds if not thousands of our boys are simply abandoned where they fall. No one brings them food, water, or warm blankets, let alone medical care.
HENRY:	Unfortunately, what you say is correct. Many of our men are indeed starving and dying from medical neglect. Many of us have tried to change this state of affairs, but the War Department is not easily moved to action.
CLARA:	Well, Senator, if conditions don't improve, the War Department won't have any troops to move!
HENRY:	You are again quite right. Let's say I could get you the necessary passes. How would your family feel about your putting your life in such grave danger?
CLARA:	My father died just a few months ago. The last time I saw him he said, "Clara, go to the battlefield, go to the battlefield." He knew what I was doing and could do if I were just given the opportunity.
HENRY:	I knew your father. He was a good and noble man, a true humanitarian. I'll use every ounce of political influence I have, Clara Barton, to get you the necessary passes and some additional supplies, as well.
CLARA:	Thank you, Senator Wilson. You have always supported me.

Scene VII: Field hospital, Antietam Battlefield, Maryland, September 16, 1862

JAMES:	Who in the world are you?
CLARA:	Clara Barton. You must be Dr. Dunn.
JAMES:	I am. What are you doing here?

CLARA: I'm here to help the wounded. I've also brought a full supply wagon.

JAMES: I can use every supply you've brought, but as far as helping the wounded, Miss Barton, this is a very dangerous place. Women are not allowed on the battlefield.

CLARA: Dr. Dunn, I have not traveled all these miles to discuss what is or is not allowed. Here are the necessary passes.

JAMES: They look official enough. But tell me, how were you able to get your wagon here so quickly? Usually the supplies don't arrive until the battle is over.

CLARA: And by then most of the wounded are dead, correct?

JAMES: Yes. How did you know that?

CLARA: I learned it at Cedar Mountain. By the time I got there, the fighting was long over and I was of little use to the wounded. They were too far gone.

JAMES: You were really at that battle?

CLARA: Yes. It was there that I resolved to be at the battle site at the earliest possible moment.

JAMES: You've certainly accomplished that here! There's still a great deal of fierce fighting going on. But how did you know where to go? Battle sites are top secret.

CLARA: I have some very useful contacts.

JAMES: Hmmm. You still haven't told me how you beat the other wagons. They must be at least ten miles away.

CLARA: When I found myself at the rear of the supply train, I realized that I had to act boldly or, as I did at Cedar Mountain, I would arrive too late to help much.

JAMES: So what did you do?

CLARA: I convinced my teamsters to travel in the dead of night to get to the battlefront. We went around the supply line, and here we are, ready and able.

JAMES: But teamsters are tough and stubborn and not easily convinced. How much did you pay them to do as you asked?

CLARA: I simply gave them an old-fashioned home-cooked meal.

JAMES: Well, you are a most unconventional person. What does the army think of your methods?

CLARA: I really don't care what the army thinks as long as they get the job done. I'm not one to wait around while men are dying, Dr. Dunn.

JAMES: I like your attitude! Are you ready to assist me with some operations?

CLARA: I'm ready.

JAMES: They can be quite bloody and gruesome. Do you have the stomach for it?

CLARA:	Dr. Dunn, I've already seen more maimed bodies, heard more agonizing cries, wet my hands with more spilled blood, and smelled more gut-churning diseases than most doctors do in a lifetime.
JAMES:	I believe you. Here, wear this gown. We have several amputations to perform. Say, how did you tear your dress?
CLARA:	A stray bullet passed through the sleeve.
JAMES:	What is that you are carrying from the wagon?
CLARA:	Special lamps for surgery.
JAMES:	Wonderful! Miss Barton, you are a resourceful person!

Scene VIII: The next day

CLARA:	Dr. Dunn, I'm going for more bandages.
JAMES:	No you don't, Miss Barton. You go and rest. Twenty-four straight hours is more than enough.
CLARA:	But, but—
JAMES:	Don't worry about anything. The wounded are settled and calm right now. You worked a miracle last night feeding them with that cornmeal you found. I've never heard it so quiet on the battlefield.
CLARA:	If only we could bring more nurses here. So many more men would be saved.

JAMES:	I know, I know. But you've done the work of ten. Do you know what one of those wounded boys called you, Miss Barton?
CLARA:	Probably Miss Cornmush, or old schoolmarm.
JAMES:	No. He called you the angel of the battlefield.

Scene IX: Freight depot, New York City, April 1912

FRED:	I'm sorry, Mr. Homgren, but I can't move your freight until tomorrow when this weather clears. My teamsters just won't go.
MICHAEL:	The burial service in Massachusetts has already been scheduled. The casket has to leave New York by today.
FRED:	There's nothing I can do. It's up to those men, and they're a tough and stubborn lot.
MICHAEL:	Let me at least have a word with them.
FRED:	Go right ahead—and good luck.
MICHAEL:	Gentlemen, is there any way I could convince you to leave now with that casket for North Oxford, Massachusetts?
JIMMY:	Not for love or money.
JOHNNY:	Tomorrow will be fine. Besides, people in caskets don't need to worry about keeping important appointments.

The Teacher's Store
16911 MIDDLEBELT RD.
LIVONIA MI 48154
Ph. no. 734-525-0720

Trn. # 23214
Date: 7/17/02

JW 04521   TS/ 20 SHORT PL   1   27.95

Total   27.95
Sales Tax   01.68

Total Due   29.63

Payment made by Check No. s455368546658

All refunds and exchange will be made
within 30 days of Purchase WITH RECEIPT
provided the goods are in good and
saleable condition except BOOKS which
can only be exchanged within 5 days
of sale.

Thanks for Shopping at Teachers Store

JIMMY:	Ha-ha—that's a good one, Johnny.
JOHNNY:	Mister, even if it were the president himself, we'd stay put, understand?
MICHAEL:	This woman knew presidents. She was a very special person.
JIMMY:	That's what they all say, "This cargo is very special and must go out right away." We're not moving until tomorrow.
MICHAEL:	Since you're not going anywhere, would you mind coming over to the casket so I can show you something?
JOHNNY:	Fine. We've got the time. Is there some special wood?
JIMMY:	Hey, how come there's a red cross on it?
MICHAEL:	Because the person in that casket founded the American Red Cross, gentlemen.
JOHNNY:	Clara Barton?
MICHAEL:	Yes.
JOHNNY:	Oh, mister, you just hit a soft spot. I come from Johnstown, Pennsylvania. She was there when we had the bad, bad floods.
MICHAEL:	After the Civil War, Clara Barton traveled all over the world helping disaster victims: Cuba, Russia, France, Armenia, Turkey, and of course the United States.
JOHNNY:	I was just a kid at the time of those floods, back in 1889. Clara Barton was right in there with all of her workers, knee deep in mud and water. My daddy said the Red Cross gave us back our lives.
MICHAEL:	She would have appreciated that thought. That's what she wanted the Red Cross to do. Say, what's the matter with your friend? He's crying like a baby.
JOHNNY:	Jimmy! Are you all right? What's wrong?
JIMMY:	I'm so ashamed! If only you had told me.
MICHAEL:	About the person in the casket?
JIMMY:	Yes—then I wouldn't have said what I did.
JOHNNY:	What on earth are you talking about? What did Clara Barton mean to you?
JIMMY:	My daddy was in the Confederate Army. He was shot in the neck at Antietam.
MICHAEL:	Confederate Army, you say? Clara Barton was a nurse in the Union Army.
JIMMY:	Didn't matter to her. She stopped him from bleeding to death. Mister, we'll take her home. No rain or muddy roads will stop us. We could never fully pay back the debt we owe her—never.

JOHN MUIR: PROPHET OF CONSERVATION

Characters (in order of appearance)

DAVID Muir, John's younger brother	LOUIE, John's wife
JOHN Muir	ROBERT Johnson, magazine editor
JAMES Butler, university professor	THEODORE Roosevelt, twenty-sixth president of the United States
J.M. Hutchings, California businessman	

John Muir

Scene I: Muir Farm, near Kingston, Wisconsin, 1850

DAVID: Hey, John! Let's go hunting for some birds' nests.

JOHN: Can't right now. I haven't done all my chores.

DAVID: But you've been plowing this field since sunrise.

JOHN: No matter. If I don't finish it, Dad will give me a whipping for sure.

DAVID: So? He always finds a reason to whip us once a day, even when we do all our chores, except Sunday, of course.

JOHN: You go on ahead. I'll catch up to you after I finish this one furrow.

(a short time later)

DAVID: Look at what I've found! These eggs are as bonnie as the ones back in Scotland.

JOHN: David, sometimes I think I could spend my whole life in the wilds.

DAVID: I know what you mean. It's the only place where we feel free. Hey! Look at all those birds flying over the lake. There must be a million!

JOHN: It's like a gray-blue cloud passing over us.

DAVID: What kind are they? They're so beautiful!

JOHN: They're passenger pigeons. I've seen them up close, and they are bonnie, bonnie birds.

Scene II: University of Wisconsin, Madison, 1860

JAMES: So you're the young farmer who dazzled the judges at the state fair with your mechanical devices. What can I do for you, Mr. Muir?

JOHN: I wish to enroll at your university.

JAMES: Tell me about yourself.

JOHN: I'm twenty-two. I know that's old to start college, but I am very eager to learn.

JAMES: Your age is not important. What matters are preparation and desire. Tell me about your formal schooling.

JOHN: Back in Scotland I went for about a year. I learned how to read and also some Latin. I came to America when I was eleven.

JAMES: Latin, you say? Hmmm. I'm the Greek and Latin professor here. Have you attended any schools in America?

JOHN: No, sir. I've had to work on our farm six days a week, sixteen hours a day.

JAMES: That doesn't leave much time for things of the mind.

JOHN: Oh, I read. My father allowed me to read the hour before sunrise.

JAMES: What kind of books?

JOHN: The Bible. I can recite all of the New Testament from Matthew through Revelation. I also read Shakespeare and some mathematics books.

JAMES: What would you like to study here at the university?

JOHN: Everything! Especially science.

JAMES: Mr. Muir, even though you lack a traditional preparation for university courses, I will recommend you for admission. I believe you will make an excellent student.

JOHN: Oh, thank you, Professor Butler. I'll study very hard. I won't disappoint you.

Scene III: Professor Butler's home, Madison, Wisconsin, early summer 1867

JAMES: John Muir! My favorite student! Come in and tell me what you've been doing these past few years.

JOHN: I've mainly been tramping about the wilds, observing nature, meeting interesting people. I even got up into Canada. It's beautiful up north.

JAMES: I heard you also worked in some factories and did quite well. Of course, we all knew you were a mechanical genius.

JOHN:	Yes, I did a lot of work on machines, but no more.
JAMES:	Why is that, John?
JOHN:	While I was in Indianapolis working for a carriage maker I had a very bad accident.
JAMES:	What happened?
JOHN:	A file tip broke off and lodged in my right eye. In a few hours both eyes had gone blind. For a whole month I had to lie still in a dark room. I thought I would never again see God's beautiful creation.
JAMES:	But your sight is fine now.
JOHN:	Yes, but with my soul's eye I see my life differently.
JAMES:	What do you mean?
JOHN:	I'm not going to spend any more time studying man's inventions— I'm going to spend my life studying God's.
JAMES:	Well, you were always very close to nature. But what exactly will you do?
JOHN:	Right now I'm headed for Louisville, Kentucky. From there I'm going to walk the thousand miles to the Gulf.
JAMES:	Be careful! Ever since the war ended that part of the country has been teeming with thieves and marauders.
JOHN:	I won't be carrying anything of value to those types.
JAMES:	What will you take?

JOHN:	My New Testament, copies of Milton's *Paradise Lost* and Robert Burns's poems, and my plant press, of course.
JAMES:	I wish I could join you. What will you do after you reach the Gulf?
JOHN:	Sail to Cuba, then South America. After that, I aim to see those beautiful mountains in California.
JAMES:	Any young lady to share your dreams and journeys?
JOHN:	Now, who would have a man who just tramps about?
JAMES:	Well, my good friend, please write me a letter now and then. And be sure to keep a journal of all your experiences.
JOHN:	Do you think that's important?
JAMES:	Indeed I do! This young country needs to learn about itself, especially its wilderness areas. You could perform a very valuable public service by writing some articles. Here's the name of someone I know who works at a large magazine in New York. You might even be able to make a few dollars. Good luck, John.
JOHN:	Thank you, Professor Butler. You've always been a true supporter and friend.

Scene IV: Yosemite Valley, California, winter 1869

J.M.:	So, Mr. Muir, I hear you're looking for some work. What kind have you been doing lately?

JOHN: A little sheepherding down in the foothills and some guide work up here in the mountains.

J.M.: Well, I need someone with construction skills. I want to build a sawmill at Yosemite Creek.

JOHN: I could build you a very good one, but only on two conditions.

J.M.: Oh, I know what you're going to say. Because there are so few skilled workers up here in the mountains, you're going to demand a hefty wage to build the sawmill and a big cut of the profits.

JOHN: No, that's not what I'm asking for. I only need a fair wage and a place to live.

J.M.: Then what are your two conditions?

JOHN: That you don't cut down any trees to build the mill or saw into lumber after.

J.M.: Hmmm. That's reasonable. Nature's felled enough. We just have to go out and get them. What's the other condition?

JOHN: That you give me time off now and then so I can explore these mountains.

J.M.: Fine, as long as that sawmill gets up and running soon. Say, what do you want to explore the Sierras for?

JOHN: To refresh my soul and to learn something about this valley.

J.M.: I've been here a long time. What do you want to know?

JOHN: How it was formed, with these rock cliffs running thousands of feet straight up.

J.M.: Earthquakes caused the bottom to drop out. That's how the Yosemite Valley came to be. Does that satisfy you?

JOHN: No, it doesn't. I think this valley was formed by slow-moving glaciers that scraped and carved out this valley over eons of time. I want to study the glaciers that still live here.

J.M.: Glaciers are just ice. They're not alive. Say, where do you come from, John Muir, to get such notions in your head?

JOHN: Here's my card—it shows my home address.

J.M.: "EARTH–PLANET, UNIVERSE." Mighty peculiar address. Well, I won't pay much mind to it as long as you build me a good sawmill.

Scene V: Strentzel Ranch, Martinez, California, April 14, 1880

LOUIE: My, my, John Muir, you are a changed man! Imagine, the famous naturalist and mountain man getting a haircut and even wearing a new white shirt! What on earth has come over you?

JOHN: Not what, my dear, but who—and that's you! Besides, I plan on getting married only once in my life, and that's today!

LOUIE: You have made the entire Strentzel family happy beyond belief. Father is very impressed with your interest in the ranch and your knowledge of raising fruit.

JOHN: I look forward to managing it for him and leading a more settled life here in the lowlands with you, Louie.

LOUIE: And I'm so excited about being your wife! But John, I never want to come between you and your love of nature. Both of us know that a big part of your heart will always dwell in the Sierras. But the mountains are a mistress I will gladly share your love with.

JOHN: Thank you. Louie, you are so understanding. But for now, as a husband, I must turn my energies to running this ranch.

LOUIE: John, the grapes don't require much attention between July and October. Use that time for your travels and writing.

JOHN: After marrying you, that's the best offer I've had today!

LOUIE: Speaking of your writing, I know the perfect place—a cozy room on the top floor. You'll have plenty of peace and quiet there, especially if someday we're blessed with children.

JOHN: Children. You know, Louie, I'm forty-two years old, and until now I hadn't given the prospect of fatherhood much hope. But now the possibility makes me more determined than ever to fight the conservation battle. To think all my travels, all my speeches, and all my magazine articles may help safeguard God's grandeur for my own precious children! Oh, Louie, thank you for marrying me!

Scene VI: Yosemite, California, spring 1890

ROBERT: John, I greatly appreciate your showing me all this, even though it's been so painful.

JOHN: Then you don't think I'm a raving madman or like the boy in the fable who cried "Wolf!"

ROBERT: Of course not. The devastation is much more widespread than I had pictured.

JOHN: What possesses men to cut down trees 4,000 years old! Do you know what they use this wood for? As supports for grape vines! Imagine, beautiful ancient Sequoias chopped up to make grape stakes.

ROBERT: Absolutely ridiculous.

JOHN: Any fool can come up here and cut one of these giants down. They must be protected for all generations. God has saved them from drought, disease, avalanches, and floods, but He cannot save them from fools.

ROBERT: But Uncle Sam can! That's why we must work now to convince the federal government to act, before it's too late.

JOHN: How? I've written hundreds of letters.

ROBERT: My magazine has a very large circulation. John, I want you to go back to San Francisco and write an article about what is happening here. Then send it along to me in New York. We'll start a groundswell of support for saving this entire region: Yosemite, Kings Canyon, and the Sequoia groves.

JOHN: What about Uncle Sam?

ROBERT: Next September the Congressional Committee on Public Lands will be conducting open meetings. I've already arranged a time for you to speak. By then, your articles will have stirred public opinion for increased wilderness protection. Hopefully, Congress will then act on our behalf.

JOHN: I'll start right away, Robert. You are a true friend of conservation.

ROBERT: Yes, but my efforts pale in comparison with yours, John Muir, especially your eloquent writings.

JOHN: I guess I was naive to think that just seeing the beauty of God's creation would be enough to convince people to protect and preserve it.

ROBERT: It isn't enough for those who can only see dollar bills.

Scene VII: Yosemite, California, early spring 1903

THEODORE: John Muir, these past four days camping out with you have been some of the most pleasant and sublime in all my life. But you've left me a bit winded, I confess. You must be thirty years older than I am, and I still can't keep up with you.

JOHN: You've done very well, Mr. President.

THEODORE: John, I never imagined how beautiful and how majestic these mountains were. Thank you for being my guide.

JOHN: I appreciate the opportunity to show them to you.

THEODORE: Nature is the greatest artist. Nothing pleases me more than experiencing it.

JOHN: That's why the government must do everything in its power to preserve it for all people, for all time.

THEODORE: I completely agree, John. The federal government has already set aside thousands of acres. Yosemite has been a national park since 1890.

JOHN: Yes, but thousands, even millions of acres more must be preserved. Fancy-talking lobbyists in Washington have found ways for the mining and logging industries to get around lots of the regulations.

THEODORE: Well, when I return to the capital, I'm going to put a stop to that and set aside even more land to be protected. These great trees must be saved!

108 *20 Plays for U.S. History Classes*

JOHN: Thank you for your support. Mr. President, I've traveled all over this great country. I know people need jobs. But they should not be at the cost of destroying the environment for our grandchildren. God has called us to be good stewards of the land, and no amount of gold or dollar bills could grow one of these trees.

THEODORE: How right you are. We must work in harmony with nature and not fight it as our enemy.

JOHN: Yes, Mr. President, because everything, including people, are hitched together in God's creation.

THEODORE: Well put, John.

JOHN: Mr. President, can I leave you with one more observation?

THEODORE: John Muir, I never tire of listening to you.

JOHN: When I'm in San Francisco, I enjoy spending time in the poorest and most neglected neighborhoods. Politicians call them slums and their children street urchins. But I regard these children as my friends. Do you know what gift from me these children have received with the widest smiles, brightest eyes, and most eager hands?

THEODORE: I suppose candy or toys—

JOHN: Flowers, Mr. President! Flowers! Don't these poor, weak children have as much right as the rich and powerful to refresh their souls in God's grandeur?

GEORGE WASHINGTON CARVER

Characters (in order of appearance)

I, II, III, IV, Voices or choral parts	Mrs. Carver
Moses Carver, a poor white farmer. George Washington Carver's "foster" father	Mary, a slave; mother of George Washington Carver
	Bentley, bounty hunter of stolen slaves

George Washington Carver

Prologue: 1864

I: Many, many years now past,

II: A boy named George was born.

III: Slavery held his mother fast,

IV: And grieved a nation bitterly torn.

* * *

I: What was the year? What was the day

II: When George's eyes first saw the light?

III: History has nothing certain to say,

IV: For his family couldn't read or write.

* * *

I: His future seemed hopeless, short and bleak.

II: As his mother held him near,

III: His small black body, sickly and weak,

IV: Held her heart in constant fear.

Scene I: A farm near Diamond Grove, Missouri, 1864

I: The air was cold and filled with dread

II: While darkness enveloped the Carver Farm.

III: As its master fretted in his humble bed,

IV: His body sensed a lurking harm.

* * *

I: On this dark night an old fear struck:

II:	Greedy men would burst upon the scene,
III:	And without warning they would pluck
IV:	George and his mother from sleep serene.

***

MOSES:	I just can't get to sleep.
MRS.:	Moses, you worry too much. You're always thinking that something bad's going to happen.
	(sound of galloping horses coming near)
MOSES:	Do you hear that? It can mean only one thing. Night riders!
MRS.:	Slave thieves. We have to hide Mary and the boys quick before the night riders get them! They'll steal them all for sure!
	(Moses runs to Mary's cabin and bangs on her door)
MOSES:	Mary! Mary! Night riders!
MRS.:	I'm coming!
MOSES:	You take baby George to the hideout. I'll look after Jim.
MARY:	I'll be right there. I just need to get another blanket for little George. Don't cry, now—We're going to a safe place. No! No! No!
	(night riders swoop down and get George and Mary as she exits)
MRS.:	Moses, what happened?

MOSES:	Those dirty rascals got Mary and little George. I got Jim to the hideout.
MRS.:	What are we going to do now?
MOSES:	I'll go to town tomorrow at first light and try to find a tracker named Bentley. I've heard he's the best there is in these parts for tracking down night riders.
MRS.:	But how are we going to pay him? We don't have much, and I'm sure he'll want a high price.
MOSES:	I'll think of something. I'll offer him anything, because Mary and her boys have been family.
MRS.:	That's right. I've always felt that Mary and I were both mothers to those boys.

Scene II: Diamond Grove, the next day

I:	Stealing slaves was a common affair
II:	In Missouri many years gone by.
III:	Families were broken without care
IV:	Or pity, for the profit was high.
MOSES:	Are you the tracker called Bentley?
BENTLEY:	Yeah. You got a problem?
MOSES:	Night riders took my slave woman Mary and her baby.
BENTLEY:	How long ago?
MOSES:	Last night just after sunset.

BENTLEY:	That's a long, long time. They could be miles from here.	MOSES:	Is that you, Bentley?

BENTLEY: That's a long, long time. They could be miles from here.

MOSES: Where do you think they'd go?

BENTLEY: Arkansas, most likely.

MOSES: Can you find them?

BENTLEY: How much they worth to you?

MOSES: I don't have much cash, but it's yours and forty acres of my best timberland.

BENTLEY: That's not really good enough, because I'll have to go so far to get them.

MOSES: How about if I throw in my fastest horse, too?

BENTLEY: What's your name?

MOSES: Carver. Moses Carver.

BENTLEY: You got a deal, Moses Carver. Here's my hand.

* * *

I: Mary was taken from her sickly child

II: Never to see him again.

III: Alone and crying in blankets piled

IV: Little George waited for this nightmare's end.

Scene III: The Carver farm, one week later

(Bentley rides up)

BENTLEY: Moses Carver around?

MOSES: Is that you, Bentley?

BENTLEY: Yeah. I've been all the way to Arkansas and back.

MRS.: Then you get down from that horse and rest awhile. I'll fix some coffee and get some pie.

MOSES: Did you find them?

BENTLEY: Mr. Carver, I'm truly sorry, but by the time I found those varmints' camp they had sold your Mary down the river. That means we'll never see her again.

MRS.: What are you holding there? You can't drink my coffee and eat my pie with your arms full like that.

BENTLEY: It's the baby, ma'am, and he's mighty, mighty sick. They couldn't sell him with his mother so they kept him till I found their camp. I offered them a little and brought him back.

MRS.: Give me little George.

BENTLEY: Mr. Carver, I'm a fair man and I don't believe in taking advantage of folks. I didn't bring back your Mary, and I don't think that baby will live much longer. So a fair wage for all my troubles will just be that horse.

MOSES: So be it, then. I'll fetch Pacer.

MRS.: Poor, poor child. What shall become of you, little George?

MOSES: For sure we'll raise Mary's boys as our own. Jim and George are Carvers now.

Youth: 1864–1890

I: Nurtured so tenderly by the Carvers' care

II: Little George thrived and grew.

III: Spurred by a curiosity endless and rare,

IV: His quick mind grasped all he did view.

***

I: Set adrift while still a teen,

II: He searched for schools far and near.

III: Earning his keep washing clothes so clean,

IV: He dodged the racists and hid his fear.

***

I: At Highland College George qualified to enroll,

II: But was shut out when they saw his face.

III: He then left Kansas more determined in his goal

IV: To find a school open to his race.

***

College and university: 1890–1896

I: In Iowa he found not all doors set.

II: Simpson College offered him a start.

III: He kept on washing to pay his debt,

IV: Studied plants and painted fine art.

***

I: Then on he advanced to Iowa State,

II: Where George's genius each professor realized.

III: He was the first Black there ever to graduate,

IV: And his plant research was greatly prized.

***

I: Then came offers of prestige and wealth

II: From universities near and far

III: To share his knowledge of plant health.

IV: He politely declined for an unseen star.

***

I: That star was the dream of Booker T.,

II: An infant school serving southern Blacks.

III: When asked to join the fledgling Tuskegee,

IV: He bravely followed his destiny's tracks.

***

Tuskegee, Alabama: 1896–1943

I: He gave to the school and world outside

II: A half century of genius and skill,

III: And patiently his science became the pride

IV: Of a farming system that had lost its will.

***

I: First he attacked the South's sad plight.

II: A land that was tired and weak,

III: King Cotton, the culprit of this blight,

IV: Needed relief from a plant unique.

***

I: George put his talents into high gear

II: To lift this curse from tradition's rut.

III: His simple cure many thought queer:

IV: "Plant all over the lowly peanut."

***

I: Few would listen until he took

II: Some Dixie acres given up for dead.

III: He planted peanuts where others forsook,

IV: And the land revived, just as he said.

***

I: Soon the farmers heeded his advice.

II: Peanuts were grown everywhere,

III: But the surplus brought a bottom price,

IV: And the rebirth of the farmers' old despair.

***

I: Back in his lab, George set his new dream.

II: He milked from that nut uses strangely new:

III: Dyes and oils, even shaving cream,

IV: And hundreds besides these few.

***

Epilogue

I: This orphaned son of a kidnapped slave

II: For fifty years gave away

III: The products that would help to save

IV: The South's great bounty to this day.

***

I: What is his legacy for history to mark?

II: A pioneer for all to laud,

III: Who conquered all that would quench his spark,

IV: A humble servant of humanity and his God.

AMERICA'S CRUSADING JOURNALISTS

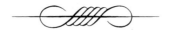

Characters (in order of appearance)

Ida B. WELLS, African-American journalist	Lincoln STEFFENS, journalist
BUYAST, urban citizen	Upton SINCLAIR, writer
Jacob RIIS, writer, journalist, photographer	REPORTER I
Ida TARBELL, journalist	T.R. (Theodore Roosevelt), president, 1901–1909
Ray Stannard BAKER, journalist	REPORTER II

Jacob Riis

Scene I: New York Public Library, 1892

WELLS: Excuse me, I need some assistance, please.

BUYAST: Ahmmmmm . . .

WELLS: Could you please direct me to the reference section?

BUYAST: Why on earth would a Negro woman like yourself have business there? This is a library, a place where people read books—serious books. I suppose you think it's just a place to sit.

RIIS: Miss, I'm headed for the reference section. Just come with me.

WELLS: Thank you.

(a half hour later)

RIIS: Can I give you a hand with all those books?

WELLS: Thank you again. They're as heavy and awkward as cotton bales back home.

RIIS: And where might home be? You'll have to forgive my curiosity, miss, but I can never seem to get away from my job. I'm a reporter.

WELLS: How interesting. I'm a reporter, too, from Memphis, Tennessee.

RIIS: You must be doing some serious research by the look of those books. What's the subject?

WELLS: Lynchings. I'm attempting to document all the lynchings reported in the last ten years. Do you realize how many of the victims were first arrested on false charges?

RIIS: I've heard that. It's a nasty and tragic business, those lynchings. Have people forgotten that we're supposed to be a nation of laws and due process?

WELLS: What is and what's supposed to be are two very different things for black people in this country.

RIIS: You could make a similar case for immigrants living in this city.

WELLS: I must confess I haven't seen much of New York yet.

RIIS: It's quite a place. How rude of me—I haven't even introduced myself. My name is Jacob Riis, and I'm so pleased to meet you, Miss—

WELLS: Ida Wells. Mr. Riis, you have been very kind and helpful. Thank you.

RIIS: Miss Wells, may I ask you a few more questions about your research?

WELLS: Of course.

RIIS: I investigate problems and issues right at the source. I walk the streets, talk with people, and enter homes and factories. I

suppose that's impossible with regards to your research.

WELLS: I wish it were not so. Three of my closest male friends were recently lynched in Memphis.

RIIS: I'm so sorry. What were the circumstances?

WELLS: The three built up a prosperous dry goods store. Unfortunately, it was across the street from a white man's business. He didn't care for the competition, so he sent some of his friends to burn down my friends' building.

RIIS: And of course they defended their property.

WELLS: Yes. They were arrested and put in jail. There was no trial. Instead, a mob was allowed to take them out and lynch them.

RIIS: What drives people to such brutality?

WELLS: Hatred and envy.

RIIS: I came to this country from Denmark in 1870. Looking back, it seemed a time of optimism and hope. What changed?

WELLS: I know what you mean about hope. Black people had it right after the war. But when the federal troops left the South in 1877, the clock turned backward for us.

RIIS: What's your personal history?

WELLS: I was born a slave in 1862. After Emancipation, I was able to get an education.

RIIS:	Who were your teachers?
WELLS:	Kind and generous Christians from the North. I even became a teacher myself in Memphis. But I was fired for writing articles that described how inferior the schools for black students were.
RIIS:	Do you still live in Memphis?
WELLS:	No. After I wrote an article condemning the lynchings of my three friends, I was forced to flee for my life.
RIIS:	You must be a very gifted writer to provoke such a reaction. This country needs more people like you to open our eyes to society's evils and injustices.
WELLS:	Thank you for your support.
RIIS:	Good luck. I so much enjoyed meeting you, Miss Wells.
WELLS:	Wait! I would like to hear about your work.
RIIS:	How about a tour instead? You said you hadn't seen much of New York.
WELLS:	But aren't you afraid to be seen walking with a black woman?
RIIS:	Not in the least! Besides, I know about every policeman in Manhattan, and I'm welcome in even the roughest neighborhoods as the Flower King.
WELLS:	The *what?*
RIIS:	The Flower King. I bring flowers to the poor kids in the slums, and they treat me like a king. Come

and see why. Mulberry Street will be a good place to start.

(four hours later)

WELLS:	It's hard for me to believe that people actually live like that in New York. It's so unsanitary! So dangerous! How many did you say lived in that small, dark room we visited?
RIIS:	Fourteen.
WELLS:	And that's common?
RIIS:	For thousands of immigrants, yes. I think you've seen for your-self why over half the babies born in this city never live to their first birthday.
WELLS:	Where do most of them come from?
RIIS:	Eastern and Southern Europe, places where life is so desperate that people risk everything to come here.
WELLS:	So desperate that they're willing to live and work like slaves? Why, even the children work fourteen hours a day!
RIIS:	Only you could compare them to slaves, Miss Wells.
WELLS:	At least we had fresh air, sunlight, and green grass. These children have no place to play except in the streets. When I was growing up, I didn't have to worry about wagons running me down or gangs of my own people beating me up. And I was able to attend school, too!

RIIS: Gangs spring up like weeds in the streets of the city, and child labor curses the future.

WELLS: Jacob, you should write a book about what we saw today.

RIIS: I have. It's called *How the Other Half Lives*. Now I'm using a camera to help document conditions.

WELLS: Jacob, we couldn't be more opposite on the outside, me being a black woman and you a white man. But inside we're kindred spirits—fighters for justice and reform.

Scene II: Ashland Hotel dining room, New York City, 1900

Ida Tarbell

TARBELL: There are few things I like better than a working lunch.

BAKER: I'll second that. Anyone else from *McClure's* coming?

TARBELL: Lincoln said he would be coming a little later with a guest.

BAKER: How about the boss?

TARBELL: Sam can't make it, but the meeting is his idea, and he's paying the bill.

BAKER: What does he want us to meet about?

TARBELL: Changing the direction of the magazine. He wants *McClure's* to be more hard hitting when it comes to today's social and political issues.

BAKER: So we're going to take the gloves off.

TARBELL: Exactly, just like a journalist I met in London a few years back— Ida Wells. Does her name ring any bells?

BAKER: Yes. She's a very influential writer in the Negro press and an expert on lynchings. Her articles have had quite an impact.

TARBELL: What do you know about her?

BAKER: As we say in the trade, she does her homework. I've never known a writer who does as much research as she does. She gathers mountains of facts, and she's a brilliant and passionate writer.

TARBELL: And a bold one. She doesn't back down for anyone, regardless of how powerful or intimidating.

BAKER: Her writing gets people's attention, just as Jacob Riis's photographs of tenement life do.

(enter Steffens and Sinclair)

Lincoln Steffens

TARBELL: Lincoln, glad you could join us. Who's your guest?

STEFFENS: Upton Sinclair. He's been at City College and now wants to become an investigative journalist.

TARBELL: Welcome. I'm Ida, and this is Ray. Sit down, please.

SINCLAIR: Thank you. It's a great honor for me to be here. Miss Tarbell, I very much admire your books about President Lincoln and Napoleon.

TARBELL: Thank you.

STEFFENS: What's the appetizer for the day?

BAKER: A discussion about changing the style and content of *McClure's*.

TARBELL: The boss wants us to strike hard and deep at corruption and injustice in our society.

STEFFENS: Sounds good to me. Our leaders have gotten into the cynical habit of ignoring or denying the dark side of America. I welcome the opportunity to expose to our readers all the dirt and rot out there.

BAKER: And I hope they find it so sickening that they demand strong medicine—reform!

TARBELL: Where would you like to start? Ray?

BAKER: The U.S. Steel Corporation. I'd love to expose that company for what it is: a greedy giant that mistreats its workers and cheats its customers!

STEFFENS: I'd like to attack corruption in our big city governments. From my brief investigations I've learned that the average citizen is fleeced by city government. Citizens are taxed and taxed but because of corruption get little in return. Sanitation and water systems remain substandard, housing is wretched, many buildings are firetraps, and the police don't do their job.

TARBELL: The public certainly needs to hear about that! I'm sorry, Mr. Sinclair, we didn't mean to exclude you.

SINCLAIR:	Don't worry about me. This whole discussion fascinates and inspires me.
STEFFENS:	Upton told me on the way here that he has a project in mind himself.
TARBELL:	Tell us about it, please.
SINCLAIR:	The meat-packing industry is rotten to the core.
BAKER:	You mean as a monopoly?
SINCLAIR:	Yes, and much more. Do you realize that there is virtually no outside control over what goes into the meat we eat? The meat-packing industry operates by two mottoes: "Let the buyer beware" and "The public be damned."
BAKER:	The same goes for just about everything we buy, including food, prescription drugs, and household gadgets. Who knows how safe these really are?
SINCLAIR:	It's certain that much of our processed meat is not safe. Some of my contacts in the packing-houses tell me that just about anything is put into sausage casings to fill them up. It's more profitable that way.
TARBELL:	Be specific. What kinds of things besides the meat?
SINCLAIR:	Dirt, sawdust, rat droppings—even dead rats!
BAKER:	How disgusting! No wonder so many people get sick!
TARBELL:	What's your plan for documenting this?

SINCLAIR:	I'll start by getting a job in a meat-packing plant myself, probably in Chicago.
TARBELL:	There's no better source for investigative reporting than first-hand experience. Mr. Sinclair, I applaud your plan.
BAKER:	Will you write an article for us?
SINCLAIR:	Actually, I'm planning to write a full length novel.
BAKER:	About the meat-packing industry?
SINCLAIR:	Only in part. Most of the story will be about the plight of poor immigrants in our big cities.
STEFFENS:	Tell them what you are considering for a title.
SINCLAIR:	*The Jungle.*
BAKER:	I like it! Short, descriptive, hard-hitting, and honest!
STEFFENS:	What about you, Ida? What dragon will you take up your pen against? Child labor, maybe? How about the hundreds, even thousands of sweatshops in the city where the workers spend twelve hours a day doing dangerous work in stuffy, crowded, and dirty rooms and get paid only a few cents an hour.
TARBELL:	Standard Oil.
BAKER:	I see a David and Goliath story!
STEFFENS:	You'll be going after the biggest bully on the continent.
TARBELL:	I know. Standard Oil must be cut down to size and be

BAKER: brought under some control and regulation.

BAKER: Right now Standard Oil does whatever it pleases. It fixes railroad freight rates and customer prices and corrupts many state governments.

STEFFENS: It's ruined many small operators in the oil business.

TARBELL: Like my own father.

BAKER: Ida, don't go after John D. Rockefeller and Standard Oil solely for revenge. Personal vendettas don't sit well with our readers. They may make an individual like you feel good, but they usually don't bring reform.

TARBELL: Your point is well taken. I'm not embarking on a private war, gentlemen. This country has some serious problems. You and I are called to be firebells to get people lined up and organized to solve them!

STEFFENS: Amen! Now, let's order lunch. I'm going to have just a salad.

Scene III: New House of Representatives office building, Washington, D.C., April 14, 1906

REPORTER I: Mr. President, can we conclude from your speech that you are now opposed to investigative journalists like Ida Tarbell, Lincoln Steffens, Ray Baker, and Upton Sinclair?

T.R.: What! Just because I called them muckrakers?

REPORTER II: Does this mean that you no longer support the reform movement?

T.R.: Hold on there! Sometimes I wonder how carefully you boys listen. Investigative journalism has served a very useful public service.

REPORTER I: But in your speech you said—

T.R.: Need I remind you of the Pure Food and Drug Act that this administration brought forth? Mr. Sinclair's book *The Jungle* had a profound influence on me. Have you forgotten how vigorously I've used the Sherman Anti-Trust Act to protect the public against monopolies? And the rights of Negroes? I've worked diligently to put an end to lynchings. I appointed a black man as customs commissioner for the port of Charleston, South Carolina, and entertained Booker T. Washington in the White House. Now, what does this all say about my support of the reform movement?

REPORTER II: Then why did you say that muckrakers can do great harm?

T.R.: Not all investigative journalists have the integrity of those you mentioned. Some have been guilty of exaggerating, distorting, and not telling the whole truth.

REPORTER I: Has that really been harmful?

T.R.: It certainly has! It's created a climate of suspicion and mistrust. Good and honorable people are scared away from public service.

No one wants to be slandered in the press, regardless of whether the accusations are false. And furthermore, if the press only writes about what is foul and rotten in this country, people will become cynical and think that it's useless to try to change things.

REPORTER II: Aren't you really worried that the muckrakers are encouraging revolution?

T.R.: I suppose so. But I'm more concerned about how they're numbing the public into apathy. There's still a lot of good in this country. But if we are led to believe that everything is bad, as some muckrakers tell us, what will be left in our society to fight the bad? If we're all pigs, who will clean out the barnyard?

REPORTER I: Thank you, Mr. President.

A MAN FOR THE HEART:
DR. DANIEL HALE WILLIAMS

Characters (in order of appearance)

I, II, III, IV, choral or voice parts	KITTIE Blake, one-time fiancée of Dan
NED, shoemaker's apprentice	Mrs. BLAKE, Kittie's mother
Daniel Hale WILLIAMS	Rev. Louis REYNOLDS, friend of Dan's
Harry ANDERSON, Dan's employer, friend, and mentor	TROLLEY, saloon patron
GUERNSEY, friend of Dan's	TILLY, saloonkeeper
HULLIHAN, father of a Classical Academy student	James CORNISH, saloon patron, stabbing victim
John HAIRE, president of Classical Academy, Janesville, Wisconsin	SANDER, saloon patron
Dr. Henry PALMER, Dan's mentor	Elmer BARR, intern to Dr. Daniel Hale Williams
Frank PEMBER, medical student	PIPER, saloon patron
James MILLS, medical student	MABEL, surgical nurse
ANDREWS, professor of surgery	Dr. William MORGAN, Dr. William FULLER, Dr. George HALL, doctors observing the heart surgery

Prologue

I: In Pennsylvania many years ago,

II: Daniel Hale Williams began his life.

III: His lineage, old and rare "Free Negro,"

IV: He proudly owned in triumph and strife.

***

I: Dan was just a lad when his father died.

II: Soon after he felt doubly betrayed

III: For swiftly his mother cast him aside

IV: To Baltimore and the shoemaker's trade.

***

Act I

Scene I: Shoemaker's shop, Baltimore, Maryland, 1868

NED: Dan! Dan! Pass me an awl! Dan! Put that book down! I need an awl right away!

WILLIAMS: Yes, yes!

NED: What's with you, anyway?

WILLIAMS: Nothing.

Dr. Daniel Hale Williams

NED: That's right. Look who does all the work. Me! I'm the only one learning this trade.

WILLIAMS: So?

NED: So? Is that all you can say? I bet you think you're just too good for this kind of work because you're so light and can pass for white.

WILLIAMS: Listen, Ned, sending me here was my mother's idea, not mine. I wanted to stay in school, but she didn't think she could afford it. Now, if you like making shoes, that's fine. I don't, and my skin color has nothing to do with it.

NED: Yeah, sure. Don't try to fool me.

WILLIAMS: I'm telling you the truth. I'm proud of all my family from way back: black, white, red. You'll never see me trying to pass for anything other than myself, Dan Williams.

NED: I'm not going to argue with you. But say, if you're not going to put your heart into this trade, what are you going to do? Just look at yourself: twelve years old, no money, no trade, and no family close by. You'd best stick it out here and learn the trade. At least you have food and a place to stay.

WILLIAMS: I know, I know. But I want something more. I want opportunity, a chance to choose the way my life will go. Pretty soon I'll be going west where I have some family. That's where I'll find some opportunity.

NED: Now, how are you going to get out there? Is there some angel that's going to pick you up and drop you down in Illinois with a hundred dollars in your pocket? Those books you read have messed up your thinking.

WILLIAMS: I'll find a way. I'll make it—somehow.

NED: Well, good luck to you. I hope you find some good trade besides making shoes, because you're not much good for cutting and sewing things, that's for sure.

***

I: A railroad man his dad once knew

II: Gave him a free ride to the West.

III: While into manhood Daniel grew,

IV: Patience was his greatest test.

***

I: He planted roots when just a teen,

II: Fixing boats and cutting hair,

III: And when Harry Anderson entered the scene,

IV: Dan found his anchor of support and care.

***

Scene II: Anderson's barber shop, Janesville, Wisconsin, 1873

(enter Mr. Guernsey)

ANDERSON: Good morning, Mr. Guernsey.

GUERNSEY: And to you, Harry. Is Dan around?

ANDERSON: Let me call him from the back. Dan! Customer! He's probably deep into one of those books you're always lending him.

GUERNSEY: Speaking of those books—Harry, I've discussed just about every one of them with Dan. And you know something? He's very bright and very smart.

ANDERSON: He plays a pretty nice bass fiddle, too.

GUERNSEY: Harry, I don't really know how to say this, you being like a father to Dan and me just a friend and customer—

ANDERSON: Speak your mind, Orrin. Have no fear of that.

GUERNSEY: Very well, thank you. I'd like to see Dan back in school preparing for a profession. What do you think, Harry?

ANDERSON: Dan's an excellent barber and helps a lot around the place, but I wouldn't want to hold him down.

GUERNSEY: I could get him into the Classical Academy, and you know what that would mean for his future.

ANDERSON: What? Orrin, my friend, have you forgotten that Dan is not white?

GUERNSEY: Harry, trust me in this matter. I know John Haire quite well, and he would not deny any qualified applicant because of skin color. If Dan is interested and can pass the entrance exam, he'll be admitted. It all depends on Dan.

(enter Williams)

ANDERSON: Dan, Mr. Guernsey thinks you would be a strong candidate for the Academy. He's willing to speak on your behalf to get you in.

GUERNSEY: You might need some tutoring in some subjects.

ANDERSON: And you would still have to cut hair to earn your keep around here.

GUERNSEY: You wouldn't have much free time.

ANDERSON: Well, Dan, what do you think? Are you up to the challenge?

WILLIAMS: Did you ever see me wasting time? The Academy? You don't

know how much I would like to go there. If I get the chance, I won't let you down. Thanks!

Scene III: Classical Academy, Janesville, Wisconsin, 1875

(enter Mr. Hullihan)

HULLIHAN: Dr. Haire, I'd like a word with you. It's a very serious matter.

HAIRE: Of course. Come in and sit down. You're Maggie's father.

HULLIHAN: That's right. And I've come here to protect her!

HAIRE: From what, Mr. Hullihan?

HULLIHAN: That Williams boy! Are you blind? He's colored!

HAIRE: Dan Williams has an excellent academic record here at the Academy, and his behavior has been nothing less than exemplary.

HULLIHAN: That's not the point! His kind don't belong with my Maggie! Don't you know what terrible things all this can lead to? Now, do you get the picture?

HAIRE: I certainly do.

(Haire reaches into his desk)

HULLIHAN: Good. That settles it.

HAIRE: Almost. Here's a full refund of your daughter's tuition, if that is your desire. But as long as I am president of this institution, Dan Williams remains. Do I make

myself perfectly clear? Now, how about your Maggie?

HULLIHAN: Give me my money!

***

I: The students liked Dan and admired his mind.

II: He mastered whatever he saw,

III: But his diploma gave him no clear sign,

IV: So he stumbled into the study of law.

***

I: But soon Dan came to understand,

II: His heart was seeking a different role,

III: A challenge that was truly grand,

IV: To make his life noble and whole.

***

Scene IV: Dr. Palmer's office, Janesville, 1878

PALMER: So, you want to become a doctor, Mr. Williams.

WILLIAMS: Yes, sir. Can you help prepare me?

PALMER: We'll see about that at the proper time. First tell me why you gave up studying law.

WILLIAMS: I found out it didn't suit my temperament.

PALMER: Oh? Can you be more specific?

WILLIAMS: Dr. Palmer, I regard the law as a heartless contest between two adversaries. One side wins, and the other is left licking its wounds. I'm not cut out for devoting all my intelligence, skill and energy to defeating someone else.

PALMER: Tell me what you think being a doctor is all about.

WILLIAMS: It's a battle, with people on one side and diseases and infirmities on the other.

PALMER: I wish it were that simple and pure.

WILLIAMS: What do you mean, Dr. Palmer?

PALMER: You must realize that medicine today is becoming more and more scientific. I view that as a most positive development. Unfortunately, many of my colleagues don't—including some very eminent ones. It's a simple case of not changing with the times. Instead of being on the side of scientific progress, they are content to stay in their ruts of tradition and throw mud at those with new ideas.

WILLIAMS: Yet ultimately, truth prevails.

PALMER: Yes, but the fights can be long and very bitter.

WILLIAMS: Dr. Palmer, I'm willing to work very hard. Will you take me on as an apprentice?

PALMER: You can be forgiven for being naive. I like your outlook and spirit. Yes, I'll take you on as an apprentice.

WILLIAMS: Oh, thank you so much, Dr. Palmer. You won't regret taking me on, I guarantee you.

PALMER: I believe you. But before we begin your formal training, I want you to be certain of a few key expectations I will have of you, with no exceptions or compromises.

WILLIAMS: Yes?

PALMER: Observe first, and then ask or comment. Study your subjects completely—take no shortcuts. Keep an open mind.

WILLIAMS: I'll certainly do what you say, Dr. Palmer.

PALMER: And as your knowledge and expertise grow, keep humble and show appreciation always to your co-workers. Now, how does that suit you?

WILLIAMS: It suits me fine, Dr. Palmer, it suits me fine.

PALMER: Excellent. In two years I think you'll be good and ready for a proper medical school.

***

I: He apprenticed there for two brief years

II: And grew in knowledge and skill.

III: He accepted each task, braving his fears,

IV: Pushing mastery closer to his will.

***

I: Medical school was the logical rung

II: Next on the ladder to true preparation,

III: So on to Chicago where his fate was flung,

IV: And science became his inspiration.

Act II

Scene I: Operating theater, Chicago Medical College, Chicago, Illinois, 1882

PEMBER: I can't wait to see old Dr. Andrews in action.

MILLS: Me too. They say he's an expert in the most modern surgical techniques.

ANDREWS: Students, before we commence with the demonstration, we'll heed Dr. Lister's antiseptic procedure. Nurse, will you be so kind—

(she sprays antiseptic all over the room)

WILLIAMS: I can't breathe!

ANDREWS: Gentlemen, please observe carefully. Scalpel—

PEMBER: What? My eyes are too fogged up to see anything!

MILLS: I'm glad that's over. Let's find some fresh air!

PEMBER: There must be a better way.

***

I: Those student years brought joy and trial.

II: Long hours for Dan was the rule,

III: And anxious was his new lifestyle

IV: As a man of color in this school.

***

I: But all liked Dan. Students and staff,

II: He earned their friendship true,

III: But at his finances none could laugh;

IV: Dan's bills seemed always far past due.

***

I: To meet his debts Harry proved able,

II: With a fatherly gift or loan.

III: For his board Dan tended a stable,

IV: And in 1883 he was on his own.

***

Scene II: Dr. Williams' Office, Chicago, Illinois, 1884

WILLIAMS: Frank, welcome to my humble office. How are you doing?

PEMBER: Just fine, Dan, just fine. My, you've certainly done well since graduation. I've heard you've become a community hero of sorts.

WILLIAMS: Oh, that's just silly talk. But I must acknowledge that the neighborhood has been most receptive to me.

PEMBER: And why not? With your skill and generous spirit, how else could

the people respond? Say, Dan, what's the practice like?

WILLIAMS: A very interesting and stimulating one. I have all kinds of patients: rich and poor and just about every color and nationality. I love the variety.

PEMBER: I see you've greatly expanded your medical library since graduation.

WILLIAMS: Like my good friend Dr. Palmer constantly preached, "We must keep up with the latest scientific advances."

PEMBER: Are you still working on cadavers?

WILLIAMS: Every chance I get. Frank, the simple truth is that we doctors are guilty of giving up too easily on our difficult internal cases.

PEMBER: Because the body is still pretty much an uncharted territory we're afraid to enter.

WILLIAMS: Precisely! Can you imagine how many lives we could save with greater knowledge and understanding?

PEMBER: It sounds like you're so busy carving and analyzing that you're destined to eternal bachelorhood.

WILLIAMS: I'm working to change that. I'm taking a trip east next month. There's a certain young lady—

PEMBER: Knowing you, Dan, you'll spend more time seeing clinics than seeing that girl.

Scene III: Blake home, Albany, New York, 1884

KITTIE: Mother, I have something very important to tell you. Dr. Williams has asked me to marry him.

BLAKE: I trust you exhibited good manners and answered him politely.

KITTIE: Of course. And I accepted his proposal.

BLAKE: Now, Kittie, dear, please be serious. We've discussed this matter many times: marriage is not a frivolous issue.

KITTIE: Of course, and I fully accept that.

BLAKE: Good. Surely you understand why you must not marry someone like Dr. Williams.

KITTIE: Surely I do not, Mother. I am in love with him.

BLAKE: That has nothing to do with it! You may not marry a colored man!

KITTIE: But we are colored, too!

BLAKE: But he refuses to try to pass for white. He's just too proud of his black ancestors.

KITTIE: Mother, Dr. Williams is a perfect gentleman. He's kind, generous, cultured, well established in his profession, and financially secure.

BLAKE: Kittie, my dear, enough of this foolish talk. Don't you realize

why we sent you to the best schools, why we so carefully arranged your social circle? You will marry only a white gentleman of the highest class.

KITTIE: But Mother—

BLAKE: The matter is closed. I expect you to inform Dr. Williams promptly of your refusal.

***

I: Rebuffed in love, he banked his heart's fire

II: To burn with a closer flame.

III: Home to Chicago and a new desire—

IV: To free a long-shackled aim.

***

I: He turned to a need so great and ancient,

II: Long buried under racism's hollow door—

III: A hospital open to every patient,

IV: Regardless of purse or color they bore.

***

I: A place to inspire his community and race,

II: Its teaching to rival the best,

III: And students Jim Crow would be welcome to face,

IV: Opportunities long suppressed.

***

Act III

Scene I: Dr. Williams's home, Chicago, Illinois, December 1890

(enter Rev. Reynolds)

WILLIAMS: Welcome, Reverend Reynolds. Please come in and sit down.

REYNOLDS: Thank you, Dr. Williams. I greatly appreciate your taking the time to see me. I know how busy you are.

WILLIAMS: It's my pleasure. And you're a busy man, too. Does your visit concern church matters?

REYNOLDS: No, it's a family issue—my sister Emma. She very much wants to enter nurses' training, but every school in Chicago has turned her down.

WILLIAMS: Is she qualified?

REYNOLDS: Yes, indeed. Emma's highly educated. She meets all the enrollment requirements except one.

WILLIAMS: The proper skin color, right?

REYNOLDS: That's right, I'm afraid.

WILLIAMS: It's the same old, tired story— denying decent and qualified people a chance.

REYNOLDS: Dr. Williams, I'm here to ask you a personal favor. You are respected and esteemed in both black and white circles. Could

	you possibly intercede on Emma's behalf?
WILLIAMS:	Reverend Reynolds, permit me to generalize your sister's plight. Is there one quality hospital in this city that people of color can freely enter?
REYNOLDS:	Only to scrub floors and the like. You know that. Say, are you trying to evade my request?
WILLIAMS:	Respectfully, no. I'm just trying to show you that there is a much larger problem at stake here. Sneaking your sister around the barriers of racism is not the solution I want to devote my energies to.
REYNOLDS:	If that's your attitude, I am sorry for coming here.
WILLIAMS:	Reverend Williams, please don't misunderstand me. I said there was a larger issue involved here, one our people have too long avoided.
REYNOLDS:	I still don't get your drift, Dr. Williams.
WILLIAMS:	It's very plain. Our people need and deserve a first-rate hospital. that will both serve and train them!
REYNOLDS:	That's a nice-sounding idea, but hardly practical.
WILLIAMS:	And why not?
REYNOLDS:	Who would build such a facility?
WILLIAMS:	*We* would, Reverend Reynolds. I have been studying and promoting this idea for some time. I

	know our community. We have the resources. All we lack are leadership and will.
REYNOLDS:	Dr. Williams, what you are saying is painfully obvious. For too long our people have believed that only whites could build such things. It's been our curse.
WILLIAMS:	And speaking of curses, it's not my vision that this hospital would be only for us. If it won't be open to people of all colors and races, I cannot in good conscience endorse it. We have enough hospitals in the city that have restrictions.
REYNOLDS:	I agree. A noble goal like this should never be underpinned by a sin like racism.
WILLIAMS:	I envision an institution of the highest quality where our people are given every opportunity to work and train. But the highest professional standards must always be maintained. Favoritism and shoddiness only corrupt and destroy what was meant to be good and useful.
REYNOLDS:	And leave only a sense of defeat and despair, just like our people feel now.
WILLIAMS:	Reverend Reynolds, I do believe you are seeing my vision.
REYNOLDS:	Yes, I am. Now, how do we get it out into the community?
WILLIAMS:	Your church and the other churches are good places to begin.

REYNOLDS: You can count on me and my congregation, Dr. Williams.

WILLIAMS: Good! Thank you, Reverend Reynolds. Let's get started right away.

***

I: This dream was launched like a bold new kite,

II: But the response was not enthusiastically clear.

III: Some tried to ground it with lethargy's might,

IV: And many looked away in fear.

***

I: In rushed Dr. Dan with words like fire:

II: "United and resolved, we'll make it fly!"

III: So the hospital became the desire

IV: Of all the people by and by.

***

I: Pies were baked and items sold.

II: The community came together—

III: Rich and poor, young and old

IV: Helped build Provident soon after.

***

I: And thus was born a place of history:

II: The first interracial hospital in our land

III: And pioneering cradle of open heart surgery—

IV: The gift and greatness of Dr. Dan.

***

Scene II: Tilly's Saloon, Chicago, Illinois, July 9, 1893

TROLLEY: Make that a real tall one, Tilly. With this awful heat you just might get my whole week's pay.

TILLY: Coming right up, Trolley. I got plenty of beer, but the ice is getting low.

TROLLEY: Then you better keep them coming real quick. Say, who's that at the end of the bar staring my way?

TILLY: Jimmy Cornish.

TROLLEY: Hey, you—Cornfish. What are you staring at?

CORNISH: Nothing. And the name's Cornish.

TROLLEY: Well, just turn your mug away from my view, Cornface. My stomach can't take cold beer and a face as ugly as yours.

CORNISH: You'd better tie your frog tongue down or Tilly will be serving your face as spaghetti to his dogs.

TILLY: Now, boys—I know it's hot, but let's cool that kind of talk. Next beer's on me.

(the two men fight; Trolley pulls a knife and stabs Cornish)

134   *20 Plays for U.S. History Classes*

TROLLEY:	That'll fix you!
TILLY:	Why'd you go and do that? We have to get this man over to Dr. Dan's right away!
SANDER:	Don't worry, Tilly. Me and Piper will get him over there.

Scene III: Provident Hospital, Chicago, Illinois, the same evening

BARR:	It sure is quiet around here, Dr. Williams.
WILLIAMS:	I think it's just too hot for anyone to move.

(enter Piper and Sander carrying the bleeding Cornish)

PIPER:	Dr. Dan! Dr. Dan! Jimmy's been stabbed!
WILLIAMS:	Bring him over here. Elmer, prepare for examination.
SANDER:	He took it in the chest.
PIPER:	Maybe even the heart.
WILLIAMS:	Jimmy, can you talk?
CORNISH:	Yeah.
WILLIAMS:	How deep did the blade go?
CORNISH:	I don't know.
SANDER:	I think it went way down, Dr. Dan.
BARR:	Dr. Dan, the external signs appear good. There seems to be little bleeding.

WILLIAMS:	Those signs can mask internal trauma. We need to find out more about where the blade cut!
CORNISH:	Dr. Dan! The pain's somethin' terrible!

(Cornish begins coughing uncontrollably)

MABEL:	Dr. Dan, I think he's going into shock.
WILLIAMS:	That's it, then. I'm going to open him up. Get word to the other doctors immediately! The surgery team needs to be ready in five minutes!
MABEL:	Yes, Dr. Dan.

Scene IV: Operating room, very soon after

(enter five doctors to observe)

MORGAN:	Dan, what's all the fuss about?
WILLIAMS:	Stabbing victim. Possible damage to the heart.
FULLER:	The heart? Why are we here, then? Aren't you just going to do the usual procedure: ice packs, opiate for pain, and send the poor guy home?
WILLIAMS:	No, he'd be dead in a few hours. I'm going to open him up and see what I can do. It's his only chance to live.
HALL:	And your chance for big, big trouble. Who's ever done such an operation? Dan, you're risking your career. This guy's alive.

	He's not a drawing or a motion-less cadaver to carve up.
MABEL:	Ready, doctor. Scalpel—

(the operation begins)

WILLIAMS: What a tangle of vessels and nerves. I'm making a little trapdoor as I cut. Serious damage to the left internal mammary artery. I'm tying it to prevent further hemorrhaging. Deep penetration by the knife into the sac covering the heart. The heart is only slightly penetrated. No signs of bleeding there. I'm going to stitch the sac and pericardium with catgut. There! We'll close him up with silkworm gut. That will more easily facilitate re-entry for checking on later possible complications. Well, that's it. Well done, team. Thank you all for your help.

FULLER: Nice work, Dan. Marvelous technique.

MORGAN: Nice work? Marvelous technique? Are you kidding? Do you all realize what we've just seen? Dan's made history! He just sewed up a man's heart!

* * *

Epilogue

I: Cornish recovered to full health once more,

II: And lived out his natural days.

III: Similar feats Dr. Dan had in store

IV: Worthy of tribute and lasting praise.

* * *

I: For years he labored both near and far

II: Teacher, leader, and surgeon renown,

III: The highest standards, his lonely par,

IV: He raised a vision too long held down.

* * *

I: A vision he challenged his people to share,

II: To see with their very own eyes

III: That none break free from lethargy's snare

IV: But those who press past bigotry's lies.

* * *

I: But all the skills of his surgical knife,

II: And the dreams of black doctors he inspired,

III: All the black hospitals he brought to life,

IV: Were all too often grudgingly admired.

* * *

I: The tragedy of Dan's remarkable career

II: Was born of politics he tried to escape

III: And jealous spite from brothers so near

IV: Who could not feel his special fate.

***

I: A fate of being black yet light

II: And a world beyond dark ghettoes;

III: Always focused in integrity's sight,

IV: Never compromised by his narrow foes.

THE DUST BOWL

Characters (in order of appearance)

STONE, a banker

CLYDE Cleary, a farmer

EDNA, Clyde's wife

JOSIE, Cleary's daughter

JODY, Cleary's son

MATSON, Cleary's neighbor and friend

SMEDLY, gas station attendant

LESTER and JIGGER, California men

The Dust Bowl

Scene I: Lawton, Oklahoma, bank office, early summer 1937

STONE: Mr. Cleary, I'm very sorry, but I have some bad news.

CLYDE: What do you mean? Don't I get that extension?

STONE: Mr. Cleary, the hard truth is that the bank cannot carry your loan another month.

CLYDE: Why not? This bank's got lots of money. And besides, I've been a good customer for over twenty years!

STONE: I know, I know, and you've been a valued customer. But we have our bills to pay, too. Business is business, I'm afraid.

CLYDE: But all I'm asking for is a little more time. When this blasted dust blows away I'll be able to get a good crop in, and then I'll be able to pay up.

STONE: Mr. Cleary, we could all be choking on this dust for a a long, long

	time. I'm sorry. We can't wait any longer.
CLYDE:	What happens next?
STONE:	The bank has no alternative but to foreclose. Your farm will be put up for public auction in thirty days.
CLYDE:	Now, isn't that something. I've given you folks over twenty years of business, but as soon as hard times come along you give me only thirty days to clear out. It's not right and it's not fair.

Scene II: The Cleary farm, one hour later

EDNA:	Josie, girl, you done all your chores yet?
JOSIE:	Yes, ma'am, all of them.
EDNA:	Good. Now, where's that brother of yours? Jody!!
JODY:	Coming, Ma.
EDNA:	I hope you fed that cow. Your pap will be home from town pretty soon now.
JODY:	She won't eat, Ma. There's too much dust in her trough.
EDNA:	Didn't I tell you to keep her in the barn? Why don't you listen, boy!
JODY:	I did, Ma, but the wind blew dust in there, too.

EDNA:	Here's your pa comin' up the road now. You best run along and clean that feed trough lickety-split!
JODY:	Yes, ma'am.

(Jody exits, Clyde enters)

EDNA:	What did they say at the bank?
CLYDE:	They won't give us any more time. In thirty days they're going to auction off the place.
EDNA:	What are we going to do?
CLYDE:	Sell off everything we can't put in the old car and move west.
EDNA:	You mean go to California like the Taylors and Hardys?
CLYDE:	Yep. Nothing left for us here, now. In California there's supposed to be some good jobs picking crops. Maybe we could earn enough to get a little place and start all over.

Scene III: The Cleary farm, two weeks later

JOSIE:	Afternoon, Mr. Matson.
MATSON:	Afternoon, Josie. Your pap around?
JOSIE:	Yep. He's over in the barn, just sitting.
MATSON:	Clyde, Clyde, you in there?
CLYDE:	Yep. Nothing but me and the dust and this milking stool. Come on in.

140 *20 Plays for U.S. History Classes*

MATSON:	I'm awfully sorry about what's happened. My, my, the place looks picked clean.
CLYDE:	We sold off just about everything: lock, stock, and barrel, as they say. How come you didn't come to the sale, Mat?
MATSON:	Clyde, we've been friends and neighbors for a long time. I just couldn't come. I don't believe in taking advantage of a friend when his luck's gone bad.
CLYDE:	I much appreciate that, Mat.
MATSON:	Ah—did you make much?
CLYDE:	Enough for gas to get us to California, I reckon.
MATSON:	That's all? Clyde, you had a good team and some mighty fine tools.
CLYDE:	I know, I know. But not many folks have money to spend anymore.
MATSON:	Did the people act respectful?
CLYDE:	They were strangers, mainly. Mat, I couldn't watch after awhile. They were like vultures, picking and tearing at the fruits of my life.
MATSON:	That's a shame, Clyde. When's the auction for the rest of the farm?
CLYDE:	End of the month.
MATSON:	You staying for that?
CLYDE:	Heck, no. We're leaving in the morning.

MATSON:	We're all going to miss you folks. You be sure to write and tell us how it is out there. Who knows, we might be following you in a few months.

Scene IV: Near Flagstaff, Arizona, mid-summer 1937

JODY:	Pa, can I get a soda pop? I'm awfully thirsty.
JOSIE:	Me, too. Please, Pa.
EDNA:	Hush, you two! I told you both we have to save our money for gas and food.
CLYDE:	Getting low on gas. I better stop and fill up.
	(they stop at the next gas station)
SMEDLY:	Yeah? What do you want?
CLYDE:	Fill 'er up, please.
SMEDLY:	Show me your money first. Okies like you have been coming through like locusts lately. I'm not in this business to go broke, you know.
CLYDE:	What are you talking about?
SMEDLY:	Okies can't pay cash for their gas so they stick me with all their junk as trade.
CLYDE:	I have money—see? Now, kindly fill 'er up.
SMEDLY:	OK, but just don't try any funny stuff, like running off without paying.

CLYDE:	What's this country coming to? What's a man got to do to get a little respect?
EDNA:	Say, mister, my man never cheated anybody in his life, so quit your worrying and start pumping.

(a short time later)

SMEDLY:	That'll be three dollars and seven cents.
CLYDE:	What? I had nearly a quarter-tank left. You charge plenty here for your gas.
SMEDLY:	Have to. That's the only way I can make up for my losses.
EDNA:	Here's three Mr. Washingtons and seven Mr. Lincolns. Get in the car, kids. We've been here too long.

Scene V: On Highway 99 near Bakersfield, California, late summer 1937

JODY:	Ma, when are we going to get to California?
EDNA:	How many times have I told you, boy? We've been in California for six days.
JOSIE:	But it's all hot and brown and dry. Pa said California would be cool and green.
EDNA:	You just have to be patient, is all. Pa, what's that up ahead?
CLYDE:	Looks like some kind of road-block. Must be working on the road.

EDNA:	In the dark? No. Looks like somebody wants us to stop. You better slow down.
JODY:	Pa, I see two men heading for our car.

(Lester and Jigger appear)

CLYDE:	What's the problem, boys? You working on the road?
LESTER:	There's no problem with this road except too many okies on it invading our state.
CLYDE:	What are you talking about? We aren't invading anything.
EDNA:	That's right. We're good American citizens just like you fellows.
JIGGER:	Is that so? Well, if you know what's good for you, you'll just turn around and head back where you belong.
JOSIE:	But mister, we haven't got a home. We lost it to the bank.
LESTER:	That's what they all say. Now, just turn this heap of junk around and there'll be no trouble. Understand?
CLYDE:	What trouble? You aren't the law.
JODY:	Pa, they got baseball bats!
JIGGER:	Hey, your kid isn't so dumb.
LESTER:	Okie, let's get one thing straight. Around here we *are* the law! So get moving!
CLYDE:	All right, all right. Just get off my running board.
JIGGER:	Now you're talking sense.

(the Cleary car turns around)

JOSIE: Those men have been drinking. They sure smelled bad.

EDNA: Pa, what are we going to do now? You said the only picking jobs were way past Bakersfield.

CLYDE: That's what I said. This is still a free country, and I mean to get us all up there.

EDNA: How are we going to get past all those men?

JODY: Are you going to get your own baseball bat, Pa?

CLYDE: No. That's not the right way, and besides there's too many of them. We'll just wait them out.

EDNA: What do you mean by that?

CLYDE: We'll go on a bit and make camp for the night. While you and the kids are setting things up, I'll be looking for a California plate in the last town.

EDNA: We haven't got any money for that. Our money's nearly gone. Besides, there's nothing open this time of night.

CLYDE: I'm not going to buy one, just borrow one from a parked car.

JOSIE: Are you going to steal, Pa? You know what the Good Book says.

CLYDE: I know, I know. But I think the Lord will understand. We have to get North where there's work. We can't go back. We can't go back.

THE LITTLE ROCK SCHOOL CRISIS

Characters (in order of appearance)

RAYMOND and JIM, Little Rock youngsters

L.C. BATES, owner of the *State Press* newspaper

Mrs. BATES, president of the Arkansas N.A.A.C.P.*

Virgil BLOSSOM, superintendent of Little Rock schools

Judge REED, Little Rock Chancery Court

THOMASON, member of Mother's League of Central High School

Earl FAUBUS, governor of Arkansas

POTTS, Little Rock police chief

Judge DAVIES, federal district court

MATHEWS, principal, Central High School

MOB I, II, III

FINE, education editor of the *New York Times*

MOB IV

Grace LORCH, white supporter of the nine

MELBA, student, one of the nine

OGDEN, white minister, supporter of the nine

CAPTAIN (Arkansas National Guard)

EISENHOWER, president of the United States

Max RABB, aide to President Eisenhower

Herb BROWNELL, U.S. attorney general

GLORIA, student, one of the nine

OFFICER (101st Airborne)

ERNEST, THELMA, MINNIJEAN, JEFFERSON, CARLOTTA, TERRENCE, students

ROMINE, director of plant services, Little Rock schools

Act I

Scene I: Playground, Little Rock, Arkansas, April 1954

RAYMOND: Jimmy! Yo, Jimmy! Let's play some catch.

JIM: Maybe later.

RAYMOND: What are you staring at?

JIM: Nothing. I was just thinking.

RAYMOND: Why are you doing that? School's out for the day.

JIM: My teacher told me that since I was so good in math and science, I could be an engineer or scientist some day.

RAYMOND: You're only in the fifth grade! Why are you thinking about things like that now?

JIM: She wishes I could go to Central High because it's the best in the state.

RAYMOND: Now, why is she filling your head with such foolishness? That school's only for white kids.

---

* National Association for the Advancement of Colored People

Little Rock Central High School

JIM:	I know, I know. But I sure wish I could go there. I'd be much better prepared for college if I did.	RAYMOND:	What did your dad say about the Supreme Court?
RAYMOND:	Jimmy, you may be smart in class, but outside you're a real dummy! Those white folks are never going to let you into that place, except maybe to mop floors.	JIM:	It can make them open up Central High to us.
		RAYMOND:	Now, how in the world can they do that?
JIM:	My dad thinks that someday the Supreme Court might make them.	JIM:	Don't you remember when we studied the Constitution? The Supreme Court decides if laws really fit with the Constitution and its Amendments.
RAYMOND:	And what if it did? Do you think it would just be reading and writing at Central? Why, those white boys wouldn't give you a minute's peace. They'd make your life miserable by always trying to trip you up.	RAYMOND:	I must have been absent that day.
JIM:	Maybe not. We all get along fine here at the park.	JIM:	Or not paying attention. Look, right after the Civil War, the Fourteenth Amendment was passed. My dad says it guarantees our rights and that all the segregation laws don't, so they should be thrown out.

         20 Plays for U.S. History Classes

RAYMOND:	It seems the white folks haven't paid much attention to the Constitution. Let's play some catch.

Scene II: The Bates's home, Little Rock, May 17, 1954

L.C.:	Daisy! Daisy! Did you hear? I can't believe my ears!
BATES:	L.C., what are you all worked up about?
L.C.:	The Supreme Court just declared school segregation unconstitutional! The vote was unanimous!
BATES:	It's been a long time coming. This is certainly wonderful news, but it's only a beginning. I hope and pray the people of Little Rock accept this calmly. But I fear there's a long and difficult road ahead for all of us.

Scene III: Community meeting, Little Rock, May 21, 1954

BLOSSOM:	For many years this school district has been diligently striving to improve the educational opportunities for all our children, Negro and white, under separate but equal programs. The recent decision of the U.S. Supreme Court had invalidated this system. The Little Rock School District will comply with the federal constitutional requirements. But until the court renders more specific guidelines, our schools will continue to oper-

	ate under their present format. Mr. Bates, you have a question?
L.C.:	Yes. Mr. Blossom, as school superintendent, are you now saying that Little Rock's schools will not begin desegregation in 1954?
BLOSSOM:	That's correct.
L.C.:	How can you justify such a delay? Why can't the schools open for the fall term on an integrated basis?
BLOSSOM:	There are many sound reasons. First of all, we need more time to complete construction of two new high schools. And, secondly, we need more time to adequately prepare our students and staff for this change. Mr. Bates, I realize my remarks will disappoint many in our Negro community. But let us not forget: we are all heading into uncharted waters. Prudence demands that we proceed slowly and carefully.
L.C.:	Mr. Blossom, with all due respect, we've heard this line of reasoning for a long, long time. Well, let's just cut to the chase. When can we expect the integration of our schools to begin?
BLOSSOM:	The two new high schools should be ready for opening in 1957.

Act II

Scene I: The Bates's home, Little Rock, 11:30 P.M., August 22, 1957

BATES:	Dear, I'm going to take Skippy out for a walk.

20 Plays for U.S. History Classes

L.C.:	Good idea. Maybe that will get your mind off all the problems and pressures of getting those students into Central High next month. I'll be going to bed. Good night, dear.
	(Twenty minutes later Mrs. Bates returns, sits down and begins reading a newspaper. Suddenly, a large rock comes crashing through the front window. L.C. comes rushing into the room.)
L.C.:	Daisy! Are you hurt? You're covered with glass!
BATES:	I'm all right—just a little shaky is all. What's that tied to the rock?
L.C.:	A message. "Stone this time. Dynamite next." It's signed "A message from the Arkansas patriots."
BATES:	Some patriots. But I'm not going to let them intimidate me!
L.C.:	I'm sure they'll try something like this again.
BATES:	Cowards always strike like this— in the dark of night when they can't be seen.
L.C.:	That's why we'll make this house a fortress if we have to. But we won't give in.

Scene II: Chancery Court, Little Rock, August 29, 1957

REED:	Mrs. Thomason, you have petitioned this court to seek an injunction against the integration of Central High School, beginning September 3. Will you please offer cause why this court should so act?
THOMASON:	Yes, Your Honor. Speaking on behalf of the Mothers' League of Central High School, we are terrified at the prospect of sending our precious children into a most dangerous situation. I have been informed that both white and Negro boys are forming gangs. Your Honor, they have guns and knives! For the safety and well-being of our children, we beseech you to stop this integration plan.
REED:	Do you have anything else to add?
THOMASON:	Yes, Your Honor. I have asked Governor Faubus to speak on our behalf.
REED:	Governor Faubus, we are honored by your presence in our court.
FAUBUS:	Thank you. I am here today to alert this court to a most perilous situation brewing in anticipation of the racial integration of Central High School. I personally know that guns have already been taken from Negro and white students.
REED:	Thank you, Governor. Mr. Potts, as chief of police, how does your department assess the situation?
POTTS:	Your Honor, my department has found no evidence of planned violence by the students.
REED:	Superintendent Blossom, what is your perspective?

BLOSSOM:	Your Honor, our staff has thoughtfully and carefully prepared its integration plan. We do not anticipate any serious problems from our students.
REED:	Chief of Police Potts, what about outsiders?
POTTS:	We cannot predict their actions.
REED:	Very well. Given the uncertainty of the present situation and the possible threat of future violence, I feel compelled to grant the injunction. Court dismissed.

Scene III: Federal District Court, Little Rock, August 30, 1957

DAVIES:	After carefully weighing the evidence presented, and mindful of this court's duties with regards to the U.S. Supreme Court's decision of May 17, 1954, I hereby overrule the injunction granted in Chancery Court. I also order the Little Rock school board to proceed at once with their integration plan beginning September 3. I am also ordering an injunction to restrain any and all persons from interfering with that plan.

Scene IV: Central High School office, Little Rock, 8:00 P.M., September 2, 1957

BLOSSOM:	Jess, school's only starting tomorrow, and you already look like you need a vacation.

MATHEWS:	Isn't that the truth for all of us? Virgil, do you really think we can pull it off tomorrow with a minimum of fuss?
BLOSSOM:	With the diehard segregationists on the march and Governor Faubus straddling on the fence, I'm not very optimistic.
MATHEWS:	If only he would publicly commit himself to enforcing the federal court order! Virgil, it's all this uncertainty that's escalating the tension.
BLOSSOM:	And that tension caused eight of the Negro enrollees to come by the office today and withdraw. No sense staying here any longer. I'm going home.
MATHEWS:	Good night, Virgil.
	(Blossom leaves and quickly returns)
BLOSSOM:	Well, the governor's definitely fallen off the political fence! He's got the whole school surrounded by the National Guard.
MATHEWS:	What on earth is he thinking! That's like putting a lighted match into a gas can to see if it's empty!
BLOSSOM:	I better get in touch with Mrs. Bates right away. She's coordinating the remaining nine students.

Scene V: The Bates's home, Little Rock, late evening, September 2, 1957

L.C.:	Who called at this late hour?

BATES:	Superintendent Blossom. Faubus has the National Guard all over Central High.
L.C.:	And what does Mr. Blossom think?
BATES:	That we should keep the nine home until the school board contacts Judge Davies.
L.C.:	What are you going to tell the kids?
BATES:	To stay home until the court acts.

Scene VI: The Bates's home, late evening, September 3, 1957

L.C.:	Daisy, I just spoke with some white reporters. They said a huge mob of segregationists spent the whole day at Central.
BATES:	They think they won because we didn't show up today. But tomorrow will be different. Judge Davies ordered that the school must be opened to us by then.
L.C.:	What did the school officials say?
BATES:	The nine are to come, but not their parents. They don't want them near the campus.
L.C.:	I don't like that. Those kids need adult protection and support.
BATES:	That's why I'm going to call up some sympathetic ministers to see if they'll accompany the nine.
L.C.:	Good idea, dear. I think you should have all the adults and students meet in one place and walk in together.

BATES:	I agree. Now, I just hope I can contact everybody in time.

Scene VII: Near Central High School, Little Rock, 8:15 A.M., September 4, 1957

(Elizabeth Eckford walking alone)

MOB I:	There's one!
MOB II:	Don't let her pass!
MOB III:	Lynch her! Lynch her!
	(The mob jostles Elizabeth. The Guard won't let her pass, and in a terrible fright, she runs to a bus bench.)
FINE:	Are you all right? I'm a reporter and I support your cause. Try not to let them see you crying.
MOB IV:	Go home, you dirty nigger lover!
LORCH:	Let me take her away from here. Come with me, dear. We'll be safe on this bus.

Scene VIII: Twelfth Street and Park Avenue, near Central High, 8:15 A.M., September 4, 1957

BATES:	Everyone ready? Are all the ministers here?
MELBA:	Where's Elizabeth? I don't see her.
OGDEN:	Ready, Mrs. Bates—two black and two white ministers, and my son, David.

BATES:	Good. Let's have the students go two by two, with a pair of adults in front and another in back.
OGDEN:	I'll walk up front.
L.C.:	Daisy! The mob surrounded Elizabeth and jostled her badly, and the Guard didn't do a thing! A white woman came to her rescue, and the two of them went off on a bus.
BATES:	Oh, that poor girl. Let's go.
	(they advance, surrounded by a jeering crowd)
CAPTAIN:	You cannot proceed any further.
OGDEN:	On what grounds?
CAPTAIN:	By order of the governor.
MOB I:	YAHOO! That's telling them!
OGDEN:	Let's go back to the cars, Mrs. Bates.
MOB II:	That's right! All the way back to where you came from!
MOB III:	And stay there, if you know what's good for you!

Act III

Scene I: President Eisenhower's vacation home, Newport, Rhode Island, September 14, 1957

FAUBUS:	Mr. President—
EISENHOWER:	Governor, Faubus, thank you for coming all this way. I'll get right to the point: I don't like what's happening in Little Rock.

FAUBUS:	No one does, except a few extremists and television reporters. Mr. President, it's a very delicate and volatile situation right now. And as governor I'm responsible for not letting it get any worse.
EISENHOWER:	Of course you are, and I'm responsible for upholding the Constitution.
FAUBUS:	I understand.
EISENHOWER:	It's not my job to get involved with matters concerning individual states, but I cannot tolerate a federal court order being ignored.
FAUBUS:	I understand.
EISENHOWER:	Governor Faubus, I want to avoid if possible a federal versus state confrontation over this issue. And, furthermore, I have no desire to be in a position where a state governor is humiliated.
FAUBUS:	I understand, Mr. President.
EISENHOWER:	I'm not ordering you to withdraw the National Guard, only to use it, if you must, to carry out that federal court order. If you do, I'm confident that the Justice Department will back off from that suit pending against you.
FAUBUS:	Thank you, Mr. President.

Scene II: Newport, Rhode Island, September 23, 1957

(the president and Rabb on the phone)

EISENHOWER: Yes, Max. What's the situation in Little Rock?

RABB: Very ugly, Mr. President, very ugly. The kids finally got in today, but they used a side entrance. Once the mob found out, things got out of hand.

EISENHOWER: Any casualties?

RABB: Three Negro reporters beaten. The entire *Life Magazine* staff down there was roughed up. And get this—three of them were arrested for inciting a riot!

EISENHOWER: What about the students?

RABB: The nine were taken home just before noon.

EISENHOWER: Thanks, Max. Keep me posted.

(hangs up)

BROWNELL: More bad news from Little Rock?

EISENHOWER: Unfortunately.

BROWNELL: Any new strategy in mind?

EISENHOWER: Yes. I'm going to issue an executive proclamation immediately stating that unless that court-ordered integration plan is peacefully and promptly executed, I will do my constitutional duty to enforce it.

BROWNELL: And if that's ignored?

EISENHOWER: There will be hell to pay!

Scene III: Newport, Rhode Island, the next day

(Rabb and the president on the phone)

RABB: Mr. President, I regret to report that your proclamation was ignored. The mayor of Little Rock says the situation is completely out of control and that violence has spread throughout the city. Mayor Mann is pleading for federal troops to bring peace and order.

EISENHOWER: Thanks, Max.

(hangs up)

BROWNELL: They ignored your order, didn't they?

EISENHOWER: Max says it's chaos down there. Herb, I want those kids in that school Wednesday morning!

BROWNELL: We'll need an effective show of force.

EISENHOWER: Of course. Let's get General Taylor to move his men in there right away. That will make those diehards pay attention!

BROWNELL: How are you going to bring this to the attention of the country?

EISENHOWER: By a live broadcast, tonight from the White House. This is too serious a matter to communicate from a vacation home.

BROWNELL:	What are you going to do about the Arkansas National Guard?
EISENHOWER:	I'll federalize it! I want it out of Governor Faubus's hands.

Scene IV: The Bates's home, Little Rock 1:00 A.M., September 25, 1957

(on the phone)

BLOSSOM:	Mrs. Bates? It's Virgil Blossom. I am so sorry to disturb you at this hour, but it's very urgent.
BATES:	Yes, go on.
BLOSSOM:	Thank you. The 101st Airborne is here in Little Rock and is ready to enforce the integration order.
BATES:	Starting when?
BLOSSOM:	This morning. We want the students ready.
BATES:	But I've already told them to stay home.
BLOSSOM:	Mrs. Bates, I don't wish to sound overly dramatic, but the President of the United States wants those nine students in school—today.
BATES:	How am I going to contact them all at this hour? They are not answering their phones because of all the threats.
BLOSSOM:	I realize that, but you are a most resourceful person, Mrs. Bates. Go to their individual homes in person, if you must.
BLOSSOM:	Mr. Blossom, if you were one of those families, would you answer

	a knock on the door in the dark of night?
BLOSSOM:	All I can say is that General Taylor expects all the students to be at your home by 8:30 A.M. That's the plan. Good luck, Mrs. Bates.
BATES:	L.C., don't fall back to sleep. We have a long, long night ahead of us.

Scene V: The Bates's home, 8:30 A.M., September 25, 1957

GLORIA:	Mrs. Bates, a station wagon just pulled up.
BATES:	Everyone ready?
	(enter an officer of the 101st Airborne)
OFFICER:	Mrs. Bates, please bring the students to our cars. They will be returned here at 3:30 P.M.

Scene VI: The Bates's home, 4:00 P.M., same day

BATES:	Well, tell us how things went today.
ERNEST:	Those army guys were all business. There must have been over twenty of them right next to us as we walked in.
THELMA:	I think we're all pretty tired.
BATES:	You have every right to be. How were you treated by the other students?

MINNIJEAN:	Pretty good. A few kids walked out, but some girls even invited me to lunch. I was even asked to join the glee club.
JEFFERSON:	You know what I think? I think they were all just as nervous as we were.
BATES:	You might be right. I want to commend each and every one of you for being so brave, so willing to keep going. But remember, we need each other; you can't think you can go it alone. Every day will present a new challenge. That's why I want us to continue meeting here after school so we can share our experiences and draw support from one another. Anything else?
JEFFERSON:	What about me trying out for the track team?
ERNEST:	Yeah, and I'd like to play in the jazz band.
BATES:	I'm sorry, but you know the agreement we made with the school officials: no extracurricular activities this year.
MINNIJEAN:	That just isn't fair!

Scene VII: The Bates's home, 4:00 P.M., October 2, 1957

BATES:	Minnijean, Melba—you both look like you had a hard day.
MINNIJEAN:	Mrs. Bates, it was bad, very bad at school today. A gang roughed up Melba and me in the corridor.
MELBA:	Then they blocked our way to class.

MINNIJEAN:	On the way to a pep rally a boy kicked me from behind.
BATES:	Was he punished?
MINNIJEAN:	I don't know, but he was taken to the office.
GLORIA:	Mrs. Bates, you wouldn't believe some of the awful names we've been called.
CARLOTTA:	Some of the girls are really nasty to us. They won't leave us alone even though we just ignore them and go about our business like you said.
BATES:	I don't know if it will make you feel any less pain, but I know what you're going through. You should see some of the letters I get. And names? I wouldn't ever repeat a one of them!

Scene VIII: The Bates's home, 4:15 P.M., October 16, 1957

BATES:	From what each of you has shared today, things are getting worse, not better, at school. I need to know who is responsible. Is it a majority of the white students?
ERNEST:	No. It's just a stubborn few.
BATES:	What about the others?
TERRENCE:	They just kind of turn their heads away when we get hassled.
CARLOTTA:	If someone bothers you, nothing happens unless you have an adult witness to back you up.

BATES:	What about the guards? There are plenty of them standing around.
ERNEST:	That's just it—all they do is stand around.
TERRENCE:	Ever since the Arkansas National Guard replaced the federal troops, the bullies are getting away with a lot more.
ERNEST:	Like today, Terrence and I were just walking down the stairs, minding our own business, when a bunch of white guys kicked us from behind.
TERRENCE:	There was a guard no more than six feet away, and he didn't do a thing.
JEFFERSON:	The other day some guys in physical education class tried to push me against the hot steam pipes, but I got away.
BATES:	Thelma, you're the smallest of the group, barely five feet tall. Have you been physically attacked, too?
THELMA:	Mrs. Bates, I've been kicked, shoved, and knocked flat on my face.
BATES:	This has to stop! I'm going to contact General Walker immediately. If something isn't done, I'll demand that he assign each of you a personal escort to stay with you at all times during school hours.

> ### *Scene IX: Little Rock schools' district office, February 6, 1958*

BLOSSOM:	Mr. Romine, what's the maintenance picture at Central?
ROMINE:	Like a war zone—fires, broken this and shattered that, graffiti all over. I tell you, Mr. Blossom, that place keeps a whole crew constantly busy just fixing things and painting.
BLOSSOM:	What an unnecessary waste of money and work. Speaking of wasted time and money, how many times have we had to check for bombs this year?
ROMINE:	At least thirty. Each incident has tied up at least ten men for six hours.
BLOSSOM:	Any major new expenses?
ROMINE:	We just replaced some of the steam radiators in the boys' restroom in the basement.
BLOSSOM:	Now how in the world could vandals break them without anyone hearing them?
ROMINE:	Mr. Blossom, I didn't say they were broken—just no longer useable.
BLOSSOM:	I don't understand.
ROMINE:	Some white boys thought it would be cute to urinate on them. Then the fumes off the hot radiators would travel up and through the whole building. The stench was unbearable.

BLOSSOM:	Disgusting. Absolutely disgusting.
ROMINE:	Mr. Blossom, before I get back to work, can I ask you a question?
BLOSSOM:	Fire away.
ROMINE:	Is it true that one of the Negro students was suspended?
BLOSSOM:	I'm afraid it's more severe than that. I'm going to ask the board to expel her for the rest of the term.
ROMINE:	May I ask what she did?
BLOSSOM:	It's a series of things. She doesn't respond like the others do. Every time she's provoked, she strikes back. There seems to be no ending to the vicious cycle.
ROMINE:	In what ways has she struck back?
BLOSSOM:	She emptied her cafeteria tray on two boys who were blocking her path. And another time, a girl threw a purse at her and she hurled it right back.
ROMINE:	That's too bad. But can you really blame her? Sounds like she's only too human.
BLOSSOM:	I know, I know.

Scene X: Little Rock schools' district office, May 27, 1958

MATHEWS:	What a week, Virgil! Imagine, Ernest Green, a Negro, received his diploma from Central High without incident. That's some accomplishment!
BLOSSOM:	Are you overlooking the spitting episode?
MATHEWS:	That was after the ceremony, and Chief Smith handled the situation very quickly and efficiently.
BLOSSOM:	That he did. Those boys were arrested and removed before any crowd could form.
MATHEWS:	And the victim, the Negro girl, she certainly helped by her calm reaction. Otherwise, we could have had serious trouble.
BLOSSOM:	Yes, we were very fortunate.
MATHEWS:	How do you think things will be next fall?
BLOSSOM:	I'm not very optimistic, Jess. You would have thought that after all we've been through during one complete year of integration, attitudes would have softened.
MATHEWS:	I've seen some positive changes.
BLOSSOM:	But not enough, especially from the adults. They're the hard-headed and hard-hearted ones poisoning the whole atmosphere, especially the ones who have no direct connection with our students.
MATHEWS:	Our so-called political leaders, you mean.
BLOSSOM:	That's right. Them and the rest of the segregationists.
MATHEWS:	You know, Virgil, in many ways those people have made our white students victims, too. Not

all the pressure was just on the Negro students. In fact, left alone, I think that most of our white students would have accepted integration without much fuss. What do you think?

BLOSSOM: How many white students did we suspend this year from Central?

MATHEWS: Over a hundred.

BLOSSOM: You and I both know that's not a normal figure. A lot of those kids had never been in trouble at school before. I think many of them were pressured by adults to hassle the Negro students.

MATHEWS: Well, whatever the cause or motivation, those Negro students took abuse constantly all year long. They were very brave.

BLOSSOM: I wish our governor would follow their example. Instead, he keeps stirring the pot, whetting the appetites of the segregationists.

MATHEWS: And what's really sad is that he's more popular in this state than ever.

BLOSSOM: I know. I'm afraid he'll pull another fast one before school starts again.

Scene XI: Playground, Little Rock, September 13, 1958

RAYMOND: Yo, Jimmy! Hear the news? The governor closed down all three high schools in Little Rock.

JIM: For how long?

RAYMOND: Maybe the whole year.

JIM: Just when I thought I could go there. I wonder when all this crazy stuff will end.

RAYMOND: Not for a long, long time.

AMERICA IN THE LAST HALF OF THE TWENTIETH CENTURY

Characters (in order of appearance)

As the story begins, all are between the ages of seven and twelve.

Boys	**Girls**
JERRY, LELAND, and SKEETS	JANICE, KATHY, and LINDA

Setting

(On hot summer days the six would perch themselves in a large almond tree they named the Batman Tree. There they would talk for hours, returning from time to time as the years passed.)

**Scene I: The Batman Tree,
Northern California, 1954**

JERRY: What should we do? How about playing war?

LELAND: Nah. I'm sick of always being on the Russian side and having to lose.

JERRY: It's got to be that way, or else Stalin will take over the whole country! He's got the H-bomb now.

JANICE: No, sir! Stalin died last year. We don't have to worry about the Russians anymore.

JERRY: How come our teachers still made us practice getting under our desks this year, smarty?

KATHY: I wonder what kids in Russia are really like. I bet you they're just like us.

LINDA: My friend Rita's mother says there are some good Russians.

JERRY: How could she say that? They're all commies!

LINDA: She said Russian soldiers saved her from being gassed to death in 1945.

JERRY: You can't believe her! She's a Jew.

LINDA: I don't care what you say. I believe her!

SKEETS:	Jerry, where do you get such stupid ideas?
JERRY:	They're not stupid! You guys are the stupid ones, thinking the Russians aren't out to get us. That's why my dad is digging a bomb shelter.
LINDA:	Now, that's really stupid! Who wants to live underground like a gopher?
JERRY:	You guys should watch McCarthy on television and then you'll learn about the commies. They're everywhere!
JANICE:	We don't have a television set yet. And if we did, I wouldn't watch that guy. My parents say he's crazy.
LINDA:	How come Billy's not here? Is he still sick?
KATHY:	Didn't you hear? He's got polio and he's in an iron lung.
LINDA:	That's awful! We should go see him.
LELAND:	I wonder if Bill will ever run again. He was the fastest guy in the whole school.
SKEETS:	He told me he was going to be like that guy in England who ran a whole mile in less than four minutes!
JANICE:	Roger Bannister.
SKEETS:	That was before Billy got so sick. I sure hope I don't get polio. My mom won't let me go swimming or to the movies.
KATHY:	My mom said a doctor in Pittsburgh named Jonas Salk invented a shot so we won't get it.
JERRY:	I hate shots.
LELAND:	We all do. But I'll get one so I don't have to end up like Billy.

Scene II: 1957

JERRY:	How come Skeets and Kathy aren't around?
JANICE:	Their families all went to Disneyland.
LINDA:	I wish our family could do that, but my dad lost his job at the factory. Well, what are we going to do?
LELAND:	I have to go home and study.

 20 Plays for U.S. History Classes

JERRY:	Study? It's Easter vacation! Besides, you always get straight A's anyhow.
LELAND:	My parents said that ever since the Russians put up that satellite *Sputnik* they're getting way ahead of us in science. Their schools are a lot better than ours—a lot tougher, and we have to work harder to catch up.
LINDA:	How can we do that? We're all on double session now. Too many kids and not enough teachers and classrooms.
JANICE:	Did you guys watch those kids going to school in Little Rock? They sure are brave.
JERRY:	Those Negro kids have no business going to that school.
JANICE:	What do you mean? It's a public school, not a private one. They have every right to go there.
LINDA:	Supreme Court said so. No more segregation.
JERRY:	We'll see. Just because nine guys in long robes say something doesn't mean people in the South are going to listen.
LELAND:	What about Montgomery, Alabama? That Martin Luther King guy got them to listen about the buses. And he did it peacefully.
JERRY:	How about coming over to my house to listen to some Elvis Presley records?
JANICE:	My mother won't let me.

JERRY:	Just because he wiggles around? He's cool! Tell your mother she better get used to rock and roll.
LINDA:	Hey! It's almost 3 P.M. *American Bandstand* is on!
JERRY:	I'm going home to listen to Elvis and smoke a cigarette.

Scene III: 1961

KATHY:	Jerry, you still mad that Kennedy's president?
SKEETS:	So what if he's a Catholic.
LINDA:	Some day we'll have a woman president.
KATHY:	Or a Negro. Have you ever heard anyone speak as well as Martin Luther King?
SKEETS:	Come on, Jerry. What's bugging you? Still dreaming about being the Marlboro Man?
LINDA:	He's upset because the Russians put the first man in space. That Yuri Gagarin—
KATHY:	Nah. It's because his mother got a job and doesn't have time to bake him cookies anymore!
JERRY:	Shut up!
SKEETS:	Touchy, touchy. Lots of women are getting jobs now.
LELAND:	They have to so they can pay for that second car everybody seems to be getting these days.
LINDA:	I know why Jerry's so mad! He just looked at his new transistor

radio and found out it's made in Japan!

JANICE: He doesn't know whether he should smash it or keep listening to it!

JERRY: Shut up! All of you!

SKEETS: The Japanese are starting to make a lot of stuff now. My dad says we'll all be driving their cars someday.

KATHY: We have an import—a VW Beetle for our second car.

JERRY: I'll tell you what's got me so upset. It's that wall the Russians just put up in Berlin!

SKEETS: So what are you going to do about it?

JERRY: Maybe join the Marines.

JANICE: Well, I don't like that wall either. But I wouldn't want any of our boys dying over it.

LINDA: It won't last.

JERRY: It will if we don't tear it down ourselves! Those commies never give up.

SKEETS: I bet you they'll end up tearing it down themselves.

LELAND: Well, Jerry, if you do join the Marines, try to learn a trade you can use once you're out. As for me, next month I'm off to college.

KATHY: What are you going to study?

LELAND: Nuclear engineering. I'm going to build atomic reactors.

Scene IV: 1968

SKEETS: Did you hear what happened to Mel down the street?

LELAND: He's not in jail again for smoking dope?

SKEETS: Nah. At the army induction center he punched the first guy he saw in a uniform. They're doing mental tests on him in some hospital back East.

KATHY: I knew he would do anything to keep from going to Vietnam.

LELAND: Skeets, how have you kept out?

SKEETS: I got married back in '65. How about yourself?

LELAND: Vital defense work—nuclear submarines. What about Jerry? Is he still over there?

SKEETS: I talked to his dad, and he said Jerry was coming home on leave. Who knows, he might show up here at the Batman Tree.

LELAND: I heard Jerry's folks split up.

KATHY: Yeah. His mother said she wanted to become independent. She's in college.

(enter Linda)

LELAND: Linda! You made it! Hop right up and find your old perch.

LINDA: I can't believe how much the old neighborhood has changed. Most of the orchard is gone.

KATHY: The cancer of suburbia has taken over.

(enter Jerry)

LELAND: I can't believe it! Jerry, you look great! Hop up.

LINDA: He can't make it up here. He's too weighted down with all those medals!

SKEETS: Jerry, you look like a Russian general at a May Day parade! Welcome back!

JERRY: You guys are something else. You're the first people besides my parents to say anything like that. At the airport some long-haired hippies cursed me. But I'm not going to take this uniform off!

LELAND: Don't take stuff like that personally. It's the war, not you, they're against.

SKEETS: If the government had listened to us back in '64, we wouldn't be in this mess.

JERRY: So you're one of the protestors.

LINDA: Me too.

KATHY: And me.

JERRY: It's you guys who have prolonged the war!

KATHY: It's President Johnson! If Kennedy were still alive, there would be peace.

LINDA: One terrible assassination has changed so much.

JERRY: One? What about King and Robert Kennedy this year? What's going on in this country?

KATHY: Lots of unrest: blacks rioting in the cities, drugs, families breaking up.

JERRY: When did those Mexicans down the street move in?

LINDA: A few years back. My little sister babysits their kids.

JERRY: Well, there goes the old neighborhood.

SKEETS: Some of that napalm get in your eyes in Vietnam? The Lopez yard looks like it's straight out of *House and Garden* magazine.

JERRY: Next thing you know we'll have Blacks moving in.

LINDA: Jerry! I thought you said you were in Vietnam. I read over half of our troops doing the fighting were either black or brown!

KATHY: And they're doing most of the dying, too.

JERRY: Kathy, I see you're driving a Japanese car. What gives?

KATHY: It's dependable and cheap to run, just like my parent's new color TV.

JERRY: Whatever happened to Janice?

LINDA: She's in the Peace Corps somewhere in Africa.

JERRY: I've got to get back to 'Nam. This place has changed too much.

Scene V: Gas station, California, 1973

SKEETS: Janice? Is that really you?

JANICE:	Skeets! Of all the crazy places to see you again. Fifty cars lined up just to get a little gas. How are you? What are you doing these days?
SKEETS:	I'm fine: wife, three kids. I just got a new job, in computers. What have you been up to?
JANICE:	After I got out of the Peace Corps in '70, I got married, but it didn't work out. I'm a real American statistic—one of the 50 percent.
SKEETS:	I'm sorry to hear that.
JANICE:	I remarried and things are fine. My little boy is in his carseat.
SKEETS:	He looks just like you! What business is your husband in?
JANICE:	He just started a recycling business. You know how much we Americans waste and throw away.
SKEETS:	Yes. You ever hear from Linda?
JANICE:	Funny you ask. Out of the blue she called me. She's a lawyer back in Washington, D.C.
SKEETS:	I suppose she's part of the Watergate Investigation.
JANICE:	We talked about that. She thinks Nixon is guilty as sin, but she's involved with some case before the Supreme Court: Roe versus Wade.
SKEETS:	That's the one about abortion. Well, it looks like we get to move a little closer to the pumps. Here's my business card—keep in touch.

Scene VI: Kennedy Airport, New York, 1986

KATHY:	Lee—Leland Wilson of California. Can that really be you?
LELAND:	Kathy! You look great! How long has it been?
KATHY:	Nearly twenty years. Are you coming or going?
LELAND:	Good question. With all this airport security, I can't tell!
KATHY:	It's a crazy world. Where are you going?
LELAND:	Sweden. The government is sending me there to monitor the fallout from the Chernobyl disaster in Ukraine.
KATHY:	Hmmm. I wonder if that could happen to one of our nuclear power plants.
LELAND:	It's highly improbable, unless some terrorist sneaks in. Say, what are you doing these days?
KATHY:	Living in Connecticut and working on Wall Street.
LELAND:	With all the yuppies, I suppose, in their power suspenders.
KATHY:	Ha-ha. Are you married? Have a family?
LELAND:	Divorced. No kids. How about you?
KATHY:	Too busy to marry, I guess.
LELAND:	No social life?

KATHY:	Oh, I have my two dogs and two computers.
LELAND:	Mind if I give you a call when I get back?
KATHY:	That would be nice. Here's my business card. I'll write my home phone number on the back. But I have to be honest, Leland, I'm on the go a lot.
LELAND:	I'll try to catch you when I can. There's my plane.

Scene VII: California-Connecticut phone connection, 1997

KATHY:	Hello?
LELAND:	Kathy! It's me, Leland. You're a very hard person to track down.
KATHY:	I'm sorry. You know how crazy the stock market has been the past few months.
LELAND:	Did you get my latest E-mail? I sent it yesterday.
KATHY:	Sorry again. I haven't been home to check it. I'm in my car headed there now. What's it about? Where are you?
LELAND:	I'm in my car, too. Jerry from the old neighborhood died. I read about it in the paper.
KATHY:	What happened?
LELAND:	AIDS.
KATHY:	That's terrible. Who would have thought? At least he lived long enough to see the Berlin Wall come down. Where are you now?
LELAND:	Actually, I just left the funeral home to pay my respects and drive by the old neighborhood.
KATHY:	Anyone I know there?
LELAND:	Janice. She sends her love. Guess what she's doing now? She's a bilingual teacher working with farmworkers' kids.
KATHY:	That's nice. Leland, could you do me a favor? Drive by the old Batman Tree and tell me what it looks like now.
LELAND:	Developers cut it down and put up a big shopping mall last year. Some of the people in the neighborhood tried to save it, but it was too sick from pollution.
KATHY:	That's awful. I wish you were here, Leland. I need someone from my past right now.
LELAND:	Kathy, I'd like to be your past, present, and future.
KATHY:	Can you get here before the Hale-Bopp Comet leaves? I'd love to share that with you.
LELAND:	I'm on my way to the airport right now.

Share Your Bright Ideas with Us!

We want to hear from you! Your valuable comments and suggestions will help us meet your current and future classroom needs.

Your name_____Date_____

School name_____Phone_____

School address_____

Grade level taught_____Subject area(s) taught_____Average class size_____

Where did you purchase this publication?_____

Was your salesperson knowledgeable about this product?   Yes_____   No_____

What monies were used to purchase this product?

____School supplemental budget   ____Federal/state funding   ____Personal

Please "grade" this Walch publication according to the following criteria:

Quality of service you received when purchasing .... A   B   C   D   F
Ease of use.. A   B   C   D   F
Quality of content... A   B   C   D   F
Page layout .... A   B   C   D   F
Organization of material .... A   B   C   D   F
Suitability for grade level .... A   B   C   D   F
Instructional value.. A   B   C   D   F

COMMENTS:_____

_____

What specific supplemental materials would help you meet your current—or future—instructional needs?

_____

Have you used other Walch publications? If so, which ones?_____

May we use your comments in upcoming communications?   ___Yes   ___No

Please **FAX** this completed form to **207-772-3105**, or mail it to: